Survivor

Follow Fatima on Twitter
@ChampFatima

Survivor

The shocking and inspiring story of a true champion

Fatima Whitbread &
Adrianne Blue

2 4 6 8 10 9 7 5 3 1

First published in 2012 by Virgin Books, an imprint of Ebury Publishing
A Random House Group Company

Some chapters of this book were formerly published as part of *Fatima:
The Autobiography of Fatima Whitbread* in 1988 by Pelham Books and
in 1989 by Sphere.

Addresses for companies within The Random House Group Limited
can be found at www.randomhouse.co.uk/offices.htm

The Random House Group Limited Reg. No. 954009

A CIP catalogue record for this book is available from the British Library

The Random House Group Limited supports The Forest Stewardship
Council (FSC®), the leading international forest certification organisation.
Our books carrying the FSC label are printed on FSC® certified paper. FSC
is the only forest certification scheme endorsed by the leading environmental
organisations, including Greenpeace. Our paper procurement policy can be
found at www.randomhouse.co.uk/environment

Printed and bound by CPI Group (UK) Ltd, Croydon, CR0 4YY

ISBN: 9780753540961

Contents

CHAPTER ONE

The Iconic Cockroach and Me

IT'S ODD TO be famous for getting a cockroach stuck up your nose. No one was more surprised than I was when the public voted that moment on *I'm a Celebrity ... Get Me Out of Here!* as the second most memorable TV moment of the year. The gold medal went to the wedding kiss of Prince William and Kate. The bronze went to the back-end view of Kate's bridesmaid, her sister Pippa, gliding down the aisle at the royal wedding.

Sports champions can be crybabies and, like Seb Coe at the Moscow Olympics and me in Helsinki, have been known to cry when we win silver instead of gold. This time, though, I was more than pleased with my silver medal, though I didn't enjoy the bushtucker trial I had to endure to get it.

I hate cockroaches and I didn't want to put on the big perspex head casket required by the task, but I did. As the cockroaches were poured in, I told myself, you only have to last thirty seconds till the buzzer sounds, thirty seconds. What's thirty vile seconds in a lifetime, Fatima? I had already survived three plastic face helmets full of other nasty creepy-crawlies, including scorpions, mealworms, spiders and snakes. But now more than 7,500 cockroaches were being tipped in.

I knew instantly that one of them had crawled into my nose and was creeping up my nasal passage. It was scary. Could it lay eggs in my sinuses or creep high enough to bite into my brain? I was counting the seconds and telling myself I had to hang on – quitting was never an option. I hung on.

As soon as the buzzer sounded and they got the helmet off, I asked for the show's medic. Dr Bob took a look and said, 'Fatima, there isn't anything there.'

'It's way up at the top.'

Dr Bob flushed a syringe full of water up my nose. Nothing came out.

He said, 'There's nothing there.'

But I could feel its legs scratching. 'Something alien is in my head. I can feel it moving.'

He looked dubious but to his credit, Dr Bob tried another syringe of fluid and then another and another. It took twenty minutes and three different solutions to flush that cockroach out. They had to edit it down for television. Finally the cockroach shot out, hitting the ground running like an Olympic bug.

One of the team put it into an empty water bottle so I could take it back to show my campmates. The Olympic cockroach was such a hit I took it home in my hand luggage, and on my first day back in Britain, I showed it on TV on *Loose Women* and *Lorraine*. A week later, this well-travelled creature was posted to a British Museum conservationist, who arranged for it to be preserved in resin. Ms Cockroach now sits in my lounge, right beside the revered BBC Sports Personality of the Year trophy.

A journalist recently asked me if it isn't humiliating for someone who has won the World Championship and two

Olympic medals to take part in undignified physical trials on reality TV. No. After five very lean years, being able to pay your son's school fees without wincing is empowering. Embarking on a new career is empowering, and meeting all the new people I have since I 're-profiled' is stimulating and great fun.

What's humiliating – well, it would have been if I had known then, now it's only sad – was revealed to me just nine days before this book had to be handed in to the publisher. While the Whitbread family were attempting to adopt the insecure, traumatised, fourteen-year-old me, they went to see the woman who gave birth to me, and that woman, who had never ever been a mother to me, saw my chance in life merely as a nice little earner. But I'll get to that.

When the *I'm a Celebrity ... Get Me Out of Here!* producer first rang and told me, 'Pack your bag, you're going,' I was delighted. I flew to Australia four days later, ready to give it my best. On the first night in the Aussie jungle, we slept outdoors on tree branches because the cave they wanted us to bed down in was so horrible and smelly and, as we would find out later, full of super-energetic cockroaches. Mosquitoes, I realised quickly, were going to be the least of it.

Now it was the morning after and I was perched on a big log, wiping sweat from my brow, and just chatting about my life; so were the others – we were getting to know each other. Because of the humidity, which quadrupled the heat, I had already switched from the ITV standard-issue safari hat to their standard-issue red-and-white bandana. So there I was, going on about myself maybe just a bit too much, when the only one of us who had ever starred in a Hollywood film said, 'Fatima, your life story is something they should make a movie about.'

I didn't take much notice. A lot of people have said that.

I didn't even take it seriously when Mark Wright from *The Only Way is Essex* and some of the others said they agreed with Stefanie Powers. Then Stef said, 'Fatima, it's the kind of life story that other people use as an excuse for their failures, but you used it as a source of strength.'

I pretended I was brushing away a mosquito, but I was trying to hide a tear. I knew they were going to broadcast a lot of what we said and did in that jungle. I didn't want red, swollen eyes in the very first programme.

A few days later, Stef said, 'Fatima, your life could be a source of strength to other people too.'

Nothing would please me more than to think what I've been through might help someone else learn how to focus and take control of their life. But I'd told Stef Powers just the bare bones of my story. She didn't know the half of it. Of all the trials we faced in the *I'm a Celebrity* jungle – and some of them were pretty gruesome – none was as bad as my early years or the heartbreak I later encountered. There were cruel twists to my life, but there were also lucky breaks – Mrs Peat, for instance. Rae Peat, the most brilliant care worker in the otherwise shocking children's home I was parked in, taught me my first great lesson in life when I was six or seven. She got me to help out with the younger children, thereby showing me, without ever saying a word, that if you look after others it also helps you.

Now that I think of it, that may be one reason why on our first night in the Australian jungle I was the one who volunteered to cut down the branches for beds and build the camp for us all. It made everybody more comfortable, including me.

My life has had astonishing high points – the thrill of breaking the world record and winning gold, going to Buckingham Palace for my MBE, falling in love. There has been the satisfaction of helping others through sport, and even the lucky accident of saving the eyesight of a stranger's child. Above all is the joy of being able to give everything I missed out on in childhood to Ryan, my amazing son.

But at first there was mainly heartbreak.

CHAPTER TWO

Careless

THE WORST DAY of my life happened very early on. I was much too young to have any memory of it, but what I have always been told is this.

In London, 1 June 1961 was wet and cold and dreary, but by the end of the first week of June temperatures were up into the twenties. The warm weather would turn out to be crucial.

That was the year Elvis Presley spent six weeks at number one on the UK charts, but the sixties had not started properly swinging yet. It would be four years before The Beatles queued up to get their MBE. Reality for most British people was newspaper-wrapped fish and chips on Friday night and barely making ends meet.

In a council flat in north London – in the sort of drab, uninspired block which Prince Charles used to be scathing about – a baby began to cry.

The baby cried and cried and cried. For the next two or three days the neighbours resisted ringing the police. It couldn't have been any longer because a baby that young left on its own wouldn't have lived any longer. Finally, when all they could hear of the baby was whimpering, someone in one of those flats picked up the telephone and dialled the Old Bill.

When the police broke down the door, a three-month-old baby was found lying in tangled sheets. The baby had been left alone in the empty flat with nothing to eat or drink. She was dehydrated, she was filthy, she was ill. That baby was me. I am told I could have died, and that if it had been colder, I would have.

I like to think that whoever it was that should have been looking after me had just popped out for a quarter of an hour, which unexpectedly stretched into an hour and then days. Anyone could be forgiven for wanting to get away from that dingy block in Matthias Road, from the sweet, cloying scent of urine in the corridors, the crude graffiti on the walls.

I want to believe that I was left unattended out of simple carelessness, not wickedness. I want to believe that I was not, as I was later told, 'dumped' and left to die. I want to believe it was a sin of omission rather than commission.

The evidence suggests that the woman who gave birth to me never wanted me. She was a Turkish–Cypriot immigrant with a beak nose, dark eyes and dark wavy hair like my own, but I do not regard her as my mother, and I am certain that as long as I live I never will.

When I was born on 3 March 1961, at Bearsted Memorial Hospital in Stoke Newington, north London, she neglected to register my birth. It was finally registered on 17 June 1961 after I had been found, when one of the social workers noticed the oversight. The birth certificate, which was not issued until three years later, on 20 July 1964, gave Adem as my father's name. But that is either an error or a joke.

I can imagine the woman who gave birth to me sitting in a DHSS office, or in the incredibly dirty kitchen I was made to scrub years later, telling an inquisitive social worker in broken English, 'The only man I know is Adem.' What the social worker didn't understand was that Adem was her three-year-old son.

At the time I was abandoned, Adem was either with his mother or perhaps it was one of the many periods when he was parked in care. As far as I can make out, his was not an idyllic childhood either, but Adem did live with her long enough, often enough, intimately enough, to learn to speak the language she spoke most easily, Turkish. He saw her throughout his childhood, he did little errands for her, ate the meals that she cooked for him. Such as she was, he had a mother. I did not.

The man who sowed the seed that created me was called Michael. He too was a Londoner and a Cypriot immigrant, but from the Greek side of the island. I no more regard him as my father than I regard her as my mother.

My mother and father are Margaret and John Whitbread. But I was not to meet them until many years later, and when I did they transformed my life in every way. Not only did they give me a home and real family love, not only did they give me a new life, but they set me on course to becoming a champion.

Suffering from severe malnutrition and neglect, the infant me was rushed from the flat in north London to a children's hospital. There I was to spend my second three months. A GP has told me that few infants have survived so long on their own without water. If you look at it that way I was, I suppose, rather lucky.

For her own reasons, the woman who gave birth to me told the authorities she would be willing to have me back.

But they felt she was inadequate, unable to look after me. On 23 November 1962, a Fit Person Order made a London council my legal guardian. I was made a ward of the court in the care of the social services, who themselves at first seemed uncertain as to what to do with me. I was housed at no less than four homes as a baby.

At last, when I was three years old, a placement of sorts was made. It was now 1964, and The Beatles song 'Can't Buy Me Love' was on more than a million lips. I was moved from the swinging London of fast music, clinging mini-skirts, and long, slow puffs of marijuana, to Hertfordshire and the green and quiet countryside. This was the best thing that could possibly have happened to me. But it was not without grave difficulties.

CHAPTER THREE

Someone Special

THERE WAS CERTAINLY nothing posh about us, the children from the home. There were more than twenty of us scribbling pictures and fitting together jigsaw puzzles in the big, high-ceilinged rooms where the paint was peeling. I will never forget the long, steep, winding staircase where I used to cause as much fuss as possible. But the house itself was impressive.

So was Cory, a skinny sixteen-year-old and the person I cared most about in all the world. The youngest assistant at the home, she had charge of the largest group of children, nine or ten of us, sometimes even more. The mornings were when Cory had very little time for me, none at all to give me any special attention. Not that the rest of her day was a doddle either – she woke us promptly at 6 a.m., she fed us, she amused us all day long, she bathed us, and when it was necessary because one of us was sobbing, she rocked us to sleep. But in the mornings she was busiest, getting all of us up, washed, dressed and fed, and delivering a few of us to the school bus.

Still a growing girl of under five foot, she had not yet noticed that she had a fashion model's figure hidden under her loose, sensible, cotton dresses and those aprons with lumpy pockets bulging with crayons and knitting wool and little bags of sweets for us. Cory had steady blue eyes and a girlish, high-pitched voice, which, despite its youthfulness, reassured me. For as long as she could remember, Cory had wanted to care for children. While other girls went out to discos after school or studied for O levels, Cory sat at home reading books on childcare. It was only occasionally that she took time out to watch her favourite pop star, Cliff Richard, on television.

Recommended by a sympathetic headmistress, she had left school specially to take this job, for which she was paid just over £2 a week. Even in those days, the salary was a pittance, a joke among her friends, most of whom earned at least £10 a week at their jobs and who worked shorter and less emotional hours. But they were often bored at their jobs. Cory loved hers, perhaps too much. Even at weekends when she was at home with her family, she worried about what would become of us.

Because she had taken over from an experienced nurse who was highly qualified, Cory had gone in at the deep end with her nine charges, including two babies in cots, a handful of children between four and six, and even one boy aged nine, who was allowed to stay on long past the cut-off age of five because his younger sister was living there. When Cory arrived at Wormley Hill House, I was three and a half, a chunky, dark-haired little girl with a will of iron. Or maybe it was a whim of iron. Thank goodness Cory realised that as well as being stubborn I was innately affectionate. I was a time-consuming charge, though not so labour-intensive as the babies, of whom there was nearly always more than one. The social services paid the matron,

Mrs Vernon, an extra allowance for every baby in the home – it was extra work.

Cory was serious-minded but also full of fun, wonderful with us children. In her tiny staff room, with its narrow bed and sparse furnishings, she continued to read childcare manuals. A bit lonely but ever resourceful, she bought a pet budgie, a blue one, who did cheer her up and seemed to enjoy looking out of the window. But after two months, Mrs Vernon decided the budgie was in the way, and it went to Hoddesdon, not that many miles away, to live with Cory's mum and dad.

The best snapshot I have of Cory shows her holding a smiling baby in the crook of one arm and holding on to me with the other. I could be clingy and unreasonably demanding, as could many of the others – we were, most of us, disturbed children. But Cory managed. She was the first person who ever showed me any love, but she had to be there for all of us and not just for me.

I remember falling and hurting myself one afternoon – I couldn't have been more than four. But even as I lay sobbing on the ground in the small playing field at the back of the house, I knew I would have to wait my turn. When Cory finally came, she examined my scraped knee with exactly the right amount of concern and she made much of me. So it had been worth waiting for. It was on the makeshift playing fields of Wormley Hill that I learned the patience which I have had to call upon so frequently during my athletics career.

The children at the home were of all sorts, English, Nigerian, Cypriot. Some of them had been born in other parts of Britain but had been taken into care in Greater

London. Some used to play joyfully. There were others who couldn't stop crying. We were a mixed bunch of sad little characters.

I don't remember many individuals. I was too young. But I do recall a blond-haired, chubby little boy called Michael. He wet the bed a lot and was always clutching a little red bus that had been brought by his mother on one of her visits. He would grab it back from anybody else who started playing with it. Michael used to hide the bus under the carpet where it made a large bulge that was easy to trip over, but he could never understand how his hiding place was discovered.

We had so little to call our own. Even our Christmas presents, nearly always donated, second-hand things, were usually shared. But Cory's mother made me a yellow dress and sewed a name tag in it. It was a pale, almost cream colour, with a pattern of little flowers. Cory sometimes had to rescue my dress from the communal laundry before it was put over the head of a girl in one of the other two play groups. With Cory's vigilance, I kept my dress, but inevitably Michael lost the battle of the red bus. His toy did become communal, and was soon broken by somebody. Although I didn't know any other way of life, like Michael I resented the fact that I didn't have anything or anyone who was specially mine. I resented always having to do things with eight or nine other children.

Every morning, still in our pyjamas, we walked in a straggly single file down the corridor to the communal toilets, where I can vividly remember the babies in their potties shuffling across the floor, whilst we bigger children tried to muster more grown-up dignity as we crouched on child-sized toilets in one of the six cubicles which had no doors. We would attend the toilets in the morning and then following lunch and before going to bed. No one got up from their toilet until they had completed the allotted task. There was no privacy.

The bathroom was on the same floor, and when we had washed our faces and hands, we were allowed to walk back to our bedrooms on our own. There some of the children would wait on their beds to be dressed, but it was important to me that I dressed myself. This bid for independence was part of my desire to be an individual. I also realised, even then, that I needed to look after myself as no one really wanted or had the time to look after me.

There was, I am sure, another reason I showed my independence. After I dressed myself, it was very nice to hear Cory tell me that I was a very good girl, which she would say even though, often as not, I put my jumper on back to front or inside out.

Once dressed, we would congregate at the top of the big staircase and make our way down to breakfast. This is where, one morning when I was feeling down, I stopped being a good girl. I was feeling particularly bleak and unwanted. The baby of the moment had colic and had taken up a lot of Cory's time. To get some attention, at the top of the stairs I began to whimper and cry and stamp my feet.

As the other children watched, eyes wide and disbelieving, I began to indulge in a tantrum, screeching and kicking my heels. Patiently, Cory tried to quieten me. But I didn't respond to her overtures, and having her hands full with the baby and seven other little ones, she was at a loss to know what to do. The din I was making was ear-piercing.

The matron poked her head out of the door of her lounge

office down below. She was a slender woman with an air of elegance. Her clothes had the classic, sophisticated look that was more stockbroker-belt Esher than the neighbouring villages. Her sophistication was beyond the comprehension of us children but, as Cory told me years later, she admired Mrs Vernon. To us, however, she was an austere presence, someone we heard talking to officials on the telephone at the little desk at the bottom of the stairs, but with whom we had little personal contact. To me Mrs Vernon seemed ancient, though she was probably forty, give or take a few years. That day, the day of my first tantrum, I was making such a disturbance that Mrs Vernon took an interest. 'Stop it, Fatima,' she said firmly.

I continued to howl and stamp my feet, if anything even more insistently. The matron came out of her office. 'Stop it,' she said again, and then to Cory: 'Whatever are you doing to Fatima?'

Cory shrugged. 'I'm not doing anything to her, but I can't do anything with her this morning.' So Mrs Vernon had to take me in hand, literally.

I watched her come up all those stairs just to see what was troubling me. 'Don't be naughty, Fatima,' she said, and gave me a little cuddle. It was a perfunctory, professional cuddle, but a cuddle nonetheless. I reduced my decibel level, but I didn't stop crying entirely, and I continued to stamp my feet. Mrs Vernon gave me a quick little kiss on the forehead and took my hand. My tantrum had worked. It had got me what I wanted – some semblance of love and attention. This was it.

'I don't want any breakfast,' I said tearfully.

'But you do want a biscuit, don't you?' Mrs Vernon smiled reassuringly. 'Come along with me. I'll give you one.'

Walking down the stairs, taking my time because it was quite a big staircase, I felt quite pleased that all the other children were going on to breakfast and I was going to Mrs Vernon's special room.

There she gave me a biscuit and stood me by the fire where it was warm. She sat down in the big armchair, put me on her knee and gave me another cuddle. I began to feel a lot better. That room was so different from the rest of the house, which was colder, more impersonal and institutional. I munched my biscuit as slowly as possible.

The next day, or perhaps it was a few days later, I had another tantrum at the top of the stairs. Mrs Vernon peered out of her office, saw what the disturbance was, and came out to the bottom of the stairs. 'Come on, Fatima, down you come, I've got something here in my office for you,' she said. It was a kiss, as perfunctory as before, and another cuddle and a lovely sugary biscuit. As I felt the warmth of the fire on my legs and prepared to bite into that biscuit, a big smile appeared on my face. I had triumphed.

This new routine, which I liked rather more than many of the other routines at the home, now became almost daily. Cory and the rest of the children would be halfway down the stairs. Cory would say, 'Come on,' and I wouldn't because I was waiting for Matron to intervene.

That first tantrum was perceived as an act of rebellion. But it was something quite different, something more important than rebellion. It was my first act of self-assertion, my first clear-cut demand for what I craved almost as much as affection – recognition. Since I had no mum and was not special to someone, I had to be someone special.

Although I was often denied the softness of cuddles when

I wanted them, although I so often had to wait my turn, I had not grown used to it. And my illogical and instinctive tantrum was a declaration that I would not allow myself to become used to teaspoons of affection when I needed cupsful, that I would not accept emotional deprivation as my lot in life. Troublesome and annoying as tantrums might be, and naughty, they were the only way I had of saying that I knew who I was.

Even though I could sense I wasn't receiving the quality of affection the matron would have given a child of her own, even though I knew she was humouring me, I responded to this special attention. It made my mornings something to get up for. It helped me get through the day. As I bit into the last of my biscuit, Mrs Vernon would say, 'Run along.'

Back I would saunter to the group, spooning up my corn-flakes quickly and downing the glass of milk in big swallows so that I could play with the others for the half hour or so it took Cory to clear up the dishes and get the big ones off to school. Then, rain or shine, came the next item on our agenda, a two-mile trudge to the nearby village of Wormley Hill. The distance was arduous for us little ones, but I think now that it gave me a head start on sports training. The purpose of our little walk, however, was to give us some fresh air, to tire us out and get us out of Matron's way.

I would hold on to Cory's skirt as she pushed the pram with the baby in it, and all the other children trotted along as close to Cory as they could get.

There was a little wood we walked past and a park with swings. Then we would come to the village. I hated our arrival at the village because the villagers knew us, knew who we were. On the other hand I loved to go there because we would see other children with their parents, their mummies and daddies holding their hands. I would grip Cory's skirt tighter. She was all I had to hold on to.

During the two years I lived at Wormley Hill, I cannot remember having one visit, not even from a social worker. But Cory tells me I was from time to time taken out for the day by prospective foster parents. Evidently, the chunky little girl with the dark eyes and hair didn't charm any of them. I was always put back on the shelf.

I did not know I had been abandoned, although I had heard things that probably I shouldn't have. I only knew I did not have a mummy like other children. Cory knew little of the details of my past, only that, as one of the staff put it, as a baby I had been 'dumped'. I don't know what makes someone what they are, but I do know that even at that age I wanted something and there was a big gap in my life, something important missing. At four years old, I was desperate.

It is my belief that I was more desperate, that I felt the loss more acutely than the other children did. But none of us was very happy. We all felt bereft in one way or another. We didn't talk about it. We were too young. Only every now and then, one of us would start to cry. Soon all of us would be crying. Cory couldn't always jolly us out of it, but one of her more successful ploys was to sit us on the window ledge at the rear of the house, so we could look out into the garden and watch for cars along the small country road which ran alongside. That distracted us.

On other occasions, I would go to the front of the house and look out of the big window, hoping and hoping that I would see someone walking up to the front door and that whoever it was was coming to take me away from my lonely existence. I used to look out of that window almost every day. If any women came to the door, I would jump up and down crying, 'This lady is going to be my new mummy!'

'Oh no, she's not going to be a new mummy,' Cory would say protectively. 'She's not come here to take anyone away. She's come here to see Mrs Vernon.' Cory knew I would find that a little more acceptable than when people came to the door to take another child away.

Then, I would say to Cory, 'Will you be my mummy?' and she would give me a kiss and a cuddle.

If not for Cory, I doubt that I would have turned out as well as I have. At the time, she was the most important person in my life. I suppose Mr and Mrs Vernon were important too, though I don't so much as remember Mrs Vernon's face and have no visual memory at all of Mr Vernon. Cory showed me the first genuine kindness I ever knew. I'll always be grateful to her for it.

Sometimes, of course, she couldn't protect me from seeing other children going away for the weekend or for a holiday with their mummies or daddies. And many parents would come to visit their children at the home for a few hours. I couldn't understand why I didn't have a mummy and daddy, and if I did, where were they?

Michael, the boy with the red bus, had a mother who loved him but was unable to take care of him properly. She was ill, perhaps even mentally ill – it may even be that she abused him. I was too young to understand the nuances. But I remember clearly one of the days she visited him at the home. She cuddled him, and they were laughing and playing together. At the end of the visit she simply took him by the hand and walked out of the back door, and kept walking very quickly towards the road.

Somebody suddenly noticed. Then Cory and a few others began to run after them, calling out, 'Wait! Wait!'

But Michael and his mother kept going. They got to the fence and went out of the gate. Cory and the others were running towards them. They eventually caught them, and Michael like me had to stay at the home.

In the mornings, on the way back from the village, I often tried to climb into the pram. I said I was tired, but in truth I wanted to be babied. I remember one very cold, dreary morning when three or four of us piled into the pram. Cory put the baby on top, and pushed us all the whole way back. On our return, Mrs Vernon said her usual, 'Did you have a good walk in the fresh air and get plenty of exercise?'

'Yes, Mrs Vernon, very nice,' we answered more or less in unison, and had a little laugh to ourselves that we had tricked her.

The routine at Wormley Hill House was simple and fairly unvaried: the daily trips into the village, lunch, drawing pictures, trying to knit – I never learned how – outdoor play in the backyard, tea, bath and bedtime. When you have so many children to care for routine is, perhaps unwittingly, used not just to pass the time but to fill the emotional spaces in the children's lives. And while on the one hand routine can get you down – it used to affect me that way – on the other hand it was our security and a substitute for love. For everything.

After our morning constitutional I would be more than ready for lunch – frequently baked beans with sausages and mash. During the blackberry season Cory augmented our diet with berries she picked either from just beyond the fence near the home or, if there weren't any ripe ones left there, from the hedgerows during our daily walks. She would put them in little paper bags in the pram and the next morning there would be a sprinkling of blackberries to cheer up our cornflakes.

Thank goodness, though, that I was not a finicky eater. I was mostly eager to eat my meal, whatever it was. But if I wasn't I knew I had to eat up anyway. I learned that the hard way from Gloria, one of the other assistants. Unlike Cory, Gloria, who was a big, strong, young woman of about twenty, did not have a gentle nature. Gloria had charge of another group of children. She bossed them around, and when she could, she bossed us too.

CHAPTER FOUR

A Bad Impression

ONE LUNCHTIME I was not hungry and could not eat my meal.

'You are being naughty,' said Gloria threateningly. 'Eat up or I will see to it that you do.'

'I'm not being naughty. I'm not hungry.' I was crying. Perhaps I was being just a little naughty, but I had lost my appetite. I was too young to realise it consciously, but perhaps my stomach was telling me, instinctively, that the emptiness I felt that day couldn't be filled by food.

'Eat up,' Gloria said. 'Or I'll make you.'

'I'm not hungry,' I repeated in a whine, expecting another entreaty.

But coaxing wasn't in Gloria's nature. Force was. Suddenly she put her body weight against me and held my arms around the back of me. As I struggled, squirming to get away, she shoved the spoon at my moving head.

Then my nose was held and food was thrust down my throat. I coughed and spluttered and spat it out, but she kept on at me. It was a rough and untidy affair in the dining room in front of everybody. The other children kept on eating. She didn't get much food down me, but she made her point. I got a few spanks too.

I don't suppose it was anything to do with the food. What does a young child do when she feels completely and utterly empty yet at the same time brimming over with the knowledge that she has to do the same thing every day and it is never the one thing she wants to do, which is be with her mummy who loves her?

The next time I couldn't eat, Gloria took it upon herself to force-feed me again. Until I learned my lesson, I would cheer myself up by running down to the edge of the garden, where the wonderful birds were. The neighbours had a splendid aviary, which we were sometimes allowed to visit. That was a treat, and one of the few bright spots in my life. There were peacocks. The colours were gorgeous and bold. I felt more at home visiting the birds than walking into the village, and I was fascinated that there could be beautiful, colourful things like that in life.

I liked our drawing sessions too, although it certainly wasn't the colour that engrossed me. With a stub of crayon clenched in my hand, I would sit hunched thoughtfully over the long wooden table, staring at a large blank sheet of paper, deciding what to draw. The drawing paper we used was the reverse side of wallpaper. Rolls of it had been contributed to the home and Cory had cut it up into smaller sizes.

Before I started my picture, I would examine the pale blue of the playroom walls, on which the best pictures from the day before were still hanging. While trying to decide what to draw, something that would merit display, I would gaze out of the window at the pink and purple of the shrubs under the grey sky. Our playroom was a room with a view, but only rarely would I attempt to draw any part of this rural landscape. Instead, I would draw the other children and sometimes Cory or the park and the swings, and the baby in the pram. Cory used sticky tape to put the best pictures on the wall. It wasn't so much the drawing that I enjoyed, it was getting my picture chosen to go on the wall. That was nice. I would think proudly, 'That's mine.' It was important to me to be acknowledged as doing something good.

I was usually a good girl during drawing, but at other times I suppose you could say that I was a handful. There were many tantrums at the top of the stairs – or elsewhere. I seem to remember that sometimes I was so naughty that I was sent to the barn. I didn't like the barn at the best of times. Even when we played there on rainy afternoons, I would much rather have been outside. The worst of times was when I was banished there.

I remember one occasion in particular when I was in there for some severe breach of discipline – at that home there was a good deal of discipline to breach – and it must have been winter, because darkness fell early. The barn suddenly seemed to me perilously far from the house. Wormley Hill was at a leafy crossroads outside the village, in the country really, and at night there was no light anywhere. The barn seemed huge, and it was pitch dark. I was four going on five.

The direst part of the punishment was that the other children were together in the safety of the big house. I was sure that the bogeyman would get me, or ghosts would, or some creepy-crawly. The barn was too far away for me to hear what was going on in the house, but I imagined I could hear them playing, Cory holding Michael or the baby on her knee. They would be having a good time, feeling secure, whilst I was out in the wilderness hearing all these windy, whirly sounds and the trees whispering dangerously.

At last I was called in for the evening meal. Bath time, which was wonderful, followed. The baths were huge and old-fashioned, made of white porcelain, with feet. They were so deep it was hard to get in and out, and so big we bathed two at a time, two girls or two boys.

We children played games – the splashing water went everywhere – and Cory entered into the fun, as she always did. But she also made sure we washed our necks and behind our ears thoroughly.

I adored water. I also remember very clearly the rare warm, fine days of summer when most of the young ones were put into buckets of water outdoors and the older children would run around the back garden with the hose pipe spraying each other.

Bath time was only slightly more sedate. When we finished our turn in the bath, the child with whom I had shared the tub and I dried ourselves while the next two were bathing. And then off we went to bed, promptly at seven o'clock.

My bed was in the rear of the room, away from the door. I felt much more secure tucked away in a corner like that than in the middle of the room.

That night, after being in the barn, I wet the bed. I woke up wet and cold. I hated to wet the bed. I knew the rules. In the morning I would have to strip the bed and put the sheets in a pile. I hoped I wouldn't do it again the next night, because if I became a regular everyone would know.

The baby's cot was near the corner where my bed was. Often the baby would cry in the night. Cory slept in the staff quarters upstairs, so I used to get out of bed and climb into the cot to see if the baby was all right. If he had dropped his dummy, I retrieved it. I was now nearly five, one of the big ones with responsibilities.

But at bedtime I would often have a cry. Other children would be crying too. Of course, there were also times when we were too sleepy to cry, or when we would play games secretly, and have something approaching a good time.

The only other house I remember visiting during the entire time that I lived at Wormley Hill was Cory's parents' house, where from time to time Cory would take me for the day, or even for the weekend. Cory never took any of the other children. I loved to go.

After she helped me on with my coat, I would pull the striped mittens, which she had knitted for me from oddments of wool, out of the sleeves where they hung by a string, and put them on. Then we went out of the back door, and through the fence.

There was a little game of pretend I used to play as Cory and I walked to Wormley village together, just the two of us, and caught the bus to her town of Hoddesdon two villages away. I imagined that I was with my mummy and we were going back to our house.

It wasn't a long bus ride to Cory's town. When we got there, we would pop into the shops to pick up a few things for our meal. There were many young children out with their mummies, and, once, as I waited for Cory to make our purchases, I remember seeing a little girl a bit bigger than me, but not much, who had Cory's colour hair and whose mummy was just ahead of Cory in the queue. The girl made a face at me and I scowled at her, but I could tell she thought I was with my mummy just like she was.

On this occasion whatever we were buying took longer to get than we expected. We had to hurry along the busy high street to visit Cory's mother at work at Hayward's, the iron-monger's shop. Cory's mother, Elsie Muddle, was a thicker-set, ever-so-slightly taller version of Cory. I liked her instantly. And Mrs Muddle, an East Ender by birth, who stood not much above five foot nothing, transmitted huge signals of warmth across the hardware counter. But we couldn't stay long. There were customers waiting, and besides Cory and I had to hurry home to prepare the tea for the rest of the family when they got home.

'Come along,' said Cory, as I looked into shop windows, enthralled by the sights of Hoddesdon, which was a town, not just a village like Wormley. 'There's no time today for dawdling. Come along, Fats.'

'Fats' was short for Fatima. I wasn't fat, and didn't even realise the implications of my nickname. I don't think Cory did either. I hurried along after her, willing to please.

But as we passed the sweet shop with its tall glass jars of loose sweets gleaming in the window – sugary chocolate marbles, jellies (my favourite) and, somewhere inside, Maltesers – I stopped dead in my sandals.

'I want sweets,' I bleated.

'You don't want sweets just before your tea,' replied Cory.

'Sweets, I want sweets.'

'We have some at home.' Cory pulled me along. 'Fatima, you can have them after tea.'

'I *want* sweeeets,' I howled. I went into one of my obnox-ious stamping of feet routines. 'Sweeeets.'

Cory was embarrassed and annoyed. 'Stop it now, Fatima,' she said.

I continued to stamp my feet and shout. After all, this was the behaviour that usually elicited biscuits. Why not sweets? But instead, to my amazement, Cory smacked my legs. To this day I remember the sting, which was not great, and my surprise, which was gargantuan. I was so startled by the fact that she had smacked me that I immediately stopped being a nuisance. Cory had never even spanked me before. Nor do I remember her ever having to smack me again.

After tea, which was a hot meal and plenty of it, eaten round a table with her parents and two younger sisters, Ann and Leona, Cory, true to her promise, gave me a little bag of jellies. I clutched them in my fingers. I still like jellies. I remember sucking my sweets as I leaned against the brick wall in the lounge, then moving further away from the oil fire, surveying this house where Cory had lived since she was four years old. Sometime later, Cory painted her fingernails and mine shocking pink.

I wish I could remember more about Leo Muddle, Cory's dad, who had blue eyes like Cory's and hair almost as dark as mine. By trade he was a wire welder, who put the delicate finishing touches on umbrella and lampshade frames, but he was a hefty fellow who towered over all of us. I was playing in the lounge on the brightly patterned carpet when he came home, and I remember him picking me up, seemingly effortlessly, and sitting me on his lap. I liked it. He was strong. He smelled different from Cory and her mother, from all the grown-ups I knew. They were all women. This was the first time I had ever received any affection from a man. It felt good.

Cory's father believed strongly that something should be done to improve conditions at the children's home. A men's club he belonged to, called the Buffs, would raise money for the home, or take us on outings.

Cory could be very effective too. At one stage the prams which were used to convey the younger children on their morning safari became so dilapidated that she placed a notice in a shop in Hoddesdon, requesting that people who no longer needed such items donate them. Overwhelmed with replies, we received a number of what to us were luxury vehicles. But the best pram, much to Cory's annoyance, was given by Mrs Vernon to one of the other play groups.

Cory was getting attached to me, as I was to her. I kept saying I wanted her to be my mummy. I never resented other children, but I never really wanted her to give the other kids the love she gave to me, because then I would feel just like all the others. I wanted to be special. It was selfish to want Cory to myself, holding my hand, putting me on her lap, taking just me out. That couldn't be.

Cory left Wormley after nine or ten months there, six months before I did. It was Cory's parents who persuaded her to leave the home, as they felt that she was not having the opportunity to lead a teenager's life. I often think that her parents may have sensed that during the time she was at Wormley Hill House she was becoming too attached to a little girl called Fatima, who constantly pleaded with her to become her mummy.

A few months after Cory had left the home to work elsewhere, her father's club the Buffs arranged a special trip to the zoo for the children at the home. Cory came along to help. It is easy to forget faces at that age, and someone else was doing Cory's job of looking after us, but almost as soon as she walked in the door, I ran up to her and grabbed her skirt, saying, 'You are my new mummy. I want you to be my mummy.' She was very good to me, but she made it clear that it wasn't to be.

Cory went on to become a nanny. Later, she and her husband emigrated to New Zealand, where her two sons were born. Now a grandmother, Cory's back in Hertfordshire. She taught fitness classes for thirty years, and works in the family coffee business. It was Cory who rediscovered *me* eighteen years after she left Wormley. Watching the Helsinki World Athletics Championships on television in the summer of 1983, she saw me win a silver medal and weep in my mother's arms. When, to her amazement, the name Fatima Whitbread flashed on the screen, she said to her husband, 'Could that be my Fatima?'

They both thought it unlikely, as Cory's Fatima didn't have a mother. But later a neighbour told Cory she had read that Fatima Whitbread grew up in a children's home.

'But was she dumped?' Cory asked.

The neighbour found the article, which confirmed I had been abandoned. Cory wrote to me, asking if I was 'the naughty little girl' she used to care for. When I replied excitedly that I was, she sent me some wonderful snapshots from those bad old days.

We met in the flesh the following year when, in the run-up to the Los Angeles Olympics, there was a television documentary about my life. Much of the programme was of me in a chauffeured limousine en route to Buckingham Palace, where I was to collect the Sybil Abrahams trophy as top achiever of the year in international events. It was the first of many times I was to win that award, one that I value highly, and it was my first visit to the palace, but I can assure you, I was just as thrilled at seeing my Cory, who is now Cory Boswell.

Seeing her was a very emotional experience. She said I was her favourite, which I knew. I grinned when I heard her say, 'Fatima was a tough little girl, very strong and very strong-willed.' Cory and I are still in touch.

One evening, just before bedtime at Wormley, I was told by Mrs Vernon that I had to be packed and ready at nine o'clock the next morning when my social worker was coming to take me to join my brother and sister in a new home. I was five years old. I had not been aware until then that I had a brother or a sister. Years later, I found out that the brother in question, Adem, who was three years older than me, was even a member of my group at Wormley for about two weeks. Cory remembers him as a troubled little boy with a chip on his shoulder. Because of 'a lesson' someone had taught him, perhaps painfully, he wouldn't call her by name, but insisted on calling her Nurse. At the time, since he wasn't staying on, the social services had felt it unwise to inform us of each other's identities. Suddenly, there seemed to have been a change in policy.

That night I could hardly sleep. Whenever I dozed I would wake up abruptly, thinking it's my last night here, I'm leaving. I didn't want to go. It was not because there was any particular child whom I would miss. We were and we weren't friends. Most of us were so troubled that we lived in our own little worlds. Besides, you never knew which of them would be gone the next day. Many of the children were transients. Some would go home to their parents occasionally or they might be fostered. They passed through. After two years there, at the age of five, I was one of the veterans. What I sensed that I was going to miss far more than the people was the feeling of familiarity and the security of Wormley Hill House.

Although it was an impersonal, creaky old house and I wasn't all that happy there, it was still the only home I could remember living in, and everyone I knew well in the world lived there. During the night, I dreamed that a scary figure in a dark cloak was walking up and down the corridor, clanging a bell and looking for me. I wet my bed.

The next morning, I stripped the sheets and blankets and placed them dutifully at the foot of the bed. I hoped that I wouldn't wet the strange new bed I would be sleeping in that night. It would make a bad first impression. As I marched with the other children in single file to the bathroom, I thought, 'This is the last time.' On the way down the stairs to breakfast, I didn't bother to make the usual fuss – stamping my feet on the floor and screeching for attention from Mrs Vernon was now a waste of time. I was leaving.

CHAPTER FIVE

Moved On

NO ONE SEEMED to notice me stirring my corn-flakes round and round in the chipped bowl instead of eating them. No one seemed to care that my stomach was in a painful knot of confusion. As quickly as possible, I left the table and was ready, as I had been told to be, by nine o'clock, standing in the reception corner of the front hall. No one had arrived to see me. I sat down on the bottom step of the staircase and, craning my head up to see the ceiling on the third-floor landing, I waited.

I had on the yellow dress Cory's mother had made me. The other personal items that I had acquired – an almost matching cardigan which came from the communal wardrobe, my toothbrush, a change of underwear and another dress from the communal pile – were in the brown paper bag beside me.

I waited and waited. Of necessity I was a patient five-year-old. I could hear all the other children playing in an adjoining room. Soon they would be departing for the morning promenade to the village. I wished I was going with them. Today there was no need for coats or to search for mittens in your sleeves. My cardie seemed an unnecessary appendage, but I had been told to take it.

It was the hot, dry summer of 1966. A summer for the record books. Not just fair, not just fine, but radiantly sunny. Sitting in the foyer was almost sinful on a day like that.

An hour that seemed like 20,000 decades passed. I felt lonely. No one came to see if I was all right. If I was leaving, I wanted to leave, and if I was staying, I wanted to be playing with the others.

The clock struck ten. Well after that the doorbell rang. Mrs Vernon brushed past me to open the front door, and I heard the social worker tell Mrs Vernon she was sorry to be late but it couldn't be helped. 'We were delayed.'

I was told that this bland, pleasant woman was the social worker who had brought me to Wormley. With her was a dark-haired woman with a gold front tooth and cloying perfume. I could smell the scent she was wearing even before she entered the house. None of the women at the home wore scent. I had never seen the woman with the gold front tooth before. I didn't like the look of her.

'Fatima,' the social worker said cheerily, 'this is your mother. She is coming with us to help you meet your brother and sister.'

The woman didn't pick me up. She didn't hug me. She didn't smile or show any affection. She was not what I had been waiting for all these years.

'She is not my mummy,' I announced with certainty. 'I don't have a mummy or daddy.'

As we walked to the car I stuck close to the social worker, taking her hand. Mrs Vernon said goodbye matter-of-factly, as if we were going on a trip to the park. I said goodbye back. I wasn't up to a tantrum. I may have looked as blank as I felt. Squeezing my hand, the social worker said, 'It will be an easy journey.' She put me in the front seat beside her. She put that woman in the back.

The journey was long and painful. The social worker kept telling me that I would enjoy myself in the countryside in Essex and to look out the window at the trees and animals as we drove along. There was no real conversation in the car. At one point the woman who they said was my mother spoke in broken English with a strong foreign accent. All these years I had wanted a mummy, but the one I wanted wasn't her. I didn't recognise her. I felt no relation to her. Nor did she seem to feel anything for me. I was crying a little.

As the car sped along, I continued to look out of the window, where the cows and horses and the fields kept vanishing. After a time, the social worker said cheerfully, 'We're almost there.' Out of the window there were flat streets crammed with small houses, each very like the other. It was a new town, like Harlow which was quite near, with a spillover of East Enders.

'It's just here somewhere,' the social worker said, driving slowly. 'Your brother and sister will be waiting for you, Fatima.'

The woman in the back said, 'I want to see them.'

The social worker turned into a street of large semis and parked the car. Pulling me past the modest front garden towards the front door, she said, in a voice that I found unconvincing, 'You're really going to enjoy being here.'

As she rang the doorbell, I stood hiding behind her, paper bag in hand, on the side furthest from the woman they said was my mother. The door was opened by the matron, an elderly lady who looked strict, and we were ushered in.

The social worker and the woman with the gold tooth

were led into the garden 'where Adem and Aliya are, your brother and sister'.

I was left alone in the hallway, wondering if I really had a brother and sister and what they might be like. I feared that further shocks might await me – a very numbed and frightened five-year-old girl – at this house, where I was to spend the next eight years of my life. During a period of less than twenty-four hours, I had been told that I was moving away from the only people and the only place I knew to a new home, and that I had a brother and a sister.

In addition, I'd been confronted with a mother who couldn't possibly be mine. She didn't look like a mother, and certainly not the one I imagined to be mine.

My whole upbringing had been that of a British girl. The songs and nursery rhymes we were taught by the assistants were traditional. The staples of our diet were sausage and mash or baked beans. The biscuit we were most frequently given as a treat was a digestive. I knew about the flag and the Queen. And the people I saw in the village and who reared me tended to have mouse-coloured hair like Cory's and snub noses. They certainly didn't wear blobs of garish lipstick or have gold teeth.

It had never occurred to me that my background was anything but British. I felt British through and through. So this foreign woman couldn't possibly be my mother. In retrospect, I think that I would have reacted very negatively to my mother whoever she was. I must have been deeply angry at having been left in a children's home. What I had been asking for was a *new* mummy, not one who hadn't wanted me in the first place.

But I doubt that I understood any of that as I stood alone

in the hallway of what was going to be my new home. The hallway was tiny compared to the one in the house I came from. This whole house was small. Compared to Wormley, it was mingy. I didn't like the look of the place. Not only that: the house appeared to be empty of children.

Returning from the garden, the stern, unsmiling matron began to settle me in, taking me first to the bedroom where I would be sleeping from now on. There were five metal beds in the room, and a small locker next to each bed. This was the girls' room. The boys' room, which was almost identical, had one bed less and was across the hall. I was given the bed under the window, which I didn't like. It was too easy for the wild, scary things in the night to get to you. They could climb in the window and you would be right there, defenceless.

The bathroom, which was further along the hallway, was much smaller than the one at Wormley Hill. Each child's toothbrush was in a plastic beaker, which had the child's name taped to it. There was a piece of plaster with my name on it and the matron attached it to a spare beaker. There were nine of them there, lined up in a row. On the way down the stairs, which weren't particularly steep or long or special, the matron gave me a little lecture about the queue for the bathroom in the mornings. It was in strict order of age. 'You must not rush to the front of the queue.' Her pinched voice confirmed my suspicion that she would be a stickler for rules, 'and always wait your turn.'

Another thing I was not to do was to enter the lounge without her permission; none of the children could. And under no circumstances could anyone except herself switch on the television. This latter bit of information was actually promising. The only TV at Wormley had been in the Vernons' flat. We children hadn't had access to it at all.

Through the open French windows of the dining room, I could see the social worker sitting in the sun. There were six or eight children out there, playing in the garden. And the woman they said was my mother was talking to two of them, a skinny, dark-haired little girl who wore spectacles and a boy who was stocky but had the same dark hair. The woman was cuddling the girl.

The matron led me over to meet my supposed sister and brother. As we approached, the girl took off her spectacles and I could hear the three of them talking in a language I did not understand.

'This is Aliya,' the matron said, indicating the girl who was blinking a little and holding her spectacles by their pink plastic frames. 'And this is Adem.' The boy glowered at me fiercely, as if to say I don't care who you are. I gave him the same unfriendly look. He was bigger and older than his sister and bigger than me. 'And this is your sister Fatima. Say, "Hello."'

We said, 'Hello.' I felt no affinity towards them, and no doubt they felt likewise.

My supposed mother told us in broken English that she loved us all and that as soon as she had enough money she would take us home to join our other brother and sister. Now it seemed I also had another brother and sister who lived in north London.

In later years I was told that Adem, who was three years older than me, and Aliya, who was eighteen months younger, were fathered by one man, that another man, one from the Greek Cypriot community, planted the seed that led to me, and that a third man fathered the two younger children, Emmie and Metin. The woman's hostility to me stemmed from the fact that my 'father's' people came from the wrong side of the island.

The social worker, whom I had found to be quite a nice person, now said that they had to be going, and that she was certain that I would be happy here. The woman they said was my mother gave Adem and Aliya each a kiss and said, 'Mum loves you.' Then she gave me a smile – the gold tooth showed – and walked off.

I wanted to hold the social worker's hand and go back with her. As for the supposed mother, well, she could go to hell. I went up to my room and had a cry.

I had always thought that when I left Wormley it would be to go and live with my new mummy and daddy in their house. It was a terrible blow to find myself at another children's home. I felt bewildered and frightened. I had to learn new house rules and make new friends. I had to start all over again. When I look back upon this period, I am convinced that the social services could have handled the situation differently.

The next morning, I found that toothpaste had been applied in a neat, thin line to each toothbrush to ensure that we all used just enough and not too much. My happiest moment was when I realised I had not wet the bed the first night.

Routine was even stricter here than at Wormley. There were fewer than half as many children, but there was less than a quarter of the space. We were packed together like pilchards in a tin. Making friction even greater was the fact that our age range was considerably larger, from a baby in a cot to, on occasion, teenagers of fourteen or fifteen. The room known as the girls' bedroom was the bigger of the two children's bedrooms, but whenever there were more boys than girls living in the house, we switched rooms.

Matron seemed to like us children best when we were out of sight and earshot. She was nearing retirement age. It may be that we were getting to be too much for her. She could not tolerate us playing in the house; we were too noisy. This was fine on dry days when we played in the garden, where there was a swing. I loved swinging.

There were fruit trees too, tantalisingly near our garden, which we were strictly forbidden to climb. But as soon as the first apples were ripe for picking, I and a couple of the others shinnied up the tree and helped ourselves. I liked climbing trees and the trophy was delicious. I wasn't caught that time, but I was the next.

The punishment for such an offence was to sit for bum-aching hours on the back porch. Matron was a keen disciplinarian. I sat and sat, bored and indignant, until long after dark, when I became frightened too. When she was ready to go to bed, Matron opened the door and let me come in. I hated the punishment but that summer I was always being caught up the tree, helping myself to the apples. Like the other kids, I was hungry.

When the weather was cold or wet, we were sent to play in the garage, which was big enough for two cars, and had not been converted in any way. Unheated, with floor and walls of concrete and large wooden doors, it made a cold, cramped, uncomfortable playroom. We put together our jigsaw puzzles, which never had all the pieces, on the dirty floor, where some hand-me-down toys and Lego were also strewn.

The younger children would often cry because of the cold and I took it upon myself to go as a deputation of one to the matron to ask if we might come indoors. I suppose I must have made it a demand rather than a request. Diplomacy was not my strong point.

'Stay there until you're called,' she said. 'I want some peace and quiet. No noise.'

When we were finally allowed into the house and had washed our hands and faces, a tea of jam sandwiches was presented and wolfed down. I enjoyed it at first, but after a while I became quite tired of jam sandwiches.

Bedtime was never later than 6 p.m., and no talking was allowed once we were in bed. But children being children there were pillow fights and obviously a lot of giggling and screeching. Within a matter of weeks, the matron, being no fool, began to shout from the bottom of the stairs, 'Fatima, you are the ringleader. Come down here!' Then I would be banished to the porch, in my pyjamas, until she decided to go to bed. As I was still petrified of the dark, this was torture. If I was lucky, I might be exiled only to the stairs inside the house, where the dangers were lesser. But these stairs were covered in a plastic material which had ridges in it and left a set of impressions on my backside.

The punishment was alternately scary and excruciatingly boring. And usually I was ravenous. Each evening before bed we were allowed two biscuits, one plain and one chocolate digestive. The matron kept count of the biscuits. We could also have a glass of watered-down, warm milk. Even though it was in addition to tea, this wasn't enough for me. I was always hungry in that house.

Matron kept all the biscuits in one big tin, which it was often my chore to take back to the kitchen and refill. One day I noticed that she kept count only of the chocolate ones in the tin. I sneaked three from the package into the bottom of the tin, where I placed them with the digestive side up. When she made her count, Matron didn't notice.

The next time I was exiled to the porch, I felt exhilarated, even though it was cold and dark and I didn't like it out there. I had a plan. I waited a good long while, fifteen minutes, perhaps half an hour, until I saw the gleam of the television on in the lounge. Matron was watching her programmes.

Stealthily, I opened the back door and crept into the kitchen. To the left of the door was the cupboard where the biscuit tin was kept. I undid the lid, rescued the chocolate biscuits from the bottom and returned to the back doorstep, where I sat happily munching away.

This became a habit. I was always being naughty. I wanted to do what I wanted to do. But I wasn't nasty.

Adem was. He and Aliya stuck close to one another and spoke to each other in that funny language. Occasionally, Adem would try to push me around. He tried to lock me in the tiny cloakroom under the stairs where there was no light. Some of the children thought it was funny to push each other in and shut the door from outside, but for me it was terrifying because of my fear of the dark. I fought him off.

'You're not our sister, our mother doesn't love you,' he would say. He was trying to bully me, but I wouldn't be pushed around. I would stand up to him. But what he said about her not loving me was quite obvious to me from the occasions when she turned up to take them home for the weekend. Even to Aliya, who was her favourite, the woman's arrival was a mixed blessing, because she would make the girl remove her spectacles and Aliya couldn't see a thing without them. The woman thought they made her look ugly.

I continued to have nightmares, triggered no doubt by some noise in the corridor in the night, but also a reflection of my inner fear. There was one nightmare that recurred over and over, which I kept on having occasionally until about ten years ago. A frightening person in a cloak was ringing a bell, and when he or she – probably he but it wasn't certain – finished, he was going to come after me. The bell was attached to a long chain, which he rang and rang. The chain was like the one that was used to flush our old-fashioned toilets.

I would wake up terrified, thinking strange creatures, ghosts, all the usual bogies of childhood, were coming to get me. I remember hiding under the bedclothes waiting for morning, often imagining that there were dangerous Red Indians hiding in the hallway, preparing to send their powerful arrows soaring through the corridor at me. I had not yet heard of a javelin.

Sometimes I did wet the bed. Bedwetters were made to feel dirty and disgusting. It was even worse here than at Wormley. You had to strip the bedclothes, of course, and the following night you were made to sit on the end of your bed until the matron was ready to retire and could send you for a final visit to the toilet. You weren't supposed to go to sleep before this, in case you had an accident. If you were a regular, you had to do that every night.

Some of the really young children couldn't stay awake in those circumstances. So what I used to do was stay awake for them, because the matron used to be very bad-tempered with them and smack their legs if they fell asleep before she said they could. I would talk to the 'culprit', whispering, because if I was heard I would be summoned downstairs. When the child fell asleep, I would try to stay half awake, so that when I heard Matron turn the television and the light off, I could wake the little girl up and tell her to sit up because 'Auntie', as we used to call the matron, was coming up. Even so, the poor little thing would be half asleep when Matron entered. She would then be shaken awake and made to go to the toilet.

The woman they said was my mother visited me before Christmas and brought me a bag of Liquorice Allsorts, which Matron immediately took out of my hand, saying they had to be kept for the proper time. Leaving the Liquorice Allsorts with Matron, who said she would return them to me at Christmas, the woman took Aliya and Adem home with her for the holiday. I never saw those sweets again.

It was my first Christmas at the home. As was the policy, we each received one present. I can't remember what I got, but I can remember a Christmas tree with lights. Among the decorations hanging on the tree were chocolates wrapped in foil, and whenever no one was looking, I would reach up on tiptoe ... but I could not quite reach high enough to pull any off. Anyway, I didn't think it would go down very well.

That same Christmas there was a bowl of fruit on the window ledge. Hungry though I was, I knew better than to eat the fruit. Matron would have been angry. But I used to touch the fruit, tempted. One evening, my finger went through the skin of an orange. It needed eating. I sucked out as much juice as I possibly could, and replaced the orange in the dish, with its puncture wound facing the window. When this crime was discovered and no one owned up immediately, we were all sent to bed. It was hours before bedtime so I decided to confess.

'You're a very naughty, naughty girl,' said Matron. 'Go and sit on the porch. The other children will stay where they are for the entire evening.' Confessing didn't help the others, it just gave Matron an excuse for more TV-watching time.

After the holiday, Aliya returned, but Adem was sent to another home.

I started at the nearby primary school during my first year at the home and I joined the local Brownie pack. School was a mixed blessing. My teacher at the infants school would sometimes sit me on her lap when she was reading a story to the class. I liked that. But seeing the other children's mummies and daddies giving them a morning kiss and cuddle before they went into school often upset me. It made me feel that I was different. On special occasions like open days and plays, when parents came to school, I felt very much an outsider.

Although there must have been many children whose parents did not deign to come to the school, or who could not come because they were working or ill, it never occurred to me that there were other children in much the same warped and leaky boat as I was. Even though I felt that the mother they had brought me when I was leaving Wormley was a nightmare instead of a dream come true, I don't think I ever realised that some of the girls and boys who lived at home with their parents might be maltreated too.

Although I still wanted a mummy, I was no longer sure I would ever have one. I had learned to survive without a mummy, but I still felt a yearning for one. And certainly after waiting for so long, I wasn't going to accept the imposter.

The Brownie pack had no drawbacks at all. Brown Owl, whose daughter was in our pack, worked in a children's home herself – it was just around the corner from where I lived – so she understood my problems of adjustment and quietly made allowances. In the area there was a cluster of children's homes full of children from London councils. If only I had been sent to Brown Owl's.

Now that I think of it, Brown Owl was stocky like the woman they said was my mother, though as a child I never took any notice, and some of my playmates had even darker skin. Obviously, it wasn't my so-called mother's size or ethnicity that I found grotesque, nor even her gold tooth – it was her complete lack of feeling for me.

Going to school and the weekly Brownie meeting were the only occasions when I was allowed outside the home, except very rarely when we went as a group to the park.

One cool, damp Saturday morning, as I lay sprawled on the filthy, concrete floor of the garage, piecing together a jigsaw puzzle with a few of the others, I got increasingly restless. Several pieces of the puzzle were missing, which added to my sense of wishing I were somewhere else.

Some of the children were arguing over who should ride the scooter in that cramped space. A few others were trying to draw pictures with their gnawed bits of crayon. It was fairly cold in there, and very boring. I threw a piece of the puzzle across the garage. It didn't go far, but further than I had expected it to. I threw another piece. Then another. A few of the others joined in. We threw the whole puzzle across the garage. What a mess. Some of the children, who were drawing, folded their paper into aeroplanes, and threw them too. I picked up one of the planes and threw it as hard as I could across the garage.

Soon we were all shouting, throwing planes and bits of puzzle and dolls. Hoops. Crayons. Whatever was at hand. It was the most fun I had had yet in the garage. Better than a pillow fight. And there was no come-uppance either. We got away scot-free.

The only better memory I have of the garage was the time I sneaked out. I was bored with chucking pieces of puzzle, I guess. Before I quite realised what I was doing, and without a word to anyone, I strolled casually over to the door, and slipped out. Keeping well down so that Matron couldn't see me, I climbed over the neighbours' wall, and hid in the shadow of the four trees till I was out of Matron's line of vision. Then I walked jauntily up the road into the park, which was quite near. It was magic. You could run and run and run without coming up against a garden wall.

I was excited to be out on my own for once, and eager to see what was going on. A group of boys, who weren't from the home and who were a little older than me, were playing on a tyre swing. The tyre was tied by a rope to the limb of one of the biggest trees in the park, and they were swinging from side to side and backwards and forwards like Tarzan. When someone gave you a good hard push, you swung towards another big tree, which you could touch with your feet.

'I want a go,' I said.

The boys told me I was too small. When I persisted, they ignored me. They knew I was one of the children from the home. One of them was big and noisy but most of them were not that much bigger than me.

'I want to have a go,' I repeated.

No notice was taken.

'Want a go, want a go, want a go!' I chanted over and over, and ran very close to where the swing was.

'Get out of the way,' the older boy said. 'You're too little. You'll get hurt.'

I wouldn't give up. I did a variation on my tantrum routine, not exactly stamping my feet, but staying underfoot. If I couldn't swing, they couldn't.

'Right,' the older one said at last. 'Have a go then. Straight away.'

I hadn't actually expected him to give in. I was a little scared.

'Straight away,' he said. 'I dare you.'

I sat down in the tyre, my legs barely touching the ground. 'Hold tight,' the boy said, and pushed me. I got a good lift and was just beginning to enjoy myself when the other tree loomed. I forgot to put out my feet – maybe I *was* too young – and crashed, right shoulder first, smack into the middle of the tree. I fell to the ground.

My pride was bruised, as were my arm and shoulder, but nothing was dislocated or broken. I didn't cry much – the boys were watching. I was trying to be brave. As soon as the boys realised nothing dire was wrong with me, they went on playing, and I ran along home.

My arm and shoulder ached for days, but I didn't dare tell anyone. At bath times I hid the few scratches and the big bruise. I knew better than to try to get any sympathy. I had to keep it a secret. If I said anything to anyone, Matron would hear of it, and I would be punished for leaving the garage.

It was not my very first sports injury. I had fallen before when running in the back garden. But this one was my first lingering injury. Over the years, there would be all too many more.

My immediate concern, however, was the changing of the guard at the home. Matron was retiring. Taking her place would be Mrs Smith, a young married woman, who was due to arrive with her husband.

CHAPTER SIX

Regime Change

THE NEW MATRON introduced cod-liver oil. Everyone had to swallow a teaspoonful each morning before leaving for school. Marmite on our breakfast toast was another unpopular innovation. But there were no complaints at all about the new swing, which was put up in the garden. I wasn't the only one who loved to play on the swings. The new climbing frame was a hit too, and we got bicycles. Some old bicycles were given to the home and some were bought second-hand. There were even some more second-hand scooters for the younger children. We were not banished to the garage anymore to play either.

It was not at all difficult to oblige Mrs Smith when she said we must call her Auntie Brenda. She also asked us to call her husband Uncle Alan. Although he had a job during the day, we were to regard both of them as our house parents. For the first time in ages, I was happy. I should have known it couldn't last.

At first, Auntie Brenda, a fairly hefty woman who wore her hair pulled back in a ponytail, was always flashing her oddly crooked smile at us. There was something the matter with the lower part of her face, which was slightly twisted, as though she had suffered a stroke. She must have been about thirty, as was Uncle Alan, who was skinnier. A real string bean who wore thick, horn-rimmed glasses, he combed his black hair over his forehead.

At about the time the Smiths arrived, we also got a white Commer van, which would hold about ten of us. Uncle Alan painted it a ghastly green colour, making the van instantly recognisable. Everyone who saw it would say, 'Here come those children from the home.' I was embarrassed whenever I had to ride in it.

This was one misery Uncle Alan caused us inadvertently. Most of the others increasingly seemed to be intentional. Indeed, our honeymoon with the new house parents was over quickly. As I remember it, as soon as Uncle and Auntie had settled in, and were no longer being scrutinised by the social services, their dispositions deteriorated rapidly.

Uncle Alan would regularly line us up in the dining room, march up and down in front of us and give a thorough lecture as to our faults. He would terrify the little ones. He didn't beat them but when he played ball with the children in the back garden, he threw the ball too hard, sometimes narrowly missing them and frightening them. When he wanted to make a point, he stood close to you, putting his nose right up to your face. He did it to some of the staff as well as the children.

One evening, almost as soon as he got home from work – he was a laboratory assistant – he lined us up, marched grumpily back and forth, and said that Auntie Brenda had told him that we had been noisy on our return from school, which had given her a headache. As a punishment, we were being sent to bed early. This was unfair. We had been no noisier than usual, and it was something entirely different, something not our fault, which had caused or contributed to her headache. I immediately said so.

Drowning out my protest, Uncle Alan said that I could not go out for a week after school hours as I had answered back.

What had put Auntie Brenda in a foul mood and then given her a headache was a little contretemps she had had with her staff and me about one of her many sins of omission, her two chief ones being that she didn't give us any affection and she didn't give us enough food to eat. It was the latter point that had caused the flare-up that morning. Tired of being hungry and beans, beans, beans, I had complained, only to find that the staff supported me. One of the assistant housemothers, Mrs Peat, a forthright cockney who often spoke her mind, supported by Edna the cleaner, gave Mrs Smith what for, complaining that the food they gave to us children was atrocious and that there was simply not enough of it to fill us up.

Mrs Smith got a headache, but instead of one tin of beans between seven children that day we had two tins of beans between seven. Imagine if we had had a full house of nine or ten.

Nor was this an isolated incident. Mrs Peat, whose job was similar to Cory's, worked at the home thirty hours a week. She and the other thirty-hour ladies often had to purchase food from the shops across the street, using their own money, because there wasn't enough food in the house to make a meal. Eventually, they would usually get reimbursed, but the money was less an issue than the lack of food, as far as Mrs Peat was concerned. She not only regularly risked her job to defend us children, she showed us consideration and love. Without Mrs Peat, whom I soon grew close to, it would have been much harder for me to survive. But I'll get to that.

My best friend Alma Riley, whom I had met at school, lived in the children's home around the corner. They always had enough to eat and appeared to be better dressed than we were. That home was entirely different from ours. Alma was happy there. And the house parents would always be kind to me when I called. I was often given a drink and some biscuits.

Alma and I did everything together. We were both in the Brownies and liked sport. I was stronger, but Alma was a faster runner than me, a real sprinter. She had lived in a children's home since her mother died when she was two, and was my friend from the time I started junior school, aged seven. I felt that Alma, who was nine or ten months younger than me, was more my sister than Aliya was. Alma was black. At school there were not many black children, but there was a lot of racial prejudice. As Alma reminded me when we were grown up, if other children taunted her with ugly names, I would take it upon myself to beat them up.

My other best friend, Wendy, who was full of fun and cheeky in the nicest possible way, was white and lived in a normal home. Her mum treated me like one of her own, giving me toast and marmalade and even coffee in the morning when I called in on the way to school, and if I wanted something – and I usually did – in the afternoon too. I was always very hungry, partly because I was always expending energy – running across the school playground, or illicitly climbing trees – and partly because we were just not fed enough at the home.

Occasionally, I would go to Wendy's after school to watch *Jackanory* on television – and have after-school tea and biscuits and sometimes even sandwiches. If I hadn't, I sometimes felt, I would have starved. It seemed to me that everyone except the children at our home had plenty to eat and adults who were kind to look after them. But we had to put up with 'Hitler', which is what we privately called Uncle Alan. And Mrs Smith, to whom we referred as 'Her'.

Even when I was still very young, Uncle and Auntie found me to be among their less tractable charges. They were not overly fond of me. To tell the truth, I don't think they really liked any of us children very much.

They certainly made sure we were not over-privileged. When it came time for the Brownies to go camping, Brown Owl had to have a special word with Mrs Smith to get permission for me to go. The Brownie leader even supplied the two blankets and sheet for my sleeping bag. I will never forget the week we girls had, following trails in the woods, singing around the campfire at night and sleeping under the stars. There wasn't a single day of rain. And there were none of the complications of my twenty-one days in the jungle for *I'm a Celebrity ... Get Me Out of Here!*

One Saturday morning, Mrs Smith told me that the woman they called my mother, and whom I thought of as 'that old cow', was coming later that day to take Aliya and me to London to stay with her for the weekend.

I didn't want to go, and said so. But Mrs Smith insisted I had to go, and confined me to quarters, that is, to the girls' bedroom, to wait. The other girls were playing outdoors. I slumped on my bed, feeling desperately upset.

Aliya poked her head into the room. 'You're not my real sister,' she said. 'My mum doesn't love you.'

'I hate you,' I shouted. 'I hate that fat old cow. I hate all of you.'

'My mum doesn't want you. My mum doesn't want you.' She took great delight in taunting me in this way. In fact, I was the only one Aliya ever caused any aggro.

She lived with the woman on and off. I never did. No one in the home or at school who hadn't been told would have thought we were related, let alone half-sisters. There was no bond, no friendliness, no closeness. We didn't even look alike, and our personalities were completely different. Aliya didn't run and play like me, so she didn't have my sturdy build. Although I was only eight or nine, I already had reasonable muscles. She was listless and quiet, and she usually did what the Smiths told her. She wasn't a fighter like me. Maybe she didn't need to be. Her attitude was that she had a family. Mine was that I didn't.

After our little shouting match, I slunk downstairs and pleaded with Mrs Smith not to send me away with that woman. 'It is clear they don't want me,' I said tearfully. 'And I don't want to be with them.' Mrs Smith did not attempt to comfort me. Instead, she seemed pleased that I was going to be away for the weekend, and hurried me off back to the bedroom, where I vented my anger and frustration by muttering 'fat old cow' over and over.

The woman they said was my mother was not that outlandishly fat, but I had to have some name for her. I wouldn't dare call the woman that to her face. In fact, I didn't call her anything. Certainly not 'Mother'.

She eventually arrived, late, as usual. I was now resigned

to going. It could even, I told myself, be interesting. There were new things to see. There would probably be more than enough to eat. And maybe, maybe, it would be all right. Aliya and I walked down the road from the home with the woman. Aliya was told to take off her glasses and put them in her bag. The woman then took Aliya's hand and talked to her in their language.

I was walking alongside Aliya, and when we reached the crossroads to turn right for the bus, the woman stopped and told me to go back. She said she didn't want me. Then, she took half a crown out of her purse and gave it to me. At first, I thought she must be joking, and that as I started to walk back towards the home, she would call out to me. But she didn't. It was no joke. I wondered why she had changed her mind. I hadn't been naughty. I hadn't had time to be. Although originally I had not wanted to go with her, I now felt completely empty.

By the time I reached the home, not only did I feel alone in the world but also ashamed and embarrassed that I had to tell Mrs Smith the woman didn't want me. When I opened the back door, Mrs Smith was shouting at one of the younger children. She stopped to ask me if I had forgotten something. Between sobs, I blurted out what had happened. I was crying out to be comforted. Mrs Smith showed no feelings and offered me no comfort. All she said was, 'Well, you didn't want to go anyway.'

Feeling totally rejected by everyone, I went to the girls' bedroom, where I sat staring at the walls. My hatred for the old cow was now complete. I was determined never to call her my mum.

In retrospect, it is still hard to follow her reasoning that day. I can only imagine that she had never wanted or intended to take me for the weekend, but that the social worker had insisted. It was easier for her to tell me 'no' than to tell someone in authority. So, the woman simply waited until no one connected with the social services was about, and then she sent me back. She gave me the half a crown to sweeten the blow. She knew it was a blow.

After that episode, I began to withdraw even more into myself and started to build a wall around me. Outwardly, I became much more aggressive and tougher. I gave Mrs Smith plenty of reason to wish I would disappear for the weekend. I kept asking myself what I had done to deserve what was happening to me. I felt in turmoil, and became obsessed with the fact that no one wanted me. There didn't seem to be any hope.

I was old enough by now to realise that all of us were disadvantaged children. But I asked myself why the two people we called Auntie and Uncle seemed to have no feelings for us. Mrs Smith had not comforted me during my hours of need. Nor did I feel she offered understanding or sympathy to any of us. But when a social worker visited the home, Mrs Smith would sit one of the young children on her knee.

Myself, I had very few visits from social workers, and little solace from them. They didn't know me well enough to be much help. They had too many cases. They couldn't be expected to concentrate on mine. But one wet summer afternoon, a new woman social worker came to the house to see me. She told me that she had traced my father and that I would soon be seeing him.

CHAPTER SEVEN

A Promise

THE MAN AND woman arrived in a big pink car. It was an amazing car, an old-style Jaguar, with great, long, undulating bumpers. The woman was driving because the man they said was my daddy couldn't drive and it was her car. He had thick, wavy hair, dark like mine, flopping over his forehead, and a foreign accent. When he got out of the pink car, the man gave me a big bag of sweets. The woman, whose name was Pamela, had long, straight hair and was thin and very pretty. She called him Michael.

Mrs Smith served cups of tea to the two of them in the lounge. Whilst he was drinking his tea, the man asked me to sit on his lap. I eagerly climbed up.

'Do you want to come home with me on a visit?' He ruffled my hair. I liked sitting on his lap.

'Yes, please.' My clothes were already packed. School was out for the summer and the social worker had long since told me that I was going to be staying with him for a week. Michael and Pamela and even Mrs Smith seemed as delighted as I was at the prospect. And Mrs Smith was actually nice.

Although I was excited as we left in that wonderful car, I was also just a little apprehensive. Leaving the home even for a visit was, in effect, leaving behind all my security. But although I was in the back seat, which Pamela said was safer, I enjoyed the journey.

However, London was a shock. It was so dirty. Michael lived in a flat on the first floor of a large old house in a run-down part of Stamford Hill in north London. There were not many trees on the street, but there certainly was a lot of rubbish, and not just on that road – all over London. I couldn't understand why the whole world didn't come to Essex to live. It was neater, tidier and cleaner, and there were trees to climb.

Nor did people bump into you on the street or push waiting for the bus, as they did the next morning as Michael and I were queuing at the bus stop. As we sat hunched together on the red bus, he confided, 'You will see, little one, three barbers work for me. I come from Cyprus with almost nothing. But in my fingers I have the first ingredient of success: a trade.' He held his right hand in front of us like an item of evidence to be examined in a trial. His fingers were blunt and well manicured, and there was a scattering of dark hair on the back of his hand.

'The second ingredient, little one, is inside here.' He touched his head. 'But hard work, little one, that is the essential ingredient of success. You remember that.'

I nodded.

'Good girl. Any honest trade is respectable. Even to work in a taverna or in a cafe.' He smiled, his white teeth glittering like a string of taverna lights. We got off the bus and onto another one, which we stayed on until we got to a big cinema. Every day he had to catch two buses and leave early in the morning to get to the barber shop on time. We had not had enough time for breakfast, but when we got to the shop, he sat me down with a big bowl of cereal, and began preparing for the customers.

Wolfing down breakfast so that I would be allowed to help, I carefully placed the towels in position, making sure they were folded, not rumpled. Michael and the three other barbers cleaned the mirrors and the razors which were clean already, as they had been done the night before. The other barbers were all foreign too, but very friendly. One who spoke good English told me that before he emigrated to England, Michael had been a policeman and then a barber in Limassol, the port city in Greek Cyprus.

To set me up for the morning, Michael took me to buy some sweets and a bottle of cherryade, which was my favourite drink. Then the customers started coming in. They were all shapes and sizes, even bald ones who came for a shave.

I spent most of the day sitting in a dirty little backroom, which had a small table with a chair and a small sink. I often looked round the corner of the door to see what was happening in the shop and the customers would wave to me. They would smile as they walked through the tiny room to go to the toilet, which was in the yard outside. But they said very little, for most of them spoke a foreign language.

One afternoon, when there were no customers in the barber shop, Michael put a wooden board across the arms of the chair and lifted me up on to it. As I sat on the board looking in the mirror, he tucked a huge white barber's sheet under my neck and draped it over my shoulders, exactly the way he draped it over the customers. But I was entirely covered; even my toes. Then he went to the back of the shop to get some special scissors. As I waited, I felt very important.

'Now, little one, I will make you a beautiful haircut.' He ran his thumb lightly over one of the scissor blades. 'These scissors are fine quality.'

He looked pleased with himself. I was beaming too, even though he hadn't yet clipped a single lock. His hair was black like mine. His hair was wavy like mine. He had a short, very neatly cropped haircut. I wanted one exactly like that.

'Like yours,' I said, twisting around in my seat and reaching out to touch his head. From my high perch, I was able to reach it. His hair was soft but springy.

'Sit up, you must sit straight,' he said, a little gruffly. 'I'm cutting.' He began to cut my hair, snip, snip, snip. 'Keep your head still.' He was concentrating. As the locks of my hair fell onto the barber's sheet or onto the floor, I watched in the mirror with rapt attention.

'There,' he said at last. 'You like?'

He had cut my hair short but not as short as his. A little bob. I loved it.

He let me sweep the hair off the floor of the shop. This gave me infinite pleasure. You hold on to the good things. I will never forget the joy I felt at looking at my new hairstyle, and knowing he had made it. As I swept the hair away, I felt almost as though I was sweeping away the loneliness of my previous life.

On the way home, this man whom I had been told was my daddy bought me some more sweets, bags full, including my favourites, which were Smarties, and another bottle of cherryade. The next evening he bought me some shoes. They were little boy's shoes.

As the week wore on, I think I became a burden. On one of the afternoons I was taken round to the nearby cinema by Michael, who bought me some popcorn and left me to watch the film, as he had arranged with one of the usherettes to send me back to the shop when the show was over.

That evening, when we returned to his flat, an elderly woman who couldn't speak any English and two younger women were there, eating a meal. They were Michael's mother and two sisters. The elderly woman gave us each a portion of rice and meat, and Michael ate some of the black, garlicky olives and a few other hot, spicy foods which I did not recognise. In deference to my British palate, the old lady had cooked me a portion that wasn't spicy.

I think they had lived in Britain for a long time, even though the elderly woman couldn't speak any English. Her clothes were entirely westernised, as were her daughters'. The family talked a lot over the meal, gesticulating lavishly and laughing, but they spoke to each other only in a foreign language. I felt homesick for the children's home because I could not understand what was being said.

During the meal, because of something one of his sisters said, the man flew into a rage, throwing food across the room. It went everywhere. He was shouting in that strange language and stormed out. I was very frightened and began to cry. The three women tried to comfort me, but could not calm me down as I was so nervous and frightened.

Later that evening, the man returned. I was relieved to see him, and stuck to him like glue until I fell asleep. I woke up as his mother and sisters were leaving, and was afraid he was leaving too. After they had gone, I would not let him put me to bed anywhere but beside him on the huge converted sofa.

Later that night, his girlfriend Pamela arrived at the flat and he took me to a little bedroom which was very cold and put me under the covers. When he told me to stay there, I did not protest this time because there was an angry edge to his voice and anyway I was three-quarters asleep.

When I woke in the morning, I ran to the other room, only to find it empty. The man and the woman had both gone. I ran upstairs to the flat above, where the woman told me he had asked her to look after me as he couldn't take me to work. She told me to get dressed and to go outside and play with the children in the street. The day seemed so long and I began to feel so lonely that I wanted to go back to the home.

The lady who was supposed to be looking after me took me to the shops and I kept asking her when was my daddy coming home. She would only tell me, 'Later.' When he finally came, I stuck to him so closely I probably got on his nerves. I was scared he was going to leave me.

He took me to the sweet shop and on the way back, just as I was beginning to feel very happy and contented again, he told me I had to go back to the children's home in the morning. I started to cry and he then told me not to worry as he would collect me again the following weekend.

That night, as I settled down to sleep beside him, Pamela arrived and I was taken to the other room, where I lay feeling completely rejected. After a while I decided to go back and join them, but when I got there they were arguing. He was shouting and Pamela was crying. When I heard my name, I listened at the door.

'But, Michael, now that you have Fatima, it doesn't matter anymore that I can't have any children.'

'It isn't enough for me.'

'But she's lovely. She even looks like you, Michael.'

'I say no. No, no, no.'

Pamela was in love with him. She wanted to marry him. She wanted me. But he wanted to live in a normal happy family with the mother of his child, his children. He wanted to watch his baby grow up. Who could blame him? He wanted a typical family, he said. He wanted what other men had. He wanted a son.

The next morning when we went back to the children's home in the car, Pamela had dark rings under her eyes and Michael looked tired and rumpled. They had spent most of the night arguing. Although I was feeling miserable, I was consoled by the fact that I was going to come back again the following weekend.

At the home, Michael did not come in but left me with Mrs Smith at the door. As he left, my feelings welled up and I began crying. I was heartbroken. I cried for a long time, but again Mrs Smith showed no understanding or sympathy and sent me to the bedroom, where I spent most of the day on my own. Mrs Smith told me to grow up and not to be silly. What I was crying out for was a hug, but instead I was sent upstairs to sort things out for myself. Occasionally, one of the other children came in to stare at me. I would tell them to go away.

During the next few days, to feel closer to him, I kept with me the few things that Michael had given me – the shoes and the empty cherryade bottle. Throughout that week, I waited for a telephone call to say what time he was coming to collect me. But if he rang, Mrs Smith did not tell me.

At the weekend, I waited hour after hour for him to arrive, and at the sound of every car, I rushed to the window. The weather was fine on Sunday afternoon, and I sat on the front wall of the house waiting. When finally I asked, Mrs Smith told me she didn't know whether or not he was coming. When he didn't, she offered me no consolation.

He didn't come the next week either.

Weekend after weekend, feeling more and more rejected and desperate, I waited for the man I had been told was my daddy. I wanted so much not to be let down again and to be wanted. Most of the children were so disturbed themselves that they did not notice what was happening to me. Only Sham, who was a few years older than me – he was the oldest boy at the home – teased me. He never missed a chance of upsetting anyone. 'Your dad is not ever coming to see you,' he said.

'He is too.'

'If he was coming, he would come, wouldn't he?' said Sham with irrefutable logic.

'He is. You'll see,' I said. I stalked off.

I shut myself in the bathroom. To hide the sound of my sobbing and my wails of frustration, I turned on the water full blast.

There were constant changes among the children at the home, with some returning to their parents and others becoming fostered by families. Aliya continued to come and go between the home and her mother. No one, however, seemed to want me. I felt utter despair. It was a feeling I had felt before, all too often, a feeling that all of us children in the home knew well.

Michael never came to see me again. But as much as that

hurt, I am now grateful that he didn't keep worrying the situation, building my hopes and smashing them again. He had tried, probably partly for Pamela's sake. He had even got his mother and sisters involved, but it hadn't worked. He didn't feel he could bring me up, so he cut the emotional umbilical cord. He had made his decision and that was it. I try to think it was a case of being cruel to be kind.

When I was about eight or ten, the woman they said was my mother took me to Michael's barber shop in Stamford Hill and sent me in to cadge some money from 'my father'. Reluctantly, and with embarrassment, I poked my head into the barber's, where he was in the middle of cutting a customer's hair. Michael did put some money in my hand. I don't remember how much because the woman or Adem immediately took it off me. Sad to say, I was not to see the man who sowed the seed that gave birth to me again till forty years later.

CHAPTER EIGHT

Auntie Rae

B Y THIS TIME, I had become very attached to the 'thirty-hour lady', Mrs Peat, who, I am convinced, kept me sane.

Rachel – 'Rae' – Whitney Peat was the embodiment of cockney grit. Snub-nosed, slender, morally sturdy, and aged about forty, she had curly hair and boundless energy. Mrs Peat had come to Essex fifteen years earlier with her husband Joe, who had a good job at Ford's in Dagenham. After raising two sons in a house around the corner from the home, Rae Peat took a job looking after the children other people had cast off. Not everything at the children's home pleased her, and as she cared deeply, and her husband was employed, she felt at liberty to say so.

She had been at the home almost as long as I had. We children called her Auntie Rae. Auntie Rae had very soft hands. She was always rubbing a pink cream called Oil of Ulay into the palms of her hands, and when she did the dusting, she wore gloves.

When she was on early shift, which began at 7 a.m., Auntie Rae's first task of the day was to wake us children up. 'Wakey, wakey, rise and shine, another day has begun,' she would chant. Most of the children would jump out of bed, smiling. Not me. I pretended to be asleep, so that she would have to come and squeeze my shoulder. Out of the corner of my eye, I would just catch sight of her pale blue overall but I would lie very still. Then she would tickle me. And as hard as I tried, I could not hold out. I would burst out laughing.

After beginning the day with a giggle, I would not have much time to wallow in my sorrows, since I had to rush off to school. If I or any of the others had wet the bed, Auntie Rae would brush over the incident, whereas it seemed to me that Mrs Smith acted as if we had done it on purpose. In my opinion, Auntie Rae should have been matron. She cared about us children and she took a lot of responsibilities home, even though, like all the 'thirty-hour ladies' at the home, she was only supposed to work and only paid for thirty hours a week.

But it never was just thirty hours. When Auntie Rae was on an early shift, some little thing would usually keep her an hour or more later than the usual time to go home, which was supposedly 1 p.m. She was not paid any overtime. The late shift, which included putting us to bed, was supposed to finish at 7 p.m., but she would be lucky to get home at a quarter to nine – and her house was only five minutes' walk from the children's home. Her husband Joe would grumble, but he cooked their evening meal if she was late.

Their house was on my route home from school. On the days when I knew her shift at the children's home had ended for the day, or if it was her week off, as I passed her house, I would wonder what Auntie was doing. I tried to imagine her putting her feet up, or preparing the evening meal for her unmarried son and her husband, or doing whatever it was you did in your own house.

One afternoon, when I was, as usual, fed up with the home, with school, with my life, I slowed down to a snail's pace, and then paused in front of Auntie Rae's little red-brick house. I could see her standing at the kitchen sink under the big window, doing the washing-up. Auntie Rae liked everything to be neat and tidy and clean, just so. She was so engrossed in her task that she didn't notice me. I knocked, tentatively, at her door.

Auntie Rae welcomed me with a hug and a big smacking kiss on the cheek, and sat me down at her carefully oiled teak kitchen table to serve me biscuits and tea. Auntie Rae placed my mug of tea on the table mat in front of me. The mat was a delicate colour, fawn. There was nice bright orange, beige and gold flowered wallpaper on the top half of the kitchen wall. The bottom half was clean paintwork.

As I dangled my short legs from her comfortable kitchen chair, waiting for my tea to cool enough to drink, I said plaintively, 'It's not fair that I have to live in the home.'

'Life isn't always fair, Fatima.'

'But my life is horrible. I feel miserable.' Actually, that wasn't, at that precise moment, quite true. I was enjoying our tea party immensely. I was especially enjoying being in Auntie Rae's kitchen. Being the centre of attention was nice too. But, since in principle it was perfectly true that I was miserable, I continued to whine. 'I'm tired of Uncle Alan saying, "Fatima, stop this" and "Fatima, stop that." And *she* is always getting at me. I hate my life. I don't know what to do, Auntie Rae.'

'Have a biscuit.'

While I was chewing it, and beginning to feel quite contented, Auntie Rae said, 'Remember this. Everything comes to those who wait.'

'I don't see why I should wait for what other children already have.'

'Just you remember,' Auntie Rae said gently. 'Now off you go, Fats, or you will be late, and Mrs Smith will give you what for.'

But I took a moment for a little look round before leaving. In the lounge, there were snapshots of her grand-children on the wall.

'Fatima, you don't have to memorise the place,' she said. She gave me to understand I could stop in for a cuppa when-ever.

And one Saturday, she invited me to go shopping with her. We went from shop to shop, and everywhere I looked, I saw other children holding on to their mother's hand. 'Can I hold your hand?'

'You're getting to be a bit big for that, Fatima.'

I put my hand in my mouth and began to suck my fingers. It was a little habit I had. Auntie Rae noticed. 'Your fingers will get distorted if you keep that up.' She took my hand in hers.

I liked walking hand in hand like that. 'Can I call you Mummy, too?'

'Fatima, I'm not your mummy. I'm your Auntie Rae.'

'But can I call you Mummy, just for today?'

'Just for today. There is no harm in that.'

'Mummy,' I said.

'Yes?'

'Just Mummy.'

On her birthday, I sneaked into the neighbour's garden and picked a huge bunch of bright yellow daffodils for her. She had so many flowers, especially daffs, growing in her own garden that I knew she must really like them. Taking the note I had painstakingly printed letter by letter in my own childish hand, I crept through her front gate, and only when I was absolutely certain that Auntie Rae was not standing at the sink and looking out of the big window did I tiptoe up to her kitchen door, and lay the daffs and my note on her doorstep. Then I knocked loudly, and ran off.

Perhaps it was a good thing that I was not there when she opened the note and read: 'Dear Auntie Rae, will you please be my mum?'

The next day, Auntie Rae explained to me very carefully that she could not be my mum but that she cared about me and would look after me whenever she could. She had her own family, she reminded me – children as well as the grand-children. Her eldest son Mick taught at my primary school. Her other son, Chris, was a lot younger. But since she was at the home so much of the time, and I was always welcome for tea at her house, we would be seeing each other, she pointed out, almost as much as a mum and daughter did.

Unbeknownst to her, when we were on a jaunt or at her house – I now went almost every day after school – I pretended Auntie Rae was my mother and that the children's home didn't exist. Then walking back to the home, the truth would hit me.

When Auntie Rae paid attention to other children in the home I would feel upset, as I wanted her to pay special attention just to me. As always, I wanted to be special, special to someone, to be wanted, to have a mum.

'Fatima,' Auntie Rae said one morning, 'please come and help me. Shay here needs looking after. Give her a big kiss for me.' I was about six or seven. Shay was a little Nigerian girl, two or three years younger than I was, and very disturbed. She was banging her head against the wall. When she was in bed, Shay would often hit her head, bang, bang, bang against the wall, and if she was sitting on the bed or in a chair, she would rock. I went over to her and put my arm around her.

'Where is my daddy?' she said. 'Want my daddy.'

'He'll come along when he can, Shay. Come out to the garden now and play.'

'Want my daddy.'

'He'll come when he can,' I repeated. 'Everything comes to those who wait.' I gave Shay a big smacker of a kiss on the cheek, just like Auntie Rae would have, and trundled her out to the garden. She began to play with the other children and forgot about her woes.

Auntie Rae was very pleased with me. 'These children need you,' she said. 'You're getting to be a big girl. The little children look to you and need the comfort you can give them.'

I had never thought of being needed before, only of being needy. Now, for the first time, I began to realise that the other children needed to be loved too. Many of them were as starved emotionally as I was. Shay was one of the worst, but Verlie used to cry all the time, too, because she wanted to go home. Her mum couldn't care for her because she had had a nervous breakdown. It was not her mum's first breakdown either. I went home with Verlie for the day once, and her dad did everything because his wife couldn't get out of bed. She was too ill. Verlie cried all the way back to the home, and her father, who was driving us, was annoyed.

Rakash, one of the Indian boys at the home, was teased mercilessly by his older brother Sham, whom I regarded as a nasty piece of work. Sham would chase him round the dining-room table, and Rakash would get into a state. He would be crying and scared. But whenever I tried to make Sham leave Rakash alone, Rakash would turn on me and defend his brother. I would get peeved. In retrospect, it is touching; it wasn't at the time.

I was entirely unsympathetic to Sham. I regarded him as a dangerous sneak and didn't at all like the way he made up to the Smiths to get extra privileges. But I suppose Sham wasn't happy either. He, like me, was a bit of a veteran.

Helping Auntie Rae look after the other children was, in fact, very satisfying. And Auntie Rae encouraged me. 'When I'm not here,' she said, 'I want you to make sure the children are all right. I want you to take over where I leave off.'

Now, instead of being jealous that she cared about the other boys and girls, I felt pleased and very proud that she was entrusting them to me. When Auntie Rae's shift was over, and she went home for the day, I would try hard to carry on where she had left off. And for the first time in my life, through the children, I began to feel needed, which is very close to feeling wanted.

I became the big sister even to children my own age. 'You're just like a little mum,' Auntie Rae said one day. I was thrilled. But she was such a clever 'child psychologist' that I never once realised what she had been up to. Auntie Rae understood more about children, and cared more than many far better educated people. She had a talent for understanding us.

Auntie Rae was the person who most shaped me from the age of six or seven through early adolescence. Those were a crucial half-dozen years, and I owe what went right about them to her. She taught me character. That was the most important thing in life. I learned that you gave as well as took, that you did not steal or cheat and you tried not to lie, but you could fib a little if people deserved it. I also learned that you worked for a living because work gave you self-respect, and you worked hard. You tried to put aside a quid or two for a rainy day, but you always had plenty of laughter and you could not have too much of that. But there was no harm either in being serious at serious moments or in telling unpopular truths. And being the best you could be at whatever you did was something to be proud of.

Auntie Rae had a lot of love in her heart. Enough to teach me – by a combination of example and gentle prodding – that love was not just wanting someone, it was giving too. I now prided myself on being almost a mother to the younger ones.

To cheer up bedtime, which was one of the worst times at this home, just as it had been at Wormley Hill, I invented my own stories about Rosie Row, a fictional rabbit. I would tell stories about Rosie's many escapades, always whispering, of course, so we wouldn't have Mrs Smith, our so-called Auntie Brenda, shouting at us. Auntie Brenda's voice seemed only to operate at a screech or a shout. Under the Smiths' regime, as in the previous one, bedwetters were required to stay awake for a late visit to the toilet. Rosie Row helped keep them awake, so that Mrs Smith, who was no gentler than the previous matron, would not have to shake them so roughly.

If the Smiths treated any of the children unfairly – and in my view, they often did – I would speak out, which made me very unpopular with them. What I called defending the little ones, Uncle Alan called answering back.

There were two main punishments at the home, and often as not, I got both for a single offence. The main punishment for all of us was to have our pocket money stopped. It wasn't a fortune to begin with, but I often wondered what happened to the pocket money we children didn't get.

I particularly remember one time when Uncle Alan had been bawling out some of the little children for no good reason, and really frightening them. I told him that it was not on. He got very cross. 'Who do you think you are, their mother?' he said.

I not only lost my pocket money that week, I got the second punishment too. I could not go out of the house that week except to go to school, which meant that I could not visit Auntie Rae on the way home from school. He knew that I lived to visit Auntie Rae.

There was no way around the punishment. I could not even go into the garden. I didn't know how I would get through a whole week when I was not only deprived of our visits, but I couldn't even play outdoors to work off my pent-up frustration. No running, no jumping, no hide and seek. 'I have to rot indoors,' I told Auntie Rae bitterly.

'Just wait it out,' she said. 'Try not to let it upset you. A week will soon pass.'

That week seemed like 20,000 decades to me. The only place I was allowed to go, thank you very much, was to school. School was not my favourite venue. I don't suppose I was the easiest of pupils either. That week, I had tons of resentment welling up inside me, and behaved even worse than usual. Not that I was ordinarily *that* bad, but at junior school I was one of the toughies.

There was a set of us ten- and eleven-year-olds who clubbed together. Wendy, my friend whose mum gave me toast and marmalade, and Alma, who lived at the home around the corner, were in our set; and Keith, who was my boyfriend. He was a very tough little kid, even smaller than me. Now he is much taller than I am. During playtime, the teachers could usually find us all at the back of the school, out of bounds. That is, until we discovered a way to disappear.

Because we were the littlest, Keith or I used to climb into the school through a small window, open the fire door, and steal into the library, where there was a TV. Nobody used the room at lunchtime, and we would sit undisturbed watching the telly and smoking the odd cigarette. But if the dinner ladies did come round, we would hide and shut the door. They never found us. They probably didn't want to.

In class, all of us were cheeky – making jokes during lessons, that sort of thing. I saw no reason not to. Most of what was on offer was a joke anyway, but I could see a reason for learning maths. For starters, you needed to be able to count your money when you went to the shops. To be honest, though, the main reason I learned my multiplication tables speedily was that you got a gold star pasted beside your name on the chart every time you learned a new one. I always tried to have more stars than anyone else. Later on, I could see a practical reason for learning how to compute circumferences and all that, even equations. I took that fairly seriously.

But learning the capitals of countries I had never heard of meant nothing to me. And reading was far less interesting to

me than running. I said so too – in a jokey way. Being bois-
terous was preferable to being bored.

I was often called in to see the headmaster, for some
infraction or other. Actually, it wasn't his fault. It was mine.
I had boundless energy. I admit that I was a bit of a villain,
not a wicked one, not a thief or anything like that, but I
knew how to be a pest. I didn't see any reason not to be. The
world was not fair: why play by the rules?

The school dinners were a horrible reminder that children from the home were different from the rest because you
had to show a pink chit to get your meal. You either lived in
a children's home or were otherwise dead poor, and everybody knew it. So there was a stigma attached. There were
only fifty or fewer of us free-lunch kids.

I would sometimes skip lunch to avoid the embarrassment of lining up with the chittie in front of the other
children. This was partly why I always had such a good
appetite when I arrived at Wendy's house or at Auntie Rae's.

On the other hand, on those occasions when I was so
hungry that I did condescend to eat the school meal, you
always knew I was there. I was one of those who would flick
peas around the room off the end of a knife. And I would
always push to the front of the queue so that if any second
helpings were available I was ready with an empty plate. I
didn't want anybody to think I was embarrassed about
anything.

What saved me from becoming a rebel without a cause
was sport. I was beginning to realise I was good at it. When
I was ten and in my last year at junior school, we had to
throw a cricket ball, and I out-threw every single boy in the
school. I threw a long way too, about 50 metres, which is

good for that age. If you consider that there were about 300 students at the school, of which about half were boys, that added up to 150 boys. My status at school rose rapidly – in the eyes of all the girls and most of the boys, although there were a few who were rather scathing. I am lucky I was ten years old instead of in my teens, or I might have worried more about having the good opinion of those boys.

What I didn't know then was that bowling in cricket has a lot in common with throwing a javelin. There is much the same whiplash motion.

Actually, I don't remember the ins and outs of that cricket competition, except that every year throwing the cricket ball was an event during track and field day. Cricket was not particularly a great love of mine, although I had already begun to realise that the sports field was my natural habitat. What mattered to me was that I had gone out there and thrown the ball myself, and no one had helped me, and when it was over, the whole school knew and was buzzing about my achievement.

One thing was crystal clear. I might not have clothes as good as some children, or as much spending money, or parents; I might be disadvantaged in every way – no, correction, I definitely *was* disadvantaged in every way – except one. Sport.

In that, it was becoming more and more apparent, I was anybody's equal. I always felt happy kicking the ball around. I would play football with the boys, but only because there were not any girls who wanted to play. With the girls, I played rounders and netball and hockey. Nor, by the way, was I too terrible at 'penny up the wall', which as I got older I played with the toughies among the boys somewhere far out of sight of the teachers. The player whose coin lands nearest the walls scoops all the money. My winnings, which were substantial – often as much as two shillings (10 pence) at a time – could be used to buy a white ticket for a school lunch instead of using the free pink chit of the poor. If we didn't have enough money for a chit, the fish and chip lady at the corner shop parade would give me and Alma a cheap bag of scraps.

PE was my best subject by far. I was picked for all the school teams and also ran at the local Blackshots stadium, where Alma and I checked out the sports clubs for kids our age. When I threw a ball, or kicked it, the ball went close to where I aimed it. It was almost effortless. One of the teachers even told me – and she must have meant it because she was angry with me at the time – that sport was my saving grace.

Auntie Rae said I was a bit of a tomboy, but she didn't seem to see anything really wrong in it, and I certainly didn't. I was one of the best marbles players in the school too. Running and jumping and throwing, all those activities of sports play, made my body feel good. And I was steadily getting stronger. It was such an entirely new experience to be better than everyone at something that it is no wonder I began to get hooked. Fortunately, the school encouraged sport, including girls' sport. If they had not believed in competition on the athletics field, I dare not think what might have become of me.

It is not bragging outrageously to say I was the star of the school netball team, which was of a high calibre. But there were so many good players in that team that I was a little surprised and very, very pleased when the other team members voted me their captain. All seven of us became very close. My friend Wendy Smith, no relation to the Smiths who ran the home, was in the team.

The teacher in charge was a serious young woman in her twenties, with dark, wayward hair. She could never quite keep her hair in place, but she had no trouble at all controlling the seven of us. And believe me that was a feat. Her secret was this: she was passionate about netball, and she communicated that passion to us. That is what made her a great coach. I no longer remember her name, but I will never forget what she did for me.

She loved her job, so she had no trouble keeping practice interesting and keeping us inspired. For once, I didn't play up. I took the game seriously. We all did, and by mid season it looked as though we had a fair chance of winning the District Schools Championship. A month before the final, we knew we were strong contenders for the title.

Then, one lunchtime, I threw a snowball at one of the dinner ladies who was a real stickler for discipline. The snowball didn't get much of a lift, but it landed smack on target – one of my most accurate throws ever. The dinner lady wasn't hurt, but her dignity was. As a punishment, I was banned from the netball team.

But there was a demonstration at school, a pint-sized 'political' demo spearheaded by the rest of the netball team. Remember, at the time demos were a way of life and had been since the grown-up student revolutions of 1968. At our demo, the netball team announced just one non-negotiable demand. They wanted me back on the team. If I wasn't on the team, they wouldn't play. This would mean that the school might as well kiss goodbye to the league title. A petition went around the school asking for me to be reinstated.

The headmaster was a decent sort. But he couldn't rescind the ban just like that. He called me into his office, and after extracting the promise that I wouldn't do any more throwing except during PE, he said I could rejoin the team – eventually – and in time for the league final. But on one condition: I had to give my school work a little more effort.

The headmaster knew how to motivate me to work hard in lessons, but he obviously didn't know anything about winning a championship. You couldn't just go out there and play without practising, no matter how good you were. If we took our netball very seriously, so did the other schools. The standard was high. But until I was officially back on the team, I wasn't even eligible to go to practice.

This problem required a little ingenuity. I persuaded the team to practise together at breaktime. During the three weeks I was banned, we had these bootleg practices whenever it was possible, and since we were keen, it was often possible. The headmaster looked the other way. So did our teacher.

By the time I was reinstated, just a week before the final, we felt that we could have taken on Arsenal if they played netball. That is, until the very day of the final. Then, like the others, I was all nerves. I was sucking my fingers when I got into the minibus, and twenty minutes later, when we arrived at Lansdowne School in Thurrock, where our opponents were waiting, I still had my hand in my mouth.

Waiting for the starting whistle, as I stood on the court in my red shirt and navy gym knickers, I almost would have preferred to be playing against Arsenal. They would have been gentler. Lansdowne would have pulled our hair if they could have got away with it. They were as tough a school team as we were, aggressive and, if anything, more determined. But we were more practised. To be honest, it wasn't entirely a game of skill. I, and the rest of our girls, did whatever was necessary to win. If the referee was looking elsewhere, we shoved a little, we fouled a little. We shouted at our opponents. Mind you, they did the same. But we won. We were the champions.

I was exhausted at the end of that match, but I was happy, elated. Back at school, we were hailed as heroines. At morning assembly, there was thunderous applause when, in front of the entire school, each girl on the team was presented with a small medal. I will never forget the thrill I felt when they handed me mine. It was just a tiny little thing, not much bigger than a two-pence piece. It came in a little see-through plastic case. The metal, which had a ball and a netball post stamped on it, was silvery in colour, but it wasn't silver. It wasn't a precious metal at all, but it was my first, a precious medal, precious to me. I had no idea it was to be the first of a long line.

That day at school was glorious. Even the dinner ladies were nice to me and seemed genuinely glad to see me – that was a change. But I couldn't wait for the school day to be over. When the final bell rang, I rushed out of the building, ran down the steps and hurried to Auntie Rae's, running most of the way. When she opened the door, I threw myself in her arms. 'I got a medal,' I exclaimed. 'Look.'

If anyone was prouder and more pleased than I was, it was Auntie Rae. As I proffered my little medal as though it were the most spectacular of the Crown Jewels, Auntie Rae looked with rapt attention and hugged me again. It was a jubilant moment.

Then I surprised both Auntie Rae and myself. I gave my medal to her. At first, she wouldn't take it, but when I insisted, she said she would treasure it. Over the years, she offered to give it back to me many times, but I got great pleasure from knowing that it was hers.

The adulation I received as the star and captain of the netball team made me feel I was wanted at last. No wonder sport was getting under my skin. What I found was that I could lose myself in any sports activity. Paradoxically, I was at the very same time finding my true self in sport. And I had adored my first whiff of the sweet smell of success. For the first time in my life, I had a place in the world.

Not long after, when I returned from school one afternoon, Aliya's social worker was there. Aliya had been on a lengthy visit to her mother – I think for some months. The social worker, who had just brought her back to the home, asked me to go upstairs to see her in the bedroom.

Aliya was unpacking her clothes and putting them in the locker beside her bed. She was crying. The woman they said was my mother was there too. Suddenly, she grabbed me by the throat and told me that unless I looked after Aliya, she would cut my throat. I was very frightened. Then in her broken English she said it twice more. 'I cut your throat, I cut your throat.' She probably didn't mean it literally, but I was terrified.

I was now nearly eleven, and in the last year at junior school. Towards the end of the final term, our class went as a group to visit Culverhouse Comprehensive, which was the school we were to start at after the summer break. It was a twenty-minute walk away, on the other side of a huge housing estate. The school looked all right until the deputy head, Miss Meredith, came up to me and said, 'We know all about you, Fatima. We're ready for you. You'd better watch your step when you get here.'

Her remark really upset me. I was by no means the worst troublemaker at junior school and I was still naughty, not nasty. I had had no idea until then that I had an unsavoury reputation, especially one that went beyond the walls of my school. That remark made me feel that I wouldn't get a fair chance and that no matter where I went nobody wanted me. Auntie Rae did her best to console me.

Soon after, the Smiths took us children in the green van to Rhyl in Wales for the summer holiday. The van was not comfortable at the best of times, and there was plenty of squabbling in the back seats. To while away the time, we must have sung The Beatles' songs 'Yellow Submarine' and 'Lily The Pink' a thousand times. We checked into a decrepit boarding house, where we were sleeping too many to a room, and then were free to wander along the seafront. Although we could walk and run along the sandy beach, it was too cold to bathe.

One of the cafes in Rhyl, a bustling place overlooking the sea, was seeking temporary help. The notice in the window said you would be paid your wages at the end of every day. They wanted girls to clear away dishes and help out in general, carrying meals to the tables and washing up. It was not a glamorous job, but as I was always short of money, I decided I was getting bored just being on holiday. Mrs Smith encouraged me to take the job.

At the end of the first day, the owner told me I would have to wait another day for my pay. After I worked the next day, he said the same. I told him I was not coming back to work as a slave in a packed cafe for no pay. I was not the only one who quit either. It turned out that he had quite a good thing going. When he hired you, he always said he would pay at the end of each day's work. Then he didn't. And he kept the job notice in the window. After two or three days, the youngsters who were working for him would twig, and walk out. In the end, he didn't pay anybody. The experience made me a little leery of the ordinary work-a-day world, where it was obviously so easy to be taken advantage of.

Shortly after we returned from Rhyl, I started secondary school. Walking on my own to school the first day, I felt as dour and dreary as my new school uniform, with its lengthy black skirt and dull grey jumper. Passing the big run-down council estate where I knew no one and no one knew me, I felt apprehensive and insignificant.

Outside the school there were hordes of pupils. Culverhouse had over a thousand of them, most of whom I didn't know, and who didn't know me, or appear to want to. I didn't like the look of them either. As I waited in the play-ground for the bell, I spat nonchalantly on the ground.

The modern, two-storey school building, which was constructed of a dark red brick and had been erected only a dozen years before, seemed to me oppressive. The big sports hall and gymnasium at the school, which had so impressed me when our class from junior school had visited, now simply didn't register. And though I couldn't possibly have failed to notice the school's huge, well-tended playing fields, even they made no ameliorating impression on my state of mind. This was obviously a school that took sport seriously, and sport, I already knew, was my lifeline. But on that first day, as I spat again on the unfriendly concrete ocean in front of the school, I thought I was going to drown.

Inside, Culverhouse was a warren of hostile corridors that all seemed to lead to the wrong room. It was a strange, bustling city, not an ocean. I now had to hurry from one classroom to another for different lessons. On the first day, I got lost three times. I felt like I was in a foreign country – like a baby who fell asleep in her pram in the local park and woke up alone in the middle of a dark forest. Not Alice in Wonderland, but Alice in Nightmare Land.

When I caught a glimpse of Miss Meredith, the unfriendly deputy head, in her tweed skirt and pale, elegant blouse which had a neat bow at the neck, I didn't say hello. What was the point? So far as she was concerned, I was already tried and convicted.

If you're called the name, play the game, the saying goes. 'Miss, Miss, Miss,' I called out in my first class that first day, and then asked a question, the same one the teacher had just answered. In the next classroom, and the next, I did the same. Pretending to the world that I felt very secure, I fell back on my old routine of playing up as much as I could. I was a pest. If I couldn't cope with school, it would have to learn to cope with me.

CHAPTER NINE

Trouble

I WAS NOW quite a well-built young lady for my age and needed to wear a bra. Mrs Smith didn't seem to notice this, although she quickly noticed even my slightest infraction of the rules. At school people did notice, and made the odd remark. I was beginning to get a bit self-conscious.

Auntie Rae had a word with Mrs Smith, who reluctantly agreed to part with some clothing vouchers. Auntie Rae and I set off for the shops to buy the bra. On the way to Marks and Spencer's, she somehow made me feel both that what was happening to my body was quite normal and that because of it, I was very special. My initial self-consciousness at this time was the only anguish I ever had over puberty.

As usual, Auntie Rae and I had a good time shopping, although, of course, we no longer walked along hand in hand. I was much too grown up. We bought a teen bra, a white cotton one, of which I was very proud.

I was now twelve going on thirteen, the oldest girl at the home. But just as I had when I first arrived, I shared a bedroom with other girls of all ages, including, whenever we had one, the baby of the moment. Changing my clothes now became an intricate, irritating manoeuvre. The little ones were fascinated by the changes in my body, and they were young enough to stare whenever I stripped off. Like most adolescent girls, I felt modest. Either I queued for the toilet or bathroom in my pyjamas and held up the rest of the queue while I stayed there to change into my white school blouse and black skirt, or I grabbed my clothes and changed surreptitiously under the blankets.

What I longed for and sometimes daydreamed about was having a room of my own. The tiny staff bedroom well down the corridor was sometimes vacant for weeks at a time, even longer. I not only wanted, but needed a single bedroom, and this one was spare. By rights, I felt it should be mine. By experience, I knew Mrs Smith might feel otherwise, and that I must broach the subject delicately. I remember waiting politely in the lounge till she had a moment for me. When, at last, she did, her welcome was brusque, something in the order of: 'What is it now, Fatima?'

'I am getting to be,' I began hesitantly, 'a young lady.' Mrs Smith understood my meaning. 'I want the room that's going,' I blurted out before I could stop myself. 'I want to have my own room. I need it, Auntie Brenda. Please.'

'I'll have to think about who deserves the room most,' she said. 'And discuss it with Uncle Alan.'

My heart sank. 'But I need my privacy.'

'Don't we all,' she retorted. She promised she and Uncle Alan would decide in due course.

I hoped and hoped, but knew better than to expect much.

The Smiths took great pleasure in allocating the room to Sham, who was the eldest boy. To be fair, he was more than a year older than me, but I was convinced they were showing favouritism. If you were slightly cheeky to a thirty-hour lady or did something untoward at school, Sham told the Smiths. He was a sneak. Mrs Smith liked him because he gave her plenty of excuses to tell whoever it was off.

One evening, as I was about to go to bed, I noticed that on the end of our row of shoes – we placed our shoes for the next morning in a line in the hallway – was a new pair of pricey leather boots. I guessed they belonged to Sham and was incensed.

My only shoes were serviceable, brown leather ones. They were ugly and the very cheapest available, their only advantage being that although they looked sturdy, they soon wore out. I despised them. All of us children in the home were badly dressed and horrendously shod. But I should have been grateful for the leather shoes I called 'honky-clonks' because before I got them, even in winter, I only had plimsolls. Those cost almost nothing and looked it. They were not at all fashionable the way trainers are today. They were an emblem of poverty, a dead giveaway to anyone on the street that I was from the home. My toes got cold too and there was no support. At one point I had high-top basketball boots, with plastic discs at the ankle, which were slightly better. But the toes of those soon wore out. Then the horrible 'honky-clonks' were foisted upon me. I was never allowed to buy the sort of shoes I wanted. It was a sore point.

I knocked on the door of Sham's room to ask him how much the boots had cost.

'Thirteen quid.' He was smirking. 'Aren't they terrific?'

Thirteen pounds. I could hardly believe it. That was a fortune for shoes at the time. I went straight downstairs and asked to speak with Mr and Mrs Smith, who were busy watching television. Mrs Smith poked her head out to say that I could not talk to them then and that I was to go to bed.

'I'm fed up with the way I get treated around here,' I said. 'You always try deliberately to upset me. But you're terrible to all of us children. It is not fair. Something ought to be done about it. Where Alma is, things are entirely different. Better. Much better. So it's not just that this is a home. It's your fault, and Uncle Alan's.' The words came tumbling out.

I knew that the Smiths were allocated a clothing allowance for each child, and it seemed to me that we could not possibly be getting all the clothes we were entitled to. 'I'm going to report you to my social worker next time he calls in' was my parting shot.

'Go to bed,' said Mrs Smith through clenched lips. 'Immediately.'

Needless to say, I got no joy on the clothing issue from either of them that night. And I did not get a new pair of shoes. I did inform my social worker, who told me that the Smiths were kind people. And then, to my amazement, he went and told them I had complained.

After that, my relationship with the Smiths deteriorated even further. There was nothing I would or could do to make them like me now. And just about anything I did made them flare up at me. Trying to be almost a mother to the younger ones, I would stand up for them – which Mrs Smith would have described as meddling. It was meddling, but I felt it was right and necessary.

Another bone of contention was the baby of the moment. I was losing an awful lot of sleep looking after her when she cried during the night. Lifting her out of the cot and cradling her till she went back to sleep was the only way to stop her wailing. But she woke up all through the night. I was beginning to look haggard, and to feel tired all the time, and irritable, but the Smiths didn't want to know.

One night, I banged on their bedroom door and demanded that they take care of the baby. When they shouted at me to go away, I kept pounding on the door until Mr Smith opened it. He glared at me and said in a tone of voice as icy as Antarctica that I must not ever knock on their door again.

But there was another, more turbulent problem looming, one that was poles apart from my difficulty with the Smiths. It began when I was summoned peremptorily one Friday morning during the Easter holidays to the dining room because the woman who they said was my mother had turned up. With her were three greasy-looking men. Aliya was there too, sitting primly next to her mother who had come to take her to London for the weekend. I wasn't at all glad to see any of them, but when I arrived, wearing the pink crimplene dress which had just been bought for me with clothing vouchers, one of the men smacked his lips and nodded at the others. I wasn't pleased either when Aliya's mother announced that for once I too was going to London for the weekend.

'I'm not going,' I said flatly.

The rest of the conversation went something like this: 'But I want both of my daughters at home.' Her tone was stagily dramatic. '*Both*.'

One of the men winked at his friend. The way those men were eyeing me up and winking was making me increasingly nervous.

'You can't make me go.'

Aliya's mother began to scream at me. 'You are my daughter. You must come!'

'Come, girl,' one of the men said to me, in accented English. 'We must go now. Is late.'

'I'm not coming with you. I'm not.'

The men began to shout at Aliya's mother in the foreign language.

Hearing virtual mayhem coming from the dining room, Auntie Rae rushed in to see what the trouble was. She took one look at the three men and at Aliya's mother and knew immediately that if they took me away, it was not going to be for my own good. She said she wouldn't hear of it. But the men glared and Aliya's mother insisted, implying that she had permission from Mrs Smith, who was away for the weekend. At last, Auntie Rae, who was getting angrier and angrier, said in a tone of voice I had never heard her use before that she had better have a little chat with Mrs Smith.

Aliya, her mother, the three men and I waited uneasily. Edna, the cleaner, came in to lend her support. While Edna wiped the table vigorously and the others jabbered amongst themselves in their language, I strained to hear Auntie Rae.

'Those men are up to no good,' she told Mrs Smith, 'but the woman says it's fine with you, for Fatima to go to London.' After an increasingly tense conversation, Auntie Rae rang off, saying, 'In no circumstances will I let Fatima go.'

Aliya's mother and the three men did not take the news well, but for the moment, that was the end of it. I was still shaking when I heard the front door slam behind them. I did not know exactly what I was frightened of, but Auntie Rae and Edna thought they knew. Years later, Auntie Rae told me I would have been lucky if it had ended there. 'I suspected those men wanted to put you on the game. They were that woman's pimps.' If they did have prostitution in mind, the woman that was supposed to be my mother either didn't notice or didn't care.

Following this incident, I asked Mrs Smith to arrange another meeting with my social worker. Nothing happened. I asked her again and again, and she always said that she had forwarded my request. But it was not until some months later, when we were approaching the school summer holidays, that the social worker visited me. Tall, dark, and earnest, Mr Walker was thirty or thereabouts, a few years younger than the Smiths and a completely different kettle of fish.

As Edna put it, Mrs Smith tried to give an upstairs-downstairs impression to everyone including the staff, who would remind her that they were not her personal servants, but were, as she was, hired by the council to look after the children. Whereas Mr Walker, who was quite well spoken, had the nervous air of a naive and very young public school boy who has stumbled into a dockers' brawl. For all I know, he may have been a coal-miner's son, but there was something of the young Robert Redford in his looks and something about his gentle, reasonable manner and his suit and tie that made you feel he had grown up in another world, one in which people who looked after children were always very well-meaning. He probably wanted to save the world; a perfectly proper aim for a social worker, I think. But he went by the book too much; he didn't use his instinct or his head.

When finally he paid me a visit, Bob Walker immediately made sympathetic noises and took me for a walk in the park. But when I told him of all my problems, he said I must be exaggerating because he had always found Mrs Smith to be a pleasant, sympathetic and interested matron.

'But she's a con artist. She puts on a show when you arrive. Don't you see?'

Now he was certain that I was exaggerating, perhaps having a bit of teenage rebellion.

'Talk to the day ladies. They will confirm my stories.'

And they did. Forthright Auntie Rae and equally forthright Edna had plenty of bitter stories of their own to tell. But the social worker just didn't want to know. To put off Auntie Rae, he warned her that if he had a serious chat with her, he would have to tell Mrs Smith. When Auntie Rae said, 'I don't mind if you tell her,' he still kept his distance.

I couldn't understand his reasoning at all then, but I do now. If he had admitted to himself that the Smiths were a problem, he would have had terrible trouble. First he would have to say to his superiors that he and they had made a big mistake in employing the Smiths. Then he would have to prove it. Imagine the attendant aggro and legal snarls, and the costs – both in time and that scarce commodity, DHSS money. And then, after all that, he would have to find a new matron or rehouse all the children. No one can entirely blame him for not being ready or able to take on the issue of the Smiths, and for telling himself that there was no issue, just a teenager's exaggeration. I shudder to think how often and to how many children this sort of thing may have happened. Isn't there something someone, anyone, can do?

I do blame Bob Walker for his next ploy. What he did – probably not realising what he was doing – was to use my so-called exaggerations about the Smiths against me. I couldn't get on with the Smiths, he felt, because what I really wanted was my mother. And he had come prepared with a solution to that. He had a surprise for me. Dear God, it was a whopper. Aliya's mother – the woman who had brought along the very men I had been complaining about to Mr Walker – wanted to make a big effort to bring the family together at last.

As we trudged through the park, Mr Walker grew hoarse trying to convince me that the woman loved me and had always loved me, but not until now had she been able to look after me properly. I knew that the idea that she loved me was rubbish. On two occasions in the past year, she'd taken me along when she took Aliya to London for the day; trips which I could not get out of. She, too, had probably accepted my presence only at the insistence of the social workers. On every visit, the woman was either 'looking after' her man or looking after Aliya and herself. I was not a top priority except when she needed someone to plead with the milkman not to stop deliveries because of the unpaid bill.

But now, according to Mr Walker, she wanted to have me at home with her. *Because she loved me!* He was immensely pleased, he said. I could tell from the sincere crack in his voice and his furrowed brow that he meant it.

Kicking a stone out of my path, I said something rude. You couldn't really excuse a social worker for being innocent as a newborn babe. It was his job to be knowing.

The plan was that I would go to stay with Aliya's mother and Aliya in London for a while to try it out. It might lead, Mr Walker said enthusiastically, to a visit of months or even forever. I could not believe that he could be so naive as to swallow that line after all these years.

'I'm not going anywhere near her,' I said defiantly.

If I was so unhappy at the Smiths', he argued, I ought to look on this as a promising development. It was desirable, he explained, again puckering his brow, that every effort be made to bring a family together. Because the woman who they said was my mother had requested it, he was bound to do it.

My heart sank. I was between the devil and the deep blue sea. And I couldn't make him understand. It looked as though my best hope was to drown. But I'm a fighter. 'I'm a ward of the court,' I said. 'I don't have to go.'

But I did.

On a hazy, humid morning early in the summer holidays when I would much rather have been arguing with Uncle Alan, Aliya and I caught a Green Line bus to London. Then we changed buses and finally got off not far from the front door.

The flat was in an unlovely block, amid other ugly blocks, edging the busy road. To me they all looked equally uninviting, but Aliya knew which was the one. We trudged up to the top floor. At each landing we saw obscene words scrawled on the walls in big letters and inhaled the stench of urine. At first, I thought the people who lived in these flats did not have toilets.

Inside the flat, the woman and her son were waiting. Nearly a man now at fifteen or so, Adem had hefty shoulders and an air of Mediterranean macho. But the anger that had always been lurking just beneath the surface was still there. Just as he had done when we were children, Adem scowled at me. I scowled back.

As soon as we got inside the front door, Aliya was hugged and kissed by her mother and welcomed by him. The three of them began to chatter in their language, which they knew I didn't understand. Ignored, I slumped against the wall of the hallway, crammed between Adem and a little table they had there near the door.

But I was not ignored for long. The woman soon set me to cleaning the balding lino on the kitchen floor. Although the kitchen, which was in a state, was minuscule, the lino was so encrusted with dirt that I thought it would take at least a week of hard scrubbing to scour it. And, she said, as soon as I had finished the floor, I was to start immediately on the greasy, chipped cooker which was missing most of its knobs and looked as though it had last been cleaned before detergent was invented.

Adem went to his room to read, and the woman and Aliya went out to do some shopping. She told me with hand signals that I must not run away. How could I? Aliya had been our navigator. I had no money and little idea of what bus to take or where to take it.

Like Cinderella, I turned my attention to the scrubbing. I found some rags and a filthy sponge to scrub with, but the only bucket I could see was full up with something thick and creamy which looked less like whipped cream than pea soup, although it was dead white. I dared not tip it out without permission.

When I asked Adem what I should do, he laughed and said that he would show me at tea what to do with home-made yoghurt. He found me another bucket, but suggested with a smile that I let the cleaning wait a moment. He had something more interesting to show me now. He was being very genial, especially for him. Maybe the years had changed him, but I was concerned that Aliya and her mother would return and find the housework undone. Not to worry, Adem said, I had plenty of time to do the cleaning. When they went out, they always stayed away for hours.

As I followed him into the recesses of the flat, however, I did feel just a bit nervous. He led me into his mother's tiny bedroom, which was scarcely big enough for the double bed. The bedstead was pushed against the wall, leaving barely enough room to walk around the bed, which had a multi-coloured quilt thrown over it. The room was tidy, almost clean – she evidently took more care of her room than the rest of the flat. It was a room with an urban view. The flat was high up, perhaps on the sixth floor. When Adem showed me out on to the tiny balcony, I could see the car park in the forecourt with Cortinas and Minis and even a taxi parked in there. Adem told me to wait there, and he rushed out and returned with a balloon full of water. Laughing, we dropped the balloon from the balcony.

I was beginning to like him. With a bright smile, he announced he had something else to show me. To my astonishment, it was a dirty magazine. The boys at school had magazines like that, but I had never paid them any attention. When Adem began flicking through the pages, urging me to look, I took a step back towards the door. But he stepped quickly in front of me, pulling my hand from the brass doorknob and pushing me onto the bed. Holding me under him, he tried to make me look at the pictures of naked men and women in the magazine.

'This is beyond a joke,' I said, hoping I sounded fierce rather than frightened and struggling to get up. 'Let me go, Adem.' I spat on the magazine, refusing to look at it.

We fought viciously. All that was going through my mind

was, I'll kill him first. Or he'll kill me. I think he got the message that it wasn't by any means foreplay. Suddenly he pushed me over, grabbed the magazine and rushed out of the room, locking the door behind him.

I banged and banged on the door and tried to pull it open. I had won, but at the same time I had lost. I felt so defeated because I was beginning to realise I couldn't win here. Adem hadn't got what he wanted, but when the woman got back she would find the floor in the same dire state as when she went out, and me in her room. It didn't bear thinking about. I lay on her bed seething with hopelessness and anger.

Shortly before the woman and Aliya returned, Adem unlocked the door.

'Don't you dare say anything,' he said, or words to that effect. 'I was just letting you have a look. I wouldn't have really done anything.'

I wondered. But I didn't have time to be upset or even angry. I rushed to get started on the kitchen. Aliya and the woman would soon be back.

On her return, the woman beat me with the flat of her hand for not having finished the cleaning. I didn't dare tell her why. Anyway, I couldn't. We could only communicate in the most rudimentary fashion and then only with Adem's help. He would do a semi-translation, and I knew he wouldn't translate any complaints I made against him.

I'm not sure she would have cared anyway. And I doubt that she would ever have told him to back off. First of all, he was menacing – perhaps, like me, she was a bit afraid of him. As a young man he was in trouble with the police. When I bumped into his sister Emmie years ago, she told me he was in prison for grievous bodily harm. And secondly, Adem helped his mother make ends meet. When one morning he came in with a bottle of milk he had stolen from the milk float while the milkman was delivering to the other flats in the building, the woman patted him on the back. Thirdly, Adem was her mouthpiece. She needed him to translate her orders to me about the housework. The woman would wave a forefinger in my face and say something I only half understood.

'Go on, do it,' Adem would say. 'Clean out the fridge.' Or 'Gather up the washing. Now!'

What I did understand when she said it, and what she took pride in saying in a dozen little ways, was, 'I don't love you.' I can only think she brought me out of the home because she needed a skivvy, someone to do the cleaning and to babysit for Aliya.

The woman had a man staying with her, a Turkish Cypriot, who came and went. He had a thick black moustache, and stubble, and he stank of booze. Stocky with a bit of a paunch, he was always coming out of the bedroom, usually with no shirt on, sometimes clad only in his underpants. He didn't ever seem to bother to comb his greasy dark hair.

During the past year on the two other occasions I had come with Aliya for the day, the man had been there. Occasionally, in the afternoon, he and the woman would disappear into the bedroom, as they did in the evening. I don't think he worked because when he was out he must have been drinking. He would come in reeking of alcohol and sit in the big armchair in the corner of the lounge, scratching at his bare, hairy chest, watching telly with us, and making silly comments about the huge photograph of the woman which was hanging on the wall above the shabby settee, where I slept at night. The photograph was a head and shoulders shot of her smiling and looking younger and much thinner. She wore a rhinestone tiara. In the photo, she wasn't bad looking. The man would make his comments in their language, but the gist of it was that he wished he had known her then. I don't think the man contributed much money to the household. Certainly not enough. The woman was always pulling pound notes out of her bra, counting them, and finding she didn't quite have enough.

At some point during the summer holiday the three of us, Adem, Aliya and I, caught a bus to the local funfair. I couldn't believe that Cinderella was being allowed to go to the fair. But we had to be home by the stroke of ten o'clock, not midnight. I rarely went anywhere interesting, and had only just got up the courage to go out on errands. When I went outside I was confused because there were so many blocks of flats in the street and they all looked the same to me. I was scared for a moment that I was lost, and certain that if I went further afield I would be. To my amazement, when I got back and I mentioned this, the woman made Adem write down the address of the flat on a piece of paper for me. She told me to make certain that whenever I went out, I had the address in my pocket.

The funfair was magic, although Aliya and I lost sight of Adem almost immediately. He was supposed to be looking after us – and he was the one who knew the way home – but almost as soon as we got there, he went off with some girl he had begun chatting up.

I was entranced by the funfair. I liked the animated

music, and the happy screeches of the children and even the adults on the rides. Aliya and I went on one of them that jiggled us about frantically and we screamed too. There were mostly young couples at the fair, walking hand in hand, although there were also plenty of dads holding on to their young children's hands. I liked the smell of the popcorn, but Aliya and I didn't have enough money left between us to buy any. What little we had, we spent on throwing hoops to win a fish. My throw wasn't good enough to win us one. At least when you throw a javelin, it doesn't have to land in a precise spot.

The time went quickly. Adem had disappeared with our return bus money, and when it became clear that he wasn't looking for us, being older, I took charge. I led Aliya into the main street, hailed a taxi cab and gave him the piece of paper with the address written on it. When we arrived the taxi driver was afraid we would run off without paying, so Aliya waited in the taxi while I hurried up to the flat to get the fare from her mother.

When Aliya's mother opened the door and saw that Aliya was not with me, she was outraged and dragged me in. Then she threw me onto the floor and began bashing me up. She was unable to understand my explanation, and unwilling even to try. 'Taxi,' I said. 'Aliya downstairs, in taxi.' As I pointed desperately towards the street, the woman picked up the little hall table and smashed it across my back and legs, again and again, until mercifully the table broke. Whatever English she possessed had deserted her, she was in such a terrible rage.

She was jabbering at me in Turkish, and I at her in English. I was frightened, and becoming hysterical myself, when she ran into the kitchen and came out with a bread knife. At this point the din was such that the man in her bed woke up, and came running out of the bedroom dressed only in his grey-white underpants. 'Polis, polis,' he said to her, grabbing the knife. 'Neighbour will phone polis.' There were pillow marks on his face, and his bushy hair was messier than ever. As usual he stank of alcohol, but I was glad to see him because his English was better than hers.

I ran to the door and pointed out the taxi's headlamps in the street. The man understood. He told her, and thankfully she did not hit me when he went to the bedroom to get some pound notes, which he put in my hand. My back hurt, but my legs were all right so, with adrenaline coursing through me, I ran down the stairs and paid the fare. The taxi driver had kept the meter going. When Aliya and I got back to the flat, I made her walk in ahead of me, but her mother and the man had disappeared into the bedroom.

Aliya and I were dog-tired. It was nearly eleven at night. She went to her bedroom in the front of the flat to sleep, and I went to the lounge. I had never felt so tired in my life. As I pulled the blanket over me on my settee bed, my mind was racing, and my body ached. Now, both my back and my legs hurt. I knew I would have bruises in the morning. My life was becoming a waking nightmare.

Just before I fell asleep, I heard the front door open and Adem sneak into his room with a girlfriend. They were whispering and giggling. Then all was quiet.

Much later, something woke me with a start. It was the door of the lounge opening. In the dark, I could sense rather than see someone walking towards the couch where I was lying. Then I could smell the booze on him as he bumped into the armchair and swore. I was frightened. I tried to call for help. Then I thought perhaps I was dreaming, as when I opened my mouth, nothing came out.

I was panic-stricken, literally frozen with terror, utterly unable to move, hoping he was just looking for something he had left in the lounge.

He found it all right.

It was me.

When he lay on the couch alongside me, I kept very still, pretending to be asleep. He moved closer.

Slowly, as though I was moving in my sleep, I inched away, into the back of the settee, creating a sliver of space between us. I hoped he would get the message and go away.

Instead, he started to touch me. He stank of alcohol and sweat. I pushed him away with my feet. He began to pull at my pyjamas, but was too drunk to get them off.

I was terrified and could not believe this was happening. I pulled away. He tried to thrust upon me from behind. I couldn't move. I was in a state of panic, but at least I was able to scream.

'No! No!' I shouted. 'Help! Someone help me!'

He tried to muffle my screams by pushing my head into the couch. With sudden strength, he pulled off my pyjamas and thrust into me. It hurt. I kept shouting and pulling away from him. I was fighting in earnest now, screaming at every possible moment, desperately hoping that one of the others would decide to come to my rescue. He clung to me tightly, panting.

Eventually, the woman came running into the front room. When she switched on the light, she saw he was stark naked and in bed with me. She glared at both of us, as though we were in collusion. Then Adem rushed in, followed by Aliya. The woman was screaming in Turkish and the only word I could pick out was *'polis'*. Two hours before, he had threatened her with the police; now she was threatening him. That got him out of the lounge and back into her bedroom.

They all went back to bed with hardly a word to me. I was sobbing, but I got out of the makeshift bed to lock the door behind them. It wouldn't lock. It was cold and I got back under the covers, a total wreck, praying for morning to come quickly.

As I lay there in the dark, wishing I could sleep, but listening anxiously to the night noises, thinking each one must be him, I wondered how the social worker could possibly have imagined that this was the family I should live in. The woman had shown me no love since I had arrived. She had more concern for the state of her kitchen floor. And now, after her lover had raped me, no doubt she blamed me.

Hours later, I heard the toilet flush, and then the doorknob being turned. I sat up with a start. I could not believe it was happening again. I hurriedly got out of the bed and hid behind the armchair. He was trying to find me again, but the woman, guessing he would make a detour, called out to him. He left to go back to her.

I knew he could come again later in the night, and I knew I couldn't face even the thought of it happening again. Timidly, I knocked on Adem's door, and pleaded with him to let me sleep there on the floor. Adem was sure the man wouldn't try it yet again, and said no. Besides, his girlfriend was still there. I went back to the lounge but I knew I didn't dare go to sleep. Leaving the light on, I sat hunched under the blanket, alone and scared.

Suddenly, I heard the door of the woman's bedroom open again. Perhaps it was her, not him. Surely Adem was right; he wouldn't dare try his luck again. I switched the light out and hid once more behind the armchair. I could hear my heart pounding. I hoped he couldn't. But, I told myself, I was a fool, scaring myself for nothing. I had to calm down – it couldn't be him.

But it was.

I could not stand the pressure of this any longer. I had to get out of that room or I would go mad. As he crept in, befuddled by the dark and the drink, I ran towards the doorway, which I could just make out in the moonlight. I ran into him as I tried to get out of the room. He stumbled as I brushed past, trying to gather himself and grab me at the same time. But it was too late; I was out of the room and pounding on Adem's door, screaming and sobbing, shouting, a mass of turbulent emotions.

Suddenly, they were all in the corridor again, the woman screaming at the man and at me. 'If you tell anyone this,' she said, 'I kill you.' I went into Adem's room and stood huddled with my back against the cold wall. The girl in his bed said nothing. When Adem had quieted his mother, he came back into the bedroom, carrying my blanket, and locked the door. He told me I could sleep in his room on the floor.

Later, when his girlfriend left, he went into the lounge to sleep and left me his bed. I locked the door and lay down exhausted in the rumpled sheets. Drained, I soon fell asleep.

I dreamt the nightmare that had followed me from child-hood. The man in the cape was ringing the bell with a toilet chain, ringing and ringing. The noise of the bell clanging was thunderous, even though the man had stopped pulling the chain and was now chasing me.

I woke with a start. I hadn't wet Adem's bed, but I knew I was beyond sleep.

Morning took what seemed like two centuries to arrive. Bedraggled physically and emotionally, I knew I had to leave that flat. I had no money, and was uncertain as to which bus to take. I only knew I was going. As soon as he was up, I pleaded with Adem to help me get back to the children's home. He told me this was my home, the place where I belonged.

'No, no, no, no,' I said, almost in a whisper, too exhausted to shout. 'I can't stay here.' He could hear the rock-hard determination in my quiet voice. He knew I didn't know the way or have the fare, but Adem finally realised that I was going to leave whatever. Then he offered to give me the bus fare if I kept quiet about what had happened.

I would have agreed to any suggestion to get away from that flat. I knew I had to get away, I had to get back to the home, which at that moment seemed like a haven.

CHAPTER TEN

The Aftermath

THE HOUSE WAS empty when I arrived. Unlike London, there was no noise in the street. Everything was quiet. Inside my head, though, there was uproar. When I thought about what had happened – what the man had done to me which could not be undone, and that terrible word, *rape*; when I thought about Aliya's mother threatening to kill me, and I could not seem to stop thinking about it – I began to tremble, my fingers twitching as though they were in the midst of a terrifying nightmare.

After unpacking from a carrier bag the few things I had taken with me – a jumper, underwear, my comb which was missing more than a few teeth, a hairbrush, a toothbrush – I went downstairs into the kitchen to make myself a hot drink. It didn't matter to me one bit that we were forbidden to enter the kitchen except when told, and I didn't give a toss that Mrs Smith might at any moment come striding in. I badly needed the warmth and comfort of a steaming cup of tea. And I needed and wanted to go to see Auntie Rae, to tell her what had happened, to get comfort from her. But I felt so ashamed.

As I put the teabag into a chipped mug and waited for the kettle to boil, my eyes welled with sudden tears. Yet I felt that I was both me and a fly on the wall watching me. I was watching myself getting out the tea things, pulling out the kitchen chair, brushing the few crumbs off the table. It was an eerie, uncomfortable feeling, as though I were coming apart into two separate bits. The hot tea warmed my shaking fingers, but it could not warm the chill I felt inside. I wanted to knock on Auntie Rae's door. I wanted to see her, and talk to her, but equally I knew I could not.

It seemed to take hours to drink the tea, and then I watched myself washing up the mug and carefully drying it so that Mrs Smith would not know that I had broken yet another of her silly rules. I stared at myself walking out of the kitchen and out of the back door, and then I realised that I was walking towards the children's home where my friend Alma lived. Because she was nine or ten months younger than me and had absolutely no idea that such terrible things happened, with Alma I could pretend that they didn't.

Turning the corner, I marvelled at the stillness of everything. In comparison with London, with its pounding heavy lorries and buses shaking the windows, Essex seemed to be a rural refuge.

At Alma's, the person that rang the bell was greeted with an enthusiastic hello. Alma was ecstatic to see me back so soon. Neither she nor any of the other children noticed the sad, weepy person that was staring down from the wall. We went in a noisy, good-natured, straggly parade to the park and threw a ball around.

Returning to the home, I slowly opened the door, willing myself to veil my feelings sufficiently to show absolutely nothing to Mrs Smith. But instead Auntie Rae was there, wiping the kitchen table. She had been on all weekend, and had just been out on an errand that morning when I had first come back. If only I had known.

'Something terrible has happened, Aunt,' I blurted out, 'but I can't tell.' Sobs racked my body; I thought I was going to burst with grief.

Auntie Rae put her arms around me. 'What is it?' I was shaking, the tears streaming down my cheeks. 'Lovie, what's the matter?'

'Aliya's mother said she would kill me if I told anyone.'

'I'm not anyone. You sit down, Fats, and tell me everything. You will feel better, love, when you do.'

I was afraid to tell her, but I was also afraid of not telling because I so needed her to know. Perching on the edge of the kitchen table, I said in a solemn but shaky voice, 'I'll tell you only if you promise not to tell anyone.'

'I won't be able to keep it a secret if it's important, love.'

I began to cry softly, and she put her arms back around me. Through my tears, my sobs of pain, the whole awful story began to pour out. Even after I had finished telling it, I continued to cry on Auntie Rae's shoulder.

Even when she said, 'I can't keep that secret. That's got to be reported,' I still felt better. Auntie Rae helped me to tidy myself up and put me to bed.

Later, she told Mrs Smith, and when nothing seemed to come of it, I felt safe.

Mrs Smith, the matron, whose duty it was, promised she would report the incident to head office. When Auntie Rae enquired the next day or the day after that, Mrs Smith said she had rung them, and that the authorities had sent someone over to the flat in London, but that the man was not there so nothing could be done. There was no official inquiry, and when Margaret Whitbread was shown my case history months later, there was no mention at all of sexual abuse.

Auntie Rae and I didn't talk about it either. What was there to say? It was not my fault, Auntie Rae had told me, there was no reason to feel dirty or ashamed. But as the weeks passed, the glum person on the wall looking down at me came more and more to the fore. The terrible time I had endured in London kept coming back to me. Even in the midst of playing ball or chatting with Alma and Wendy and my other friends, I would suddenly, for no apparent reason, drop into a state of deep gloom. This would alternate with feelings of rage.

I started to smoke. My increasingly frequent arguments with Mrs Smith and her husband became increasingly bitter. I will never ever forget my shock and feeling of utter hope-lessness, which quickly turned to anger, that terrible morning when she told me, 'It's obvious that no family will ever want *you*.' It wasn't the last time she said it either.

But I have to admit, I gave them as good as I got, and by the time I got to school I was in no mood to be told anything by anyone. And certainly not to be asked some stupid question about Shakespeare or the capital of the Sudan. Not surprisingly, I was always in trouble at school. I was lippy to the teachers. At that school, they were used to it. They were ratty back to me, and I accepted it. But I wouldn't take anything from the other pupils, no matter how big they were. Anyone who was snotty with me had trouble to answer to.

There was a brawny lad who was a brutal, verbal bully. He was big-fisted and in the leather-jacket set, but it was his loud mouth that bloodied. He called me a bastard and made certain everyone knew he meant it literally. He knew I lived in a children's home and told everyone in the school, humiliating me relentlessly.

He towered over me, but at the first opportunity in the playground I stood up to him and, nervous though I was, snarled, 'You were cheeky to me in Maths and now you are going to get what I said you'd get.'

He pushed me away.

'I said now you're gonna get what I promised you.'

'I don't fight girls,' he said, looking at me like I was nothing. 'Fuck off.'

Instead, I let rip. I had to jump up to hit him, he was that much taller than me. He hit back, but he was making it clear that he was trying not to fight because I was a girl. That was even more infuriating. He had got away with denigrating me in the classroom and now, by not fighting, he was humiliating me again. I hit and hit and hit him. A teacher had to pull us apart.

Only on the hockey pitch at Blackshots, where I played for the local Thurrock Colts team, could I turn my frustration and aggression into something worthy of applause. There was only one of me, but that one was all over the field, wielding a hockey stick with a vengeance. 'Stay out of my way' was the message.

With netball, it was much the same story. It may have been a girls' game, but I was anything but a ladylike player. On the court there was no gloomy me; no person watching from the sidelines or like a fly on the wall; I felt no sense of being split. There was only the one person, but that one had the strength and speed of seven. Little did I realise that sport was going to be my passport to the future. Even though I sensed that sport was now the only thing keeping me from drowning in despair, I didn't think about it much. To be absolutely honest, my life didn't really seem to be worth saving.

And then, for the first time, I began having trouble with PE lessons – that is, with country dancing, if you can call it PE. Not that I had any problems with dancing per se; but what we did at the disco on a Wednesday night was a far cry from country dancing. We wiggled and twisted and shook it up and down. Country dancing was all prim and pre-set, with movements just so; no life in it, no fun. I agreed wholeheartedly with Pete Townshend of The Who, who prescribed rock and roll, where the music inspired you to dance your troubles away.

The teacher was the same stern, be-bunned deputy head, Miss Meredith, who had soured my impression of the secondary school when I'd come with my junior school class to look it over. Some years later, this same Miss Meredith, who, Mum tells me, was a good teacher and who had a lot to put up with in me, explained that my moods were a trial to her. Either I was feeling high, or terribly, terribly low – no in between for me. That I believe, but I have to say too that country dancing as it was taught there was such a stupid bore that I did my best to avoid it. One out of every three lessons would find me smoking in the girls' loos. And when I did turn up, I did my very best to disrupt the class, by making awkward remarks and dancing the wrong steps. If it was fast, I would move slowly; if it was a slow step, I would be lively. Miss Meredith got fed up. She would have had to be more than human not to.

During one lesson, she showed us a new country dance. I did it in ultra slow motion. Miss Meredith first coaxed me, and then, having grown pale with frustration at my behaviour, she shouted, 'Move faster!'

Of course, I didn't.

'Move,' she said in an uncharacteristically fierce tone, 'move, move!' She swatted my legs with her open palm, hard. I moved all right.

'Move, move!' Her words were in time to the music. 'Move!' She slapped my legs again. I moved, and properly too.

'No more nonsense,' she said. She slapped again. 'Keep moving. It is time you condescended to join our class.' In her heart of hearts, like most of the other teachers I was giving a hard time to, she must have wished that I hadn't condescended to turn up.

The authorities were eventually alerted that something was deeply wrong. I was deemed intolerable. A summit meeting was convened to discuss what could be done about me. The school was on the verge of expelling me.

Mrs Smith didn't throw any official light on the reason for my troubled and troubling state, perhaps because she wanted me out of her house. She often said how pleased she would be when I became sixteen. I'd be too old for a children's home and would be sent to a hostel in London. I was terrified of going to London, not just because of what had happened to me there, but because I knew that that was where lone girls got trapped by drugs and prostitution and poverty. It was the last place I wanted to go. Not that I was even consulted.

My fate was to be determined by a summit conference in

which I did not even take part. Miss Toomey of the district social services came from head office, accompanied by Bob Walker. As a pair they were utterly contrasting. She was a mousey, middle-aged, well-intentioned spinster whom it was easy to underestimate. She looked as though only saccharine ran in her veins, but she had the experience and the nous to suss out a problem quickly, and when the situation called for it, she had a surprisingly sharp tongue. That day the situation would call for it.

Bob Walker and his heart-breaking caution, I have already described. But together Toomey and Walker made a fairly formidable pair. That day, when they sat down with one of the teachers I didn't know very well and Mrs Smith, I was fortunate that they were batting for my side.

Before the summit, Miss Toomey had a little chat with Auntie Rae, who was not invited to the meeting, but who did after all know me the best. The conversation went something like this:

'But what's the matter with Fatima? Why can't the Smiths get on with the girl?' Miss Toomey asked.

'Because Fatima believes in justice and fair play.'

Miss Toomey did a double take. 'But at school she's a troublemaker too.'

'By the time she leaves here in the morning, the child is so wound up, it's only her good nature that keeps her from setting the place on fire. You would be too, Miss Toomey, if you had Mrs Smith snarling at you, not to mention him, Mr Smith, on at you too.'

Auntie Rae was shooed out as the others arrived, and the meeting began, with the social workers, Toomey and Walker, arguing that I should stay at the home, largely on the grounds that I had been there a long time and had friends in the neighbourhood. It was a sort of 'better the devil you know' argument, based on the social workers' theory that what I seemed to need at the time was something to hang on to, stability – plus what Bob Walker thought of as Mrs Smith's benevolent influence and what Miss Toomey knew to be the lack of a suitable place for me in London. The decision was, I could stay on at the Smiths' and stay in school – provided I went to see a child psychologist.

Even the idea of it embarrassed me. But with the threat of London looming and the glum, weepy person on the wall getting gloomier and ever more in attendance, I agreed to try it once. Really I had no choice. With my fingers in my mouth and Auntie Rae at my side, I boarded the Green Line bus for the journey to Grays. After what seemed like hours, we arrived. I felt tense and slightly nauseous, and Auntie Rae, who had been trying hard to keep my spirits up, must have been exhausted.

CHAPTER ELEVEN

No Messing About

'LET'S JUST GO home,' I said when we got to the grimy, red-brick building which housed the council's special medical services. The sky had darkened. It was going to rain. 'I'm not crazy. I don't want to see any child psychologist.'

'You're not in the least bit crazy.' Auntie Rae's tone was reassuring. 'But you do need help. Come along, Fats. We must do what we must do.'

As we procrastinated in the rain, a septuagenarian on mismatched crutches brushed past into the building. 'He's a little old, isn't he?' I said. 'Aren't we supposed to be seeing a *child* psychologist?'

'They take the lame of all sorts here, Fats. Likely he has come to see one of the other doctors or for a new pair of crutches.'

Somewhat relieved that the passers-by could not know for certain why I was there, I followed Auntie Rae into the perfectly ordinary waiting room, which was much in need of paint, and slumped into an uncomfortable little chair. But I was too restless to sit still for long and began to suck on my fingers again and to prowl about, feeling hostile and extremely embarrassed. I knew I wasn't crazy, just angry and confused – and with good reason.

I didn't want a stranger messing about with my head.

Dr Dano motioned us into her office, where Auntie Rae and I sat stiffly on the hard little chairs opposite the doctor's ugly but imposing desk, Auntie Rae with her coat in her lap and me holding on to my jacket as if it were a life preserver. On the desk was an odd little contraption, a pole with a chain attached to it and a small ball suspended from the chain, which vaguely reminded me of the toilet chain in my recurring nightmare.

To break the ice, Dr Dano, a woman of sixty who was quite unlike anyone I had ever met, flashed a gentle smile and quietly muttered some pleasantry on the order of, 'I am pleased to meet you.'

My hands began to shake. Another foreign accent. She was from Eastern Europe, I think, a tall, angular woman with glasses and lank, iron-grey hair pulled back in a pony-tail. She had on a tweed skirt, with the matching jacket slung over the back of her chair. She was an Eastern European bluestocking, someone utterly foreign to me. I didn't want to talk to her. So I didn't.

But the doctor was resourceful. Pointing to the ball on the chain on her desk, she asked me to hit it hard. 'Actions are plainer than words,' she said, 'aren't they?'

I swatted the ball. It spun on its chain just a bit.

'You can do much better than that, can't you, Fatima? Try now to think of someone you dislike, and then strike the ball again.'

Thinking of Mr Smith, I hit the ball so hard that it pulled the chain nearly to breaking point.

The doctor was impressed. 'You must really dislike that person.'

I nodded.

She seemed to feel that we had accomplished something, and said we would talk more at my next appointment.

'This is a waste of time,' I told Auntie Rae on the bus back to the home. 'I can't talk to that woman.'

'Do try, love.' Auntie Rae patted my hand. Out of the window there were grey skies. 'It may help, and unless your behaviour improves, I think you will be moved to a different children's home and a different school.'

That was my worst thought. It meant I would have nowhere and no one. Tears welled in my eyes again. But I held them back because I certainly didn't want strangers staring at me on the Green Line bus.

'Look on the bright side,' Auntie Rae said. 'This woman doctor is here to help you feel better, that's all.'

My next appointment was to be in three weeks.

'It's a waste of time seeing her. I could be doing some training.' After school, if there wasn't a school team practice, I played netball or hockey for one of the local Thurrocks clubs at the Blackshots sports centre.

'Even without training you're the best athlete in the school, right? No one can take that away from you.'

My spirits rose. Auntie Rae was a brilliant psychologist.

'Seems to me, Fats,' she said, certainly not referring to the weather, 'there is sunlight on the horizon.'

But Auntie Rae wasn't with me most of the time, to bolster my spirits in that special way she had. She was only at the home thirty hours a week, and she couldn't always defend me against the Smiths' snipes and denigrations. She couldn't accompany me to school, where I put on a loud, defensive front and tried not to show how much the schoolchildren's digs and the teachers' dismissive comments hurt me. She wasn't there at night, as I lay alone in bed with my thoughts, which turned always towards what had happened in London, even as I tried desperately to think of other things.

Some situations simply cannot be fixed by jollying along, and the psychologist wasn't much help either. She asked me what I liked best about school. When I said, 'Sport,' she told me to play a lot of it. I could use sport to get rid of all the anger that was welling up inside me. 'You have good reason for the anger,' she said, 'but try to let it go. Over time, you'll feel better.'

But what did she know? It had been such a grating struggle just getting to be thirteen. I felt I couldn't face another thirteen years more, let alone the twelve months ahead. Was I going to spend the rest of my wretched life being horribly messed about? Would I always alternately seethe with rage or feel hopelessly, drearily bleak?

Even my lifeline – sport – was keeping me only barely afloat. Sport, at which I excelled almost without even trying, made me feel I was somebody. And the aggression-releasing cut and thrust of netball, the bounding and the screams on court kept my feverish emotional temperature just below danger point. But with one thing and another – the aggro at school, the Smiths, the horrible experience in London – my spirits sank lower and lower until I reached rock bottom.

Aliya's mother's only interest in me, and it still hurt, seemed to be as a skivvy. She had not protected me from her son's or her lover's unwelcome sexual advances. What happened to me in her flat, that horrible experience, was something I would never entirely get over. My anger kept boiling over.

I remember feeling on the day of a netball match that our school was playing against St Chad's School that I was getting to the end of my tether. If I could just get this bloody match over with, I felt I would just quietly lie down and wait for the rest of my wretched life to be over.

About half an hour later, I met Mrs Whitbread, the no-nonsense umpire with attitude who so utterly changed my life. She was, I now realise, the spitting image of me, except for her colouring – the wan complexion which was typically English, as were her blue eyes and cropped, mousy hair. Sturdy for her five-foot four-inch frame, chubby but with muscle under the skin, she was a PE teacher at St Chad's, who were our main rivals for the league title; yet girls from our school were supposed to accept that she was impartial when it came to umpiring this match.

Our own teacher, who lacked the one thing really necessary in a netball umpire, a loud, carrying voice, had let St Chad's do as they liked during the first half of the match. But when it was Mrs Whitbread's turn, suddenly we had to behave on court like convent girls at prayers. It was beyond a joke.

As the second half got underway, I loudly challenged her calls, giving her a lot of lip. I knew precisely how to be difficult and disruptive. Having no mainstay, no direction, no prospects, I saw no reason not to take it out on everyone, and Mrs Whitbread, the voice of authority, was a natural enemy. What I didn't know was that on the drive over to Culverhouse in the St Chad's minibus, Mrs Whitbread, who was shepherding a team of seven toughies, had kept hearing, 'I hope she isn't playing, Miss. I hope Fatima isn't playing. I hope she isn't playing, Miss.'

Mrs Whitbread was none too pleased when she found out that this very Fatima was the one who kept disagreeing with her calls. I played netball the way, I later found out, she played hockey: aggressively, relentlessly, with a bit of a killer instinct. When it came to netball, I wasn't a brilliant skills player, but I had a touch. I played centre, which meant I was the fulcrum, the one who set up nearly every goal. Every moment of that match was cut and thrust, every goal hard-earned. Anyone could see that I knew how to read a netball game. They could also see that I knew how to open my vitriolic mouth.

But she wasn't taking anything off me. She wouldn't put up with my verbals at all. 'Stop giving stick to other players on your team, and stop querying my decisions,' she said, in a voice loud enough to drown out fourteen noisy players including my own protest of innocence. 'Stop it, or I'll send you off the court. Now.'

I kept it down till near the end of the match when my temper reignited. Wanting to see what I could get away with, and wanting my team to win – it was a very close match – I questioned another of her calls. The umpire sounded her whistle and motioned to me to come over.

I wasn't going to go to her, and as Mrs Whitbread stared at me open-mouthed in disbelief, I held my nose in the air. One of her toughies, Donna Kempster, who played netball for St Chad's but also played with me on the Thurrock Colts, the local junior hockey team, said, 'You'd better play along with her, Fatima, or she will ban you from the match. That's one teacher who means what she says.'

Impressed, I shut up for the remainder of the match. But my team didn't win. The game was a draw – 16 all. I wouldn't remember it otherwise but, as I realised much much later, that match was a crucial turning point in my life.

Weeks later, on a Saturday afternoon when the girls on the Thurrock Colts hockey team found their match had been suddenly cancelled, some of us, still in our gold jumpers and short black skirts, stayed on to watch the club's first team play. Mrs Babs Bannister, who managed the Colts and had stood up to Mrs Smith for me when I was late coming home from matches, was goalkeeper on the senior team.

During the warm-up one of the Thurrock players, whom I vaguely recognised, motioned to me. 'Keep your eyes on me,' she said, 'and you might learn a trick or two.'

The player was the very woman who had umpired the netball match. As the match wore on, I was impressed by the standard of her play, but what amazed me was that the woman who had told me to shut up during play now gave more stick to her team-mates and had more to say during the match than the other players put together.

Not long after, Alma and I went to Blackshots one afternoon. As Alma went off to do some running, I noticed a javelin lying on the field. To be perfectly honest, what I noticed first was a javelin thrower, David Ottley, who was practising throws. He was twenty years old, blond-haired, and well-muscled. To thirteen-year-old me, he looked like a bit of all right.

'I'd like to try the javelin,' I said, picking up the one lying on the field.

A training assistant rushed forward. 'First you have to get the permission of the coach,' he said. 'She's not here yet so please get off the field.' But I could sit in the stands and watch Dave practise until the coach arrived, and I did.

It was a sharp surprise to find out that this same Mrs Margaret Whitbread was the javelin coach at Blackshots playing fields.

Because I was known to be a troublemaker, Margaret Whitbread seemed far from delighted to see me. But I kept coming back. If I wanted to learn to throw a javelin – and I did, for more than one reason – then I had to cope with her, outspoken and strict though she was, and she had to cope with me, a smart-arse troublemaker. She began by taking me to one side and telling me very firmly I would be welcome in the javelin group only so long as I behaved. It was precisely the sort of school-teacherish threat that always got my back up *and* it came from a woman who as a player was a bit of a villain herself.

My answer to her, to my own amazement, was something in the order of, 'I'll behave, Miss.'

My friend Alma and I now went to Blackshots stadium twice a week, Wednesday after school and every Sunday morning; going by bus on weekdays, but walking to and from the track on a Sunday. Walking took a long time but it saved the bus fare, which we used to buy cigarettes. I had tried most sports on offer at Blackshots, finding the long, hard sessions at the athletics club a help in burning off the white-hot anger that was otherwise always with me. Alma was focusing on sprints and I on the javelin. Over time, I grew to know Mrs Whitbread well.

Margaret Callender Whitbread had grown up in Essex, the only child of a brawny chief petty officer who had boxed and played hockey for the navy and been an Amateur Boxing Association judge. Mrs Whitbread's mother Marion had sprinted for Essex way back in 1935. No one in the family was surprised that at sport Margaret was, as her father often bragged, 'a natural'. His only disappointment was that she was not much of a boxer.

The sport she was passionate about was the javelin. Before marrying, she threw for Great Britain, continuing to coach even after bearing two sons. As an athletics international, she had travelled to glamorous cities all over Europe. At sixteen, in 1956, she was British under-17 champion, and at just eighteen she came fifth in the Empire Games (now the Commonwealth Games) at Cardiff. She is still fond of Cardiff.

Margaret Callender never won a major international javelin championship; partly because javelin throwers mature like wine – she retired at age twenty-two to work as a coach and PE teacher – and partly because the Easten bloc had the unfair advantage of full-time athletes, many of whom were taking illegal drugs. She decided to learn the very best coaching techniques so that one day, without using the drugs that the East Germans and others were taking, Britain could at least give the Eastern bloc a run for their money.

Sport was – as her husband John Whitbread, a tall, wiry docker, liked to say, grinning from ear to ear – her second love; a close second, too, but not too close for comfort. On Saturdays, in the afternoon, she played county-level hockey. But Saturday nights she was home with him.

Mrs Whitbread was someone close up I could emulate. There were also the shining examples of the pentathlete Mary Peters and the horsewoman Princess Anne. At the Olympics in Munich in 1972, the summer after my eleventh birthday, Mary Peters not only won the gold medal, she also set a new world record. Because the pentathlon was five events in one, including running, jumping and throwing (the shot), Mary Peters had to train and train and train, building plenty of muscle on her sturdy frame. She was far from the traditionally feminine ideal, but nevertheless she was a much-loved, much-admired British heroine. Like everyone else's in Britain, my eleven-year-old spirits had been lifted by her achievement. I dreamed of becoming an Olympic athlete.

The year before that, Princess Anne had won the European Championship. That was thrilling. Of course, there was no chance of my becoming a three-day eventer like Anne: I lived in the wrong world; almost everyone did. But it was possible for me to become an athlete.

What with one thing and another, particularly my luck in finding an expert coach and my schoolgirl crush on Dave, I began to focus on the javelin. Some credit for my choice of sport must go to the javelin itself. It is not only a magical event, it is a beautiful one. The flight of the javelin is a glorious sight and, as I very soon discovered, letting go was a fantastic feeling. If only television used its nous and spliced the javelin competition together, showing it as a whole instead of in bitty, disjointed pieces, it would make trans-fixing viewing. You would feel the tension of the competition building and care, as I do, each time the javelin soars.

Even before I had acquired much skill, I loved the event, as my new coach certainly sensed. But if I really wanted to throw the javelin, Mrs Whitbread said, I must get my parents to buy me one and some proper javelin boots. I couldn't face telling her that I didn't have any parents, but I kept coming along to practice, albeit without the proper kit. Occasionally, she asked if my parents were still planning to get me the boots and javelin. My answer was always a vague nod.

When she found out that I lived in a home, she immediately gave me a pair of used javelin boots that she got from an athlete who had outgrown them. Making a joke of the fact that the boots were hand-me-down, she said, 'They will be easier to break in.' The suede was not as blue as it had been, and there were other signs of wear, but they were my first javelin boots. I was as excited, proud and happy as if they had come in a gift box from Harrods. The boots were a little too big, but at Mrs Whitbread's suggestion, I stuffed the toes with paper and wore them.

And she gave me a javelin.

I was, if anything, even prouder of it.

Back at the home, the first person I saw was Ingrid, the German student who was working there for a year. Nothing else would do: I had to demonstrate my new javelin. It took me two throws to get up to the cabbage patch at the end of the garden, which is such a paltry distance I probably shouldn't admit it, even now. Ingrid politely oohed and ahhed.

'One more throw,' I said, retrieving the javelin. To my horror, the next throw was much longer than the others and sailed right through the French windows, landing with a loud tinkle of glass well inside the dining room. Fortunately, there was no one in the room at the time.

Ingrid panicked. What would Mrs Smith say? I can't say I was Miss Cool myself. I hid my javelin in the closed cupboard near the back door – convenient for a quick getaway. When Mrs Smith returned, she was absolutely livid and, as soon as she heard it was Fatima, ignored Ingrid's explanation that it had been an accident. Uncle Alan, she said, would see to me. I was sent to my room to wait until he had unloaded the car. They had been away for the weekend at a house they owned in Aveley village, not that far from the home, and where they went on what they called their weekends off, which I regarded as my weekends off too. No aggro. No arguments. No bickering.

Now they were back and we were back to punishments as usual. My punishment this time was that I could not go out after school for a month. That meant that javelin practice at Blackshots was off-limits, as was any visit to Auntie Rae. My pocket money was to be cut for one month to help to pay for the damage. Ingrid tried to speak on my behalf but they refused to listen.

Secretly, I did pop into Auntie Rae's anyway after school. Her house was near enough. As I began to tell her everything I knew about the javelin, which was not much, and everything I knew about the javelin teacher, my spirits rose a little.

But I couldn't get to Blackshots. Depressed and angry, I spent much of my extra free time smoking in the bathroom, putting my head out of the window to exhale the smoke.

So that Mrs Whitbread wouldn't wonder why I had defected as soon as I had got my boots and javelin, I decided to smuggle a note out to her. All I could find to write on was an airmail letter, which I stealthily removed from a cabinet in the dining room. The only place where there was enough privacy to write the note was the toilet. Not knowing her home address, I addressed the air letter to St Chad's School, where she read it in the staff room. Explaining that I had accidentally hurled my javelin through the French windows and that I was being punished, I said that I hoped she would let me rejoin her javelin group when I could because one day I was going to be the best javelin thrower in the world.

After what seemed a century, my term of punishment was over. This time Mrs Whitbread was pleased to see me. But there was to be no messing about.

CHAPTER TWELVE

New Possibilities

JUST LIKE MRS Whitbread's star javelin thrower Dave Ottley – who was, as I have said, a strong reason for my initial attraction to the javelin – I had to get right down to work. It turned out that Dave wasn't just handsome, he was helpful and very nice. Aside from the blushing, I think I largely managed to hide my crush. But I was much too young for him. Later, we would both win Olympic medals.

Meanwhile, just getting to grips with the javelin – by which I mean, actually learning how to hold it – was a matter of trial and a frustrating amount of error. There are three main grips: an index finger and thumb hold, a middle finger and index finger hold, and mine, in which my middle finger and thumb held the javelin tightly behind the cord grip, while my index finger was lightly (or not so lightly) folded around the shaft of the javelin. For further support, I would wrap the rest of my fingers around the grip.

The run-up was the other headache. To throw, you run holding the javelin aloft until just before the line when you let it go. The number of strides and the angle of the javelin are crucial. A good throw requires speed, rhythm and explosive release at the right moment. Put your toe over the line and your throw doesn't count. That first season, as I was a novice, Mrs Whitbread told me to have the front end of the javelin pointing slightly downwards. It made no sense to me, as I was trying to make the thing soar. But with Mrs Whitbread alternately coaxing me gently and screaming in my ear, I did as she said.

In July, when Auntie Rae came to see me compete at Blackshots stadium, and when I won with a district record of 39 metres which still stands, it was hard to tell who was prouder – her, Mrs Whitbread or me.

Then, after delicate negotiations, of which at the time I was entirely unaware, Mrs Smith agreed that I might have a meal at Mrs Whitbread's house in Chadwell St Mary, which was about twenty minutes' drive away.

After javelin practice one afternoon, we got into her battered, mud-coloured Mini, and finally pulled up again after a ride which involved many turns and much screeching of the brakes, giving me an inkling as to why the Mini was so battered. We were in the alleyway at the back of a two-storey brick house. Walking past the modest back garden vegetable patch where the straggly green onions and yellowing parsley were in need of picking, I was brimming with anticipation. I had never before had a meal at a teacher's house; never even been asked. And this teacher was more than a teacher. She was a coach, the best in all Essex, which so far as I was concerned meant the world.

As she began to unlock the back door, which was mostly glass, it was opened from inside by curly-, brown-haired Gregg, Mrs Whitbread's eldest son, who was four years old. His jovial nan had been looking after him and his brother Kirk, who was two and a half years younger, straight-haired and blond.

While Mrs Whitbread and her mother-in-law were saying goodbye, I had a look around. Smaller than the children's home, their house was a bit bigger than Auntie Rae's, and like hers had a homey atmosphere. There was a big, cheerful, gold dralon corner settee in the lounge and two matching easy chairs under a huge picture window. I plopped onto the settee and gazed out of the window at the small front lawn and the other houses in the street. I felt I could sit there forever.

But someone had to look after the boys while Mrs Whitbread prepared the tea. Playing piggyback in the garden with Gregg and Kirk was far from a chore, the three of us cavorting and giggling like three-year-olds, enjoying ourselves. When Mrs Whitbread's handsome husband John arrived home from the Purfleet docks, the boys jumped happily into his arms. Hugging them warmly, John Whitbread, whose hair was the same brown as his son Gregg's, flashed me a friendly grin.

The five of us sat down at the kitchen table for tea. Putting a huge platter of ham salad on the green velour tablecloth, Mrs Whitbread began to dish up. 'Would you like some beetroot, Fatima?' she asked.

My cheeks flushed as red as the stuff on the table as I admitted hesitantly that I didn't know what beetroot was. We had never had it at the home.

'I suspect you may find you like it,' John Whitbread said. 'Would you like to try some?'

I did, and Mr Whitbread was right. I do like beetroot, although not the way I now like prawn cocktail, spaghetti Bolognese, or my own recipe for baked monkfish, all of which I had never even heard of and certainly never tasted at that time. It is hard to imagine now just how narrow my culinary and cultural horizons were, beetroot being only one of countless things that were beyond my experience.

'Disadvantaged' is precisely the right word for us children who grow up in institutions. But as I learned from John Whitbread, it is no embarrassment to encounter something for the first time. It can be an adventure.

During the meal there was a lot of laughter. There were many visits to the Whitbreads' after that first one, and always much laughter and fun. The only sad part was having to go home. I had fallen in love with the Whitbread family and they had fallen in love with me. Even the boys felt the tie. One evening, as Margaret picked up the keys to the Mini and got up from the table to shuttle me back to the home, little Gregg told me what he had already told his parents, that he wanted me to become his big sister. Then he blurted out what he thought was a brilliant idea: why didn't they just buy me from the shop instead of borrowing me and having to return me at night?

John Whitbread replied, 'It's not that simple, but Mum and I would like Fatima to be part of the family.' He then turned directly to me and said: 'We want to adopt you, if you want it.'

It was what I had always dreamed of. Oh, you should have heard my 'Yes'. It was loud and clear.

But getting adopted wasn't that simple. No, not simple at all. As a first step, the Whitbread family came to visit me at the home. Mr and Mrs Whitbread made certain they got on with Mrs Smith. Gregg and Kirk loved having so many children to play with, and the afternoon passed happily. But I felt sad for the young ones who lived at the home and who had to endure the moment of the boys leaving to go home with a mummy and daddy. To those left behind, it felt like a scab being pulled from a raw, festering wound. I could still remember the sharp, incomprehensible pain I had felt as a little one at being left on the shelf.

It had taken me thirteen years, but now I had found a family who had enough love in their hearts for another child. And they wanted me.

'Be good,' Margaret Whitbread said as they crammed into the Mini. 'Try to stay out of trouble. That will help. But one way or another, John and I are going to get you out of here.' Immediately regretting that she had raised my hopes, she patted me on the shoulder and tried not to show her anxiety. Suppose they wouldn't let her foster me. Suppose something went wrong. So many things could.

My behaviour did improve, and Mrs Smith may well have wondered why it was that whatever Mrs Whitbread told me to do I would do quite happily, but if anyone else told me anything, I dug in like a donkey. Confirming that Mrs Smith had it in for me – and was never one to get things jogging along anyway – Auntie Rae quietly told Margaret Whitbread that to move mountains, in this case, it was best to start at the top. 'Ring head office,' she counselled.

Miss Toomey at head office, who didn't make the best of her looks but who always took the trouble to say what she thought, was the one who put the show on the road. Things began to move quickly although Miss Toomey had warned there would be ages and stages and plenty of red tape. There had to be investigations, references, approvals by my social worker and by head office.

But with Auntie Rae, unbeknownst to anyone, even me,

giving Mrs Whitbread the gen behind the scenes, things began to gallop – even though the woman who gave birth to me would not cooperate. Since I was a ward of the court, where I lived was ultimately up to the social services. But the woman who said she was my mother, whose consent to my being fostered would have made my new placement easier, banged down the telephone when Margaret Whitbread tried, at the social worker's suggestion, to talk to her. Social services had had no luck either. When, on another day, Mrs Whitbread tried again and Adem answered, he was hostile too. How could I ever get adopted if she wouldn't even co-operate with fostering? I was in a state of anguish and I was deeply afraid that with all the aggro, the Whitbread family would just give up on me.

Then, one afternoon, Mrs Smith sat me down at the kitchen table and told me that if I went to live with the Whitbreads, if I allowed them to foster me, if I became a member of their family, I would be betraying Auntie Rae. How could I do such a thing to her?

The last thing I wanted was to hurt Auntie Rae, who had kept me going for so long. Even though I yearned to move in with the Whitbread family and to become a part of it, I did not want to do it at the expense of wounding Auntie Rae. Sitting with my head in my hands, tears brimming, I considered giving up all hope of adoption.

'You have to learn to think of other people,' Mrs Smith said, or words to that effect. Then, whilst Mrs Smith sat in silence, letting what she had suggested to me sink in, and a tear spilled onto my cheek, Auntie Rae, whose shift was starting, sauntered in.

Seeing the gloom, Auntie Rae said, 'What's this then?'

'A problem with Fatima, of course. I didn't want to tell you, but Maggie Whitbread wants to foster her.'

'Why, that's wonderful.' Auntie Rae's face lit up with joy. 'Then she's been on to Miss Toomey like I said, and it's to go through.'

I have never in my life felt such relief. Mrs Smith had the decency to look embarrassed. I don't know what she had been playing at. I now found out how Auntie Rae had given Margaret Whitbread all the gen on how to arrange with officialdom to foster me.

But it wasn't over yet.

CHAPTER THIRTEEN

Stupid Regulations

WHAT HAPPENED NEXT still makes me upset whenever I think about it. It makes me angry for the children who are still stuck in uncaring and under-funded children's homes. Because of social services, I almost didn't get fostered. The social workers seemed to be trying to ruin my life. Even Miss Toomey, who was a caring woman, and who had no ulterior motive, tried to throw a spanner in the works. I'm sure she and my social worker Mr Walker meant well, but they could easily have ruined my life.

What happened was this. Bob Walker, who really didn't know me or the Whitbreads, told them that taking me into their home just wouldn't work because I had lived in children's homes for too long. He said I was too institutionalised for family life. That was 'the department's view'.

Even if I got along at the Whitbreads' at first, he predicted, 'the honeymoon period' would soon end. Then there would be unhappiness and heartache. Maybe even mayhem.

Showing Margaret Whitbread the records of my case, he pointed out that my life had been a series of raised hopes and disappointments, which I had countered with hostility. I had a chip on my shoulder. The Smiths saw it and at school they were aware of it.

'But that's them, not John and me,' Margaret Whitbread argued. 'I get problem children in my class all the time. Because they play up with another teacher doesn't mean they will play up with me.'

'It's not just another teacher,' he told her. My whole record was trouble.

Mrs Whitbread told him that all I needed was a family and I would be all right. Thank goodness she was a school-teacher and *knew* that she knew children, or she might have been swayed by the 'authorities' who had read in some book that 'institutionalised' children could not adapt to family life and so wanted to deny me my chance. As Margaret put it, the social worker had labelled me as 'beyond help' because I had been institutionalised too long. Things haven't changed much. Only 3 per cent of the 3,050 looked-after children adopted in 2011 were between ten and fifteen years old.

Then they played the race and religion cards.

One of the social workers pointed out that my skin tone would be noticeably darker than that of the Whitbreads' other children, and said that I was Muslim and should go to a family like the one I was from. But there weren't enough such families looking to adopt. Even in 2011, only 10 per cent of those 3,050 adopted children were of mixed ethnic origin. Clearly, it was an issue for social services, who wondered if it would be a problem for the Whitbreads too.

Margaret said, 'We are C of E, but we are not church-goers, so no that won't be a problem for us. And if Fatima wants instruction in that faith, we will get it for her.'

But no one had ever told me I was Muslim before, and

actually I wasn't. My birth father was a Greek Cypriot. As far as I know he wasn't religious, but he had been born into the Greek Orthodox Church, which is Christian. Those few times that I had been in the flat of the woman who gave birth to me, scrubbing the floors and trying to stay out of the way of her lover, I never heard a word about religion, and I never saw evidence of religion of any kind.

Most heartbreaking of all, we now found out that when I was a baby, a couple had wanted to foster and adopt me, but social services had refused even to let them take me home for an initial visit because they were the wrong religion – they weren't Muslim.

The Whitbreads had to supply references as to their good character. A judge and a policeman wrote letters for them. The police sergeant was Andy Norman, who had run for the Metropolitan Police Athletics club, which he now managed. Since the 1970s, he had also been actively organising Southern county amateur athletics events, which is how Margaret Whitbread knew him; she coached for Southern counties. Both were unpaid volunteers. As it happened, Andrew Norman would later loom very large in my life.

Fostering a child usually takes longer than it took the Whitbreads. Mrs Whitbread urged Mr Walker, who seemed to be in no hurry, to get on with his investigations of the family so he could do the required home visit. To encourage him, she was often on to head office, where Miss Toomey was kindly but cautious.

Meanwhile, I sneaked into the dining room, where the case records of us children were kept, and took a look at my file in the big pine bureau. I am not sure if they were the exact same papers that Margaret Whitbread was shown, but they told the same sad story. I remember dropping the file, the facts of my case were so upsetting, and bending down quickly to gather up the pages before Mrs Smith or one of the others came in. They mentioned all the homes that I had lived in as a baby, as a toddler, as a child. I had never had a real home.

At last, the personal investigation and references were deemed acceptable. We were up to stage three. Bob Walker was to do the official visit – he would inspect the Whitbreads' house and examine the room that would be the foster child's, i.e. mine. My own room. I barely even dared to think of it.

But the room the Whitbreads had for me, as they knew only too well, was a problem. Not only was it minute – only six feet by nine, if that – but 'my room' was literally the vestibule through which anyone entering the house by the back door had to walk. And the back door was the one the family usually used because they could park the car behind the house.

Mrs Whitbread wrung her hands, knowing the social worker would be within his rights to say the room was unsuitable. But it was all they had. In their two-bedroomed house, the boys were sharing a room, sleeping on bunk beds, while John and Margaret had the other room. Mrs Whitbread and her friend Mrs Lynn Mays spent a whole weekend decorating my room to try to show it off to the best possible effect, putting up pink velvet curtains and washing down the woodwork. Compared to my dormitory, it was paradise.

Margaret and John waited nervously for Bob Walker to arrive. Then they took him on a tour of the house, culminating with the tiny room. The house was tidy and spotless, not a fibre of the cream carpet out of place, and unnaturally quiet – the boys' grandad was looking after them at his place.

Taut and nervous, the tour completed, the Whitbreads led the social worker into the lounge and awaited his verdict on the little room. As he sat sifting through his briefcase, it was evident Bob Walker was not completely satisfied. Margaret Whitbread could not contain herself any longer. 'What's going to happen to Fatima?' Her voice was shrill with anxiety.

There was no immediate reply.

'Is the room, in your view, suitable?' John Whitbread asked quietly.

Ignoring the issue of the tiny room, Mr Walker said he was not at all certain they would be suitable foster parents.

Margaret gasped. 'But why?'

What he said, to their absolute astonishment to this day, was that there must be something wrong with the family because there were no family photographs on display. In fact, there was nothing on the walls but a clock. The family snapshots were kept in photo albums at Grandad's. The Whitbreads were not surprised when the social worker then spoke again about it being too late for me to be adopted because – as he had told them before – in his opinion, I was too institutionalised. But photos on the wall?

Evidently, he was going by the book – some textbook he must have read as a student and taken all too literally. Margaret and John proceeded to tell Bob Walker exactly what they thought of him.

'I have had enough of petty bureaucracy,' John said. 'The child needs a home. We have one for her.'

'It's ridiculous for Fatima to be subjected to the Smiths,' Margaret said, 'when there is a loving home she can go to.'

There was much more of the same in a heated discussion.

Picking up his briefcase, Mr Walker said he could see that they were concerned. He would consult with head office and inform them of the social services' decision just as soon as he could.

After two weeks of anxiety, there was a semi-happy ending. The Whitbreads were told that I would be allowed to spend the school summer holidays with them 'on trial'. Margaret Whitbread's answer was, 'Absolutely not.' She and John felt it would distress me too much to feel 'on trial'. No matter what, they would make it work – they both knew how desperate I felt about further rejection. And they were confident all would be well. But the social worker still felt I was unsuited to life with their family.

The best the Whitbreads could get from head office was the agreement that I move in with the family for 'a holiday'. After those three weeks, Miss Toomey, Mr Walker, and their boss Mr Butcher, who was very experienced, would meet with Mrs Smith and Mrs Whitbread. Once again, there would be a summit to decide my fate.

Rushing home on the last day of term, I picked up my few belongings, which I had already packed the night before, and – with my friend Alma to see me off – I danced back to school. I had arranged with Margaret Whitbread that she collect me there on that sunny day, 25 July 1975, because I didn't want to be met at the home.

Alma was a little sorry to see me go, but she was happy for me. As we got near school, she looked off the other way and said, 'I'll miss you, Fats.'

'Alma, I'll miss you too.' My voice cracked. 'You know I will.'

Then we hugged each other, right there on the way to the school.

As we arrived, a few minutes early, I saw Mrs Whitbread's Mini turn the corner and pull up with a screech. Hugging Alma once more, I got into the car.

'Everything OK?' Margaret Whitbread asked.

'Yes, Mum.' I grinned.

'Not Mum,' she said gently. 'Not yet. We've got to get past that meeting with head office. But don't worry. If anyone can do it, we will.'

'I know,' I said, repeating silently to myself: 'I know, Mum.' For the moment, I was still Fatima from the children's home and she was Mrs Whitbread, but in my heart I was sure that she was eventually going to become my mum. But she didn't want to hurt me by counting our chickens before they had hatched. That was understandable. Suppose at that meeting with head office something went wrong! My heart nearly stopped at the thought of it, and my hand went to my mouth.

Flicking a glance at me as she drove, Margaret Whitbread said firmly, 'Fatima, everything will be all right.'

I nodded. It *had* to be all right. I would look on the bright side, which was already very bright indeed – for starters, that very night I would be sleeping in my own bed in my own room in the Whitbread family house. The thought of it made me feel jubilant. All the way to Chadwell St Mary I kept on grinning. I couldn't stop smiling, I was so happy.

When we got to the house, the boys couldn't stop holding my hands and giving me a kiss. I had saved up my winnings from 'penny on the wall' to have presents for each of them: a gleaming black model of the John Player Special Grand Prix racing car for Gregg and a bright plastic London red bus for Kirk.

When John Whitbread came home from work, he hugged me. Then we all sat down – Mum and Dad, my two brothers, and me – to have our evening meal.

That weekend, we went to the family caravan at Creek Sea for a two-week holiday. The eight-berth caravan had every possible mod con – flush toilet, electricity, TV, etc. – yet it was set in a secluded rural spot with a spectacular view of the River Crouch. We took bikes with us, and played croquet, marbles, darts, cricket, badminton, tennis and bowls. We went swimming, on outings to Maldon, to the Southend Festival and walked along the seashore. We seemed to have time to do everything.

Fishing was the best. My father and brothers and I would sit beside the lake for hours waiting for a bite. There were other fishermen dotted about, quite a number of them, sitting in rapt silence. The lake was peaceful. But one morning, growing restless, I climbed up to the little foot-bridge about a hundred yards away, and cast my line. I got a bite almost immediately. The boys were thrilled and cheered excitedly, which the other fishermen did not appreciate because it scared the fish away – or so they believed. Dad and I got a few more nibbles and more cheers from the boys, who even pulled in a couple of carp and some eels them-selves. Try telling children to keep the noise down when they are holding a wet wriggling fish.

After what was our first family holiday – and it had been a roaring success – Mum and I took off for Crystal Palace, the national sports centre on the outskirts of London. There, Mum was to be one of the coaches for the seven days of the Guinness School of Sport, which was offering intensive training in all Olympic sports. I was one of the trainee athletes.

I'll never forget my first impression of Crystal Palace. The grass seemed to be greener and the playing fields bigger than any I had ever seen. Not only that, there was a new Tartan track. You could have floated a javelin on my enthusiasm.

And not just mine. So many fine young athletes together created a perennial high. But exciting though it was to live in the dormitory with the others – for once, the communal living felt like a privilege – to eat meals with them, to train together till the sweat became a salty river running down our necks; satisfying though it was to learn some new skills and to hone others; pleased though I was at all that, what I really wanted right then, more than anything, was to be living with my new family in my new home.

That I would ever be able to do so on a permanent basis was by no means certain, of course. The big meeting with Mr Walker, Mrs Smith and head office was looming. But Mum kept me focused on sport that week, and when the day came, I was so engrossed in the afternoon training session I didn't even notice she had gone.

When Mum got to the home, fortunately it was Auntie Rae who opened the door. She gave Mum a warm drink and some confidence. Then the social workers arrived. Bob Walker, Miss Toomey and Mr Butcher, the top man from head office, sat down with Mum and Mrs Smith to decide my fate.

Mrs Smith made it more than plain that she felt I should stay at the home. This was odd to say the least. For years, it had been clear to Auntie Rae and me, even to Edna and to casual visitors like the Thurrock Colts' manager Babs Bannister, that Mrs Smith had little or no love in her heart for me. In fact, she appeared to regard me as a festering thorn in her side. The year before, Mrs Smith had pressed for me to be moved to London. Now that a family wanted me, she was insisting I stay at the home. It made no sense.

Miss Toomey said that the social services were in the middle. They had to do what was best for everyone concerned. They were worried that Margaret and John Whitbread might be making a mistake that would harm both the Whitbreads and me.

'Fatima is at a difficult age,' Miss Toomey said, 'and you and your husband have two young sons. It could possibly be too much to handle.'

'John and I know what we can handle. Fatima likes being in our family.'

'Yes, you're getting on well now, but even someone as experienced as Mrs Smith has had problems with Fatima. What concerns me is what will happen when the "honeymoon period" is over. It could get rather nasty. You and your husband might find you no longer want her, and she will begin to feel about you the way she feels about the Smiths.'

Years later, Mum told me that at that moment she felt like punching Miss Toomey. But instead she said, as calmly as possible, 'We know what we're getting into. As I told you before she came to live with us a month ago, we want Fatima. We still want Fatima. We will always want Fatima no matter how naughty or troublesome she is. I know what Fatima can get up to. John knows. But we love her and want her as our daughter. Our sons love her. It would be cruel to take her away from us and bring her back here where she has been so unhappy. It would be cruel to her.' Mum almost couldn't go on. 'And cruel to us.'

'Being emotional isn't really what we're here for,' one of the three social workers in the room said.

'Isn't it?' said Margaret Whitbread. 'A girl's future is at stake. Her whole life.'

'We do understand that,' another of them said.

Then Mr Butcher, the top man from head office, put in another word on the Whitbreads' behalf. His words carried the day. It was decided there and then that I could be fostered by them. If things went wrong, well, fostering was reversible.

In one final effort to jeopardise my future – or so it seemed to Mum and me – Mrs Smith said that she wanted me at least to spend the last week of the summer holiday at the home, just so I could experience living there again and see if I really did prefer to be part of a family.

Mum objected, but Mr Butcher thought it a fair compromise. In view of Mrs Smith's long-standing service – in view of everything she had done for me over the years – coming back to live there for a week was, he thought, a way I could say 'thank you'. The idea of it still makes me want to spit.

Mum drove home to Chadwell St Mary to tell the boys and Dad that I was going to live with them permanently. They were very happy and excited. To Dad, alone, she explained that there was a 'clause' to the agreement. After the Crystal Palace course finished, I would come to live with them, but at the very end of the summer, I was to have a final week's 'holiday' at the children's home.

'More red tape,' Dad said angrily. 'It will choke Fatima. It is down to us to make certain somehow that it doesn't choke her to death.'

It was a few days later, on our journey home to Chadwell St Mary after the Guinness School had finished, that Mum told me about the clause.

'I'll never go back there. I hate it there. I'm not ever going back to the home. Why should I?' I cried.

In a very calming voice, Mum tried to explain that if I didn't, it could jeopardise my future with them. I felt very sick inside. Mum did too. But Mum told me I could do it. So did my friend Alma. She visited me at the Whitbreads', and we had a great time making terrible remarks to each other about Mrs Smith.

The day came for me to go back to the home, a Saturday morning; I would be back at the Whitbreads' the following Friday night. The whole family was very, very upset, but Mum and Dad told me it would be the last time we would be apart. They reminded me I had Auntie Rae, who was on my side, living just around the corner and that I could ring them and reverse the charges on the telephone whenever I wanted.

As I got out of the car at the home – I wouldn't let Mum accompany me inside – she said to me, 'Fatima, just remember two things: that we love you and that it is very important that this week you behave.'

The Smiths were not even there when I arrived. The student on duty couldn't understand why I had come back. No one had told her. The Smiths were away for the weekend at their house. I phoned home. 'The Smiths aren't here. You can come and get me.'

Mum said I must stay in case they were just out.

'They're away for the weekend.'

But Mum said she couldn't come for me, much as she wanted to, because it was a head office decision that I stay a week and we must abide by it. Auntie Rae said it was a scandal but that I should look on the bright side. If the Smiths were not around, I wouldn't have any arguments with them. 'Count your blessings, Fats,' she said, ruffling my hair.

The Smiths returned on the Sunday afternoon. Ignoring me, they went straight to their room until later that evening. When I rang to tell Mum, she said I must not misbehave, reiterating that no matter what, we had to abide by the head office decision.

Throughout the week the Smiths more or less pretended I wasn't there. To be more exact, they were cool, barely civil, even hostile at times. I remember phoning Mum every day and telling her I didn't see any point in staying. But by then I knew I had to stick it out.

Meanwhile, I helped Auntie Rae with the two babies and a newcomer, a little one of five who kept knocking his head against the wall. In the short time I had been away, some new children had arrived, and many of those I had known had moved on. I had not realised quite how disturbed most of the children were while I lived amongst them. They were in their own little worlds, as I had been in mine. With so many children coming and going from the home over the years, we children were used to seeing others leave and rarely said goodbye.

On the last day, I went outside to sit on the fence and wait for Mum. I sat, my legs dangling, almost a nervous wreck, when Mum screeched up to the kerb. She had come, with the boys, to take me home. While Gregg and Kirk played on the swings, Mum and I had a chat in the garden with Auntie Rae.

The Smiths had gone out. Auntie Rae was appalled that they had made no effort to see me off, even though I had given them the pound of flesh they wanted. 'You were good and brave to stay the week, Fats,' Auntie Rae said. She said again how happy she was for me. She even thanked Mum for giving me the family I had always wanted.

Then it was time to go.

As we Whitbreads piled into the Mini, Auntie gave me a big smacker of a kiss and told me to get on with my new life. But we promised to stay in touch – and we did.

Margaret Whitbread put her key in the ignition and turned over the engine.

'Off we go,' she said to me. 'Ready?'

'Ready.'

'Do you want to take a last look?'

'I've seen too much of the place already. Let's go.'

She stepped on the pedal. I was fourteen years old, and I knew I was going to become a Whitbread. The elation I felt is impossible to describe adequately. Never had I felt so joyous. It was the most important thing that had ever happened to me and – despite all the wonderful and terrible things that have happened since, with just one exception – it still is.

CHAPTER FOURTEEN

Revelations

I HAD HAD to wait until I was fourteen to get what most people have from the start – a family. But at last the heartbreak of not belonging anywhere was over. No longer was I an unwanted stray at the pound. At last I had found a foster mother – and a foster father and two brothers, even a grandad and a nan. For the first time in my life, the gods had smiled on me, and they were grinning ear to ear. If it became possible, the Whitbreads told me again, they wanted to adopt me. Fostering was not enough: what they wanted was to make me officially a member of the Whitbread family. It goes without saying that that's what I wanted too, and I wanted it badly.

I cooked meals for the family whenever Mum was working. She didn't mind one bit; she hates cooking. I adore it. I ironed Dad's shirts. I kept my little room clean and tidy and neat. Life at the Whitbreads' was ordinary life. It was wonderful.

Every meal was an adventure. Often as not, I would cook something I had never eaten before. It would be a couple of years before I got to the point of perfecting recipes – I had so many basics just to try out. But my spaghetti Bolognese is now almost as good as you get in Italy. I've never been to Bologna, but I can speak for Rome.

When I had first come to stay with the Whitbreads, even before Crystal Palace, Mum had bought me a brown leather jacket I had wanted ever since junior school. A fabulous soft, leather jacket with a good quality zip and roomy pockets, to me it was the height of fashion. It was warm too. I wore it with a green polo neck that it set off, and I thought I looked stunning.

I wore that outfit for days at a time, which was a bit of a problem because it was really too warm to wear indoors, and unless there was a family outing, I rarely went out – even to school, despite the fact that my new school, Torells, was just 800 metres away. At Culverhouse, I'd had near perfect attendance, but I so loved being in my family's home, I didn't want to leave it. How different it felt to say 'home' when it meant the house I lived in with my family, and not the children's home, which was merely an institution, and not a home at all.

I never missed a javelin practice, nor any of the running or weight training I now did to build my strength though. My friend Jill Burroughs, a sprinter with fine, straight, dark hair, often trained with me at Blackshots, and played truant with me from school. Sipping coffee with Jill and dragging on a cigarette seemed far more stimulating than lessons. But Jill and I were the most wholesome truants in the world. When we skipped school she would happily sit there watching, or sometimes help me bustle about the Whitbread kitchen, baking cakes as a surprise for the family. Or I would iron the boys' fancy T-shirts. Batman, Robin Hood and *Star Wars,* in those wee sizes, made me smile each time I smoothed them into place on the ironing board. This was far more ironing than the Whitbreads were used to, and once it was even too much. I burned a hole in my father's shirt. Not certain how he would react, I got into a state, which Dad couldn't understand the reason for at all. 'But it was an accident, wasn't it?' he said.

The only screaming and shouting came when we both began to play cowboys with the boys, who were being Indians that day.

I loved the boys. Their little faces always lit up when they saw me. My bigger one glowed too. I taught the boys to swim. They taught me the role of big sister. It was a level of bonding that would have been impossible in the children's home. You couldn't bond with the kids in the home because of the overwhelming feeling of emptiness and the lack of love in all our lives. Momentarily, you could be a substitute mother, a temporary surrogate, but that was all. No ongoing, deepening relationship was possible as it now was with my new brothers.

In the mornings, they would wake me up with their favourite new game called 'Jump on Fatima'. Mum would get Gregg off to school and I might take little Kirk to nursery on my bicycle. On Saturdays, I chaperoned them to the matinees at the cinema. As often as possible I sat on one of their bunk beds, listening with rapt attention to their record books of *Thomas the Tank Engine* and *The Jungle Book*.

When five-year-old Gregg started having sleepless nights and worried school mornings, he confided that a boy in the class above was bullying him. Big sister intervened in a rather different way than a big brother would have. A big brother would have threatened the bully or punched him himself. I urged Gregg, who was quivering in his grey school shorts at the thought, to go up to the bully and warn him bluntly that if he didn't desist, Gregg would hit back. It may be that my scowling face helped, or it may just have been Gregg's bravery, but that was the end of it.

Despite my happiness and security in my new home, I was still having fearful nightmares, and would awaken sobbing and terrified. The man in the cloak became ever more menacing. Mum or Dad would come into my room and sit with me late into the night, listening and comforting me as I revealed all the things that had happened to me before I came to them. Happy though I was in that family, the recurring nightmares continued. I was in a fragile state.

That's why, at the time, Mum didn't dare reveal to me that she had been to see my so-called biological mother. She thought the truth of that visit would hurt me too much. The memory of what took place was very painful for Mum, but she knew she had to tell me about it eventually, and finally did so, just nine days before I had to hand this book in to be published.

What happened is this. She and her dad, Grandad James, drove up to London to see the woman who had given birth to me. And that woman, who had abandoned her baby and let me grow up in dire children's homes, who had failed to protect her twelve-year-old daughter from being raped in her 'mother's' flat, and who did not even comfort me afterwards, that woman saw my chance for a good life as her chance for some easy cash.

'Money,' she said, snapping her fingers. 'Money, money.' They were in the untidy lounge of her London council flat. She'd agree to the adoption, she said, for £2,000, equivalent to £16,420 in today's money. Unless she was paid the money, she would not cooperate.

Right: A snapshot taken when I was nearly four, at Wormley Hill House. These two pictures here, and the image used on the front cover, are my only 'baby pictures'.

With the other Hill House children. I am in the middle. My beloved Cory is far right, holding baby Julie.

A school photograph of me, aged eleven. The year after this was taken, I was sent to live with 'the woman' and her boyfriend.

With my javelin coach and adoptive mother, Margaret Whitbread, on the day I won the Victorix Ludorum at the 1977 District Schools Championship.

A family at last: with Mum and the boys, holding the Victorix and another athletics trophy.

Too cool for school: me in the leather jacket Mum bought me when I first came to stay with the Whitbreads.

Mum, Dad, my brothers and me on holiday in Lanzarote.

Winning the European Junior Championship, my first great victory, in Poland, 1979.

This is the photo I sent to Steve.

European champion and world-record holder, Germany, 1986.

Throwing for gold at the World
Championships in Rome, 1987.

The famous victory 'wiggle'.

I had to bite my gold medal to believe it was real.

A dream come true: in my polka-dot dress with my BBC Sports Personality of the Year Award.

With Nigel Mansell and Margaret Thatcher at a reception at 10 Downing Street.

Andy and me on our wedding day.

The best thing that has ever happened to me: me with my son, Ryan.

Ryan's first day at the Brentwood School. Being able to give my son everything I missed out on as a child is one of the greatest joys of my life.

Entertaining the Soweto township children at our hotel in South Africa.

That moment: with my head in a helmet full of cockroaches on *I'm A Celebrity, Get Me Out of Here!*

On the red carpet at the National Television Awards, January 2012.

Peter Andre came to support me when I was filming 'Fatima's Fat Fight' for *This Morning* in spring 2012. He's a good friend.

The Whitbread family en masse. Gregg is far right, next to Ryan; Kirk is at the back with his fingers in the air; Mum is in the floral dress. I am at the front, surrounded by family. I never thought I would have so many relatives to call my own.

Above left: Proud: holding up my MBE, with my European Championship, World Championship and Olympic medals before me, and (*above right*) me with my son. It is hard to believe that the little girl born with nothing has come so very far.

Well, she wasn't paid. Not only was the idea unseemly, she just had no right to put a selling price on my head. There was also a practical reason: the Whitbreads didn't have the money.

Mum and her dad had also been to see my biological father. Social services had supplied both phone numbers and addresses. Michael said he wasn't bothered if I was adopted – and that's all he said. He didn't say he was pleased that I'd finally have a home. He didn't say he wished me well. Mum says seeing the woman was a nightmare. Seeing the man was distressing. She couldn't speak of either incident for more than thirty years, not until I was fifty-one years old.

She couldn't speak of the ride back from London either. Witnessing a man, her dad, sobbing all the way home was horrible. Grandad James had been torpedoed twice and survived in World War Two, and had also fought in the Korean War, where he saw his mates blown up before his eyes. He was a tough cookie; he was a docker and he boxed. But he said that the attitude of those people regarding a child they had created blew every sense of common decency out of the water. It literally made him weep.

It still makes Mum weep. So does the fact that I couldn't be adopted. Everyone thinks I was adopted. Well, I never was. But the man from head office at social services suggested a way around it: deed poll. I had been fostered formally, and just before my fifteenth birthday, I went with my new parents to a local solicitor's office and changed my surname to Whitbread officially, by deed poll. The man from head office now also advised us to say I was adopted. Since we had all decided it was a permanent arrangement, it would give the right impression, even though it wasn't quite so.

And actually, because my name was now Whitbread, most people just assumed, in the years that followed, I'd either been born into the family or adopted. In the first few years of being in the public eye, I did tell a few journalists the full facts in an attempt to keep the record straight, but they always put 'adopted' in the paper anyway, so in the end I stopped correcting them.

When we finally received all the deed poll paperwork, I was absolutely thrilled. I just kept looking at the words FATIMA WHITBREAD for days. I got excited when I received any letters addressed to that new person, Fatima Whitbread, whom I now had the right to be.

I remember mostly the joy of being part of a family, and the novelty of feeling safe, but I was still so disturbed that it took nine or ten years for me to feel totally secure. Until then, some small, scared part of me still believed that one day I would wake up and the Whitbread family would have disappeared, leaving me to return to somewhere as bad as the home.

Although I had been rebelling against those in authority since well before my teens, I was so pleased at having parents that I had none of the usual teen set-tos with them. We have had our ups and downs, like any family, but no major battles. Family life was to me sweetness and light, peaches and cream, lovey-dovey stuff. Perfect.

When Dad came in unexpectedly and smelled cigarette smoke, he didn't make a scene, but told Mum. Little by little I was weaned from the weed. When I burned the steak, there was no to-do about it. It was an accident, wasn't it? We all ate up, and whenever they could, they complimented me on my cooking.

Except for those nightmares and my own occasional bursts of temper, it was a placid life. How I loved my new family! What I had expected in a family was a fantasy of perfection, a kind of Cinderella's dream. It was very unlikely that I would ever get such a thing or that such a family as I imagined it even existed. Yet I had found it.

All was relatively blissful until Mum received a phone call from my deputy headmistress to find out why I was never at school. Mum was still teaching at nearby St Chad's, and she knew all the Torells staff. Mum told her the truth, that I liked it at home.

'She'll have to come to school, Margaret. It's the law.'

I went in for a day or two, now and then.

The deputy head persisted. She felt it was important. Mum urged me to attend more frequently. But what really got me back to school was the lure of sport. One day, as I was ironing, and my friend Jill folding the laundry, we decided that we were going to play county hockey. The only way to do that was to come up from the school hockey team. On practice days, Jill and I now went in to school late, attended one or two classes, and then went to hockey practice, which was in the afternoon.

Without much difficulty, we made the school team. I still played truant a lot, but I went in for most of the school matches and especially whenever I knew we had a difficult match. Depending on the season it might be netball or hockey or athletics. The matches were in the afternoon after school.

My pride in my achievement was dampened just a bit when one or two people goaded me, saying I had no right to the place on the hockey team because I had not been at Torells from the first year. One of them got quite nasty. I will never forget her saying, 'We don't want you at this school, Paki.' It was the first time in my life I had ever been the butt of a racial slur. And when the girl shouted 'Paki' at me, I almost turned my head to see if she was talking to someone else. I had always thought of myself as thoroughly British. I still do.

Outspoken Miss Bullock, the sports teacher, told me not to worry, my detractors were jealous of my considerable talent. I had never thought of my ability at sport as a talent until then. Nor had I realised it was 'considerable'. That sounded serious. As for the aggro in the gym, what I could do to help her and the situation, Miss Bullock said, was to avoid fights even when someone else was picking them. Holding my temper back wasn't always easy, but I tried.

Eventually, though, it had to happen. Things boiled over when one of the girls who had made unpleasant comments pushed me during practice, and I pushed her back. We ended up in a fist fight; Miss Bullock had to part us. In the changing room after practice, Miss Bullock threatened to drop us both from the team. The other girl blurted out, 'But it's not fair for Fatima to play for the school when she's just arrived here.'

'On the contrary,' replied Miss Bullock, 'because Fatima certainly isn't eligible to play for some other school, is she?'

If either of us wanted to continue on the team, Miss Bullock said, we had to shake hands and get on with it. That girl and I became reasonably good friends after that, and Torells won the league.

The Saturday that Virginia Wade won Wimbledon in the Queen's silver jubilee year, I was awarded the Victorix

Ludorum at the 1977 District Schools Championship. That is the prize that goes to the girl who is the overall champion in a sports competition, and I was the outstanding competitor on the day, winning four events: hurdles, sprints, high jump and javelin. My triumph mattered only to my family, teachers, to my opponents and to a few friends. Yet my joy and pride at my accomplishment may well have been as great as Virginia Wade's, and her Wimbledon victory fired my imagination. If only, like her – I couldn't help thinking – I might some day win something that excited the whole nation!

Mum told me she had never before had so dedicated a young javelin thrower to coach. Never had I felt so dedicated to any task as much as I did to winning with my javelin. It now became my whole focus. I did study sometimes, but mainly at home. I passed GCSEs in History, Art, Maths, English and Cookery, before dropping out to train full time at the end of the school year in which I turned sixteen.

I left school with my parents' blessing. I had made the decision to become a full-time athlete. With my mother-coach behind me, I now began the journey that I hoped would take me to the very top of the javelin world.

CHAPTER FIFTEEN

Rivals and Admirers

TO BUILD MUSCLE, I trained hard from day one. Part of the training we made into a family game: I would run with a rope tied to my waist, while my brothers would run behind, hanging on to each end of the rope. They were so much slower than I was that it made for good resistance. I did proper weight-training five times a week. I did a lot more besides in three hard sessions a day, six days a week.

There was also our technical work. For example, Mum would throw me a four-kilo medicine ball over and over again at exactly the right angle, so that I could catch it using the muscles of my arms, back and legs in a way that is similar to throwing a javelin.

My debut as a senior international was at Crystal Palace when I was sixteen, just after I quit school. I was now more dedicated than ever, training hard, getting ready for what I knew would be a long haul: Mum had warned me repeatedly that javelin throwers mature with age.

Javelin throwers are always hungry, too. Sport makes you ravenous. Living with my family, there was always milk in the fridge and plenty of food on the table. Even though they were not rich and had two growing boys, there was never any pressure put on me to contribute money to the housekeeping. But becoming a world-class athlete is an expensive process. Just paying the food bills can be ruinous. Thank goodness that when I was about seventeen a meat-packing firm that had read about me in the local newspaper decided to sponsor me with monthly deliveries of their product. Steaks, legs of lamb, chops – they were full of the protein I needed to build muscle.

It is well known in sports circles that many young athletes live on the dole. Some start training to get over the boredom of no job, and some have no job because they are so busy and so tired after training. I never went on the dole. I don't begrudge the others, not at all, but it just wouldn't have felt right for me, and I was lucky enough to have the Whitbreads' support.

And that support came in many ways. By now, Mum had worked her way up from the Southern counties coaching position to become Britain's national coach. It was an unpaid role that allowed her to realise her ambition to take British athletes to the top of the international athletics scene. Luckily for me, it meant she was always by my side as I found my feet as a full-time athlete.

As team manager to six athletes, Mum travelled to competitions in Dusseldorf and Milan, where she shared a room with Tessa Sanderson, the British javelin number one. They got on well. Tessa, a Jamaica-born Brummie, had her eye on the 1980 Olympics. No one considered she could be threatened by me any time soon. Certainly not Mum. Least of all Tessa. When Mum mentioned in passing that her daughter Fatima, five years younger than Tessa, was coming on and that she had talent and might one day be a danger, Tessa laughed. Mum shrugged, 'It's years off anyway.'

Tessa was my inspiration. When I learned, aged eighteen, that I was going to Canada on the 1978 Commonwealth team as the British number two behind her, I was elated. Tessa was not yet a direct rival to me. At that time, she was more of a role model.

In Canada, we roomed together. In the mornings we used to go out on bikes, cycling around the town. In the evenings, before the competition, we went to the disco. We danced, danced, danced with lads of all nations. When she is in high spirits, Tessa can be silly with the best of them and great fun. We had a lot of laughs. She won the Games with a throw of 61.34 metres, three metres less than her British record, and I was actually pleased with sixth place and 49 metres.

Not long after we got home from Canada, the well-known sports photographer Tony Duffy phoned Mum to suggest he photograph me. Many of the shots, he said, would find their way into the media because of my striking looks. He did a photo shoot of me training at Crystal Palace, and said he would keep on photographing me over the years as my career blossomed, which he was sure it would. Some of his pictures are in this book.

Tony is still an eminent photographer of serious female athletes, and his interest in me at the time was indicative of my growing presence on the sporting stage.

In fact, everything in that winter of 1978 went precisely as it should have. Mum and I were beginning to think that, despite all the Eastern Europeans, who dominated the javelin scene, I might even hope for a medal at the 1979 European Junior Championships coming up that summer.

Then, on a damp, foggy morning at Crystal Palace, where the international squad was training, one of the younger coaches made us train vigorously indoors where it was warm, and afterwards go outside immediately and start to throw. Too inexperienced to remember that damp weather means danger, he gave us no warning against throwing flat out straight away. And I, equally inexperienced, gave it my all.

On virtually my first throw, I hurt my back and had to lie down. At lunchtime, I met up with Mum, who had been coaching another group of throwers, and together we popped in to see the squad's physiotherapist. He said I would be all right in a couple of days. I had merely over-stretched. But the next morning my back was so painful that Mum took me to the casualty department of our local hospital. The X-ray showed that I had fractured a vertebra.

For the next eight weeks the pain was so sharp that I couldn't even bend across the bath to turn the taps on. I could swim, which I did at the Blackshots swimming baths, but just getting into the car to go to the baths was a major achievement. This was my first serious sports injury. Unfortunately, there would be more.

When I resumed training after nearly two months' 'holiday', all I could manage was some very lightweight working out while sitting in a chair, and a spot of jogging. When I tried the javelin, I couldn't throw more than 30 metres without being in agony. Even a shrug could elicit sharp pain. Physios, doctors, acupuncturists – none of the experts could say with certainty when I would get over the injury, which I continued to aggravate by competing. The damaged vertebra had healed with adhesions of gristle around it. Even having heat treatment and manipulation every day hadn't stopped the pain. The injury hurt me most when I threw, and it reduced the range of movement I had in my shoulder.

There were those who suggested I give up my sport. But that wouldn't have been the answer. There was no proof anyway that desisting from sport, giving up, retiring from the javelin almost before I had begun, would make the injury go away. Cutting myself off from competition now would have been like cutting off a limb. You amputate when you have to. But only when you have to.

There was, as I say, no proof that retiring – aged eighteen – would help. And if I was staying in the sport – and I was – I had to compete. Competing, as I had by now learned, is practically the only time you throw flat out; in practice you take fewer chances, holding something in reserve. But you can't ever be razor-sharp without competing. You can't win if you don't throw and the European Junior Championships were on the horizon.

They were taking place in a sleepy little Polish industrial town near Auschwitz in a place called Bydgoszcz. We Brits immediately renamed it 'By Gosh'. I was grateful for the good-luck card that Tony Duffy had sent me, but I knew that no British girl had ever made the final for a throwing event in these championships, which were open to under nineteen-year-olds. In fact, no British woman in history had ever succeeded in winning a throwing event in any major European competition; not even Tessa, the Commonwealth champion. Because the Eastern Europeans and the Finns took the javelin so seriously, the standard in Europe was far higher than in the Commonwealth. State aid, sports science, and every possible medical and sports facility had long been there to support the women behind the Iron Curtain.

The competition didn't start well. On the very first day, I was almost obliged to withdraw entirely. Mum and I found, to our amazement, that the Poles didn't have any Apollo javelins. According to international rules, the full range of javelins commonly in use should be available at a major championship like this one. But the only Apollo in Bydgoszcz, I was told, was the one I had brought along for informal practice.

This was a blow. I didn't want to have to start learning to use another sort of javelin in the midst of the European Junior Championships. Thankfully, Sir Arthur Gold, the Briton who headed the European Athletic Association, was at the stadium. After I explained to him about the javelins, and after he then consulted his committee, he came back to say that if I was prepared to sell my virtually new Apollo to the Polish Youth Federation for a nominal fee, the javelin would be made available for me and all the other competitors for use in the championship. I was paid the grand sum of one Polish zloty.

Then, with the Apollo, I qualified: the first British girl *ever* to do so. Now I was in the final with the cream of Eastern Europe.

I was a very young eighteen-year-old when it came to international competition, and I awoke on a sweltering 19 August 1979, the morning of the final, with my stomach aflutter. Breakfast was a few crumbs of toast and a spoonful of boiled egg. I couldn't eat; my stomach was in knots. The close escape of the day before, when I had so very nearly not been able to compete, made me even edgier than I otherwise might have been.

We took the team coach to the stadium. All those smiling British faces made me feel more confident. But on entering the changing room, my face fell. At nearly six foot, the East

German thrower Katrin Strobel towered over my five feet four and a half. The other throwers were all taller than me. As I smoothed on my white vest and white shorts and began to pull on my red GB tracksuit, the Eastern Europeans chatted easily to each other.

As we made our way outside, my nerves increased. In the stadium were dozens of athletes, not just in the javelin, who were busy stretching, jogging on the spot and taking little practice throws. I did a few stretches too, but after nearly being hit by a stray javelin, I knew I needed a quiet place to warm up. Wearing my GB tracksuit, I walked a fair distance with my coach, Mum, before finally stopping at a small grassy area near the railway line.

I jogged off to do some striding and stretching, then came jogging back. 'Mum,' I said, 'my back hurts and my stomach is a wreck and the Eastern European throwers think I am less than nothing.' I began to rattle off every worry that entered my head.

Mum just chatted away about the wind, which was getting a little stronger, and how that might affect the javelin.

'You aren't even listening, Mum.' I was annoyed. 'Everything is terrible and you don't even ...'

Mum interrupted sharply. 'You are only going to throw in a competition, Fatima. Not that many years ago, more than a million Jews were packed into the trains that ran on this railway, and travelled past this very spot to Auschwitz, to their deaths. That is something to be upset about. Competing in a championship is not. Fatima, you can only do what you can do.'

Pulled up short, I nodded. Mum was right. 'But, Fatima,'

Mum added, lest I mistake her meaning, 'you've worked hard. Give it everything you've got.'

We walked back together. Then, just before she had to leave me to it, Mum said, 'Good luck.'

I would need it.

Before the real throwing starts, you get a few warm-up throws. There, on the Tartan javelin runway, was Katrin Strobel taking a throw with my Apollo javelin. Then she ran and collected the javelin, to have another go. If I wanted to use the Apollo, that was my problem. She wasn't letting go. This sort of psyching out, I would soon learn, was common enough at big meets. Muscle is only half of winning; mind is the other 50 per cent. After her next throw, I made certain I got to the javelin before she did. But when I picked it up, she actually tried to take it from me. I didn't let go.

'Clear off,' I said. 'It's my go.'

'*Nein*, I throw now.' She gave a tug on the javelin to pull it out of my hand.

'Leave off.' I gave a yank back. 'It's *my* javelin.'

'I throw now.' It was turning into a tug of war.

Pulling on the javelin, I said defiantly, 'Me first!'

Strobel began shouting in German and I in English. Each of us had one hand on the javelin. Now I clenched my other fist. Surprised, Strobel backed off momentarily. In that moment, I gave a decisive yank and walked off with the javelin.

I had won that battle, but what about the war?

Glaring at her when she took the javelin for her first throw of the competition, I realised that now she was barely even noticing me. Her mind had switched focus entirely to concentrate intensely on the athletic feat she was about to perform. I watched with trepidation and some admiration as Katrin Strobel thundered up the runway, unleashing a lightning bolt that soared 56.02 metres.

That was a fine opener, only a few centimetres below my personal best.

The three other throwers who preceded me came nowhere near 56 metres. I didn't expect to win the competition. How could I? But I would break my back before I would let the European Junior Championship title, a coveted title, go to that argumentative East German. I gave my opener everything I had. It landed, exactly like Strobel's, at 56.02.

Things hotted up in the third round. The talented young Bulgarian, Antoanetta Todorova, threw 57.58, which Strobel topped with 58.02. Strobel did a little war dance of delight, and raised her arms over her head in victory.

But the cardinal rule of competition is that you don't put a medal around your neck until you have won it. It is not only bad form – it may lead to defeat. It made me angry to see Strobel lording it over all of us like that. Who did she think she was? Snatching the javelin from the stand, I strode back to the runway for my throw, tension and anger in every pore.

Mum, in the stands, was chain-smoking and muttering under her breath, 'Relax, relax. Remember your technique.' When I looked to the stands, I couldn't find her. But I heard the British 200 metres runner Mike MacFarlane call out clearly, 'Come on, Fatima.'

I took a deep breath and let the tension flow out of me; like water through a colander, Mum's favourite analogy. I looked down the red Tartan runway to the green field beyond, which was dotted with tiny markers where I would have to throw my javelin. Really, it was just like the field in Essex where I practised; just like the field where I had won my first schools title on the same day that Virginia Wade had won at Wimbledon.

Wrapping my mind round the javelin, visualising the perfect shot, one in which every muscle was instructed correctly and did as it was told, I held the javelin aloft and began to run. Then, whipping my arm forward, I let the javelin go.

The roar from the British contingent massaged the spasm of pain I felt from my damaged vertebra. The scoreboard was flashing 58.20 metres. I was in the lead.

There were two more rounds of throwing, but Strobel's face showed she did not believe she could beat my throw. At that moment, inside her head, Strobel settled for second place – and that's what she got.

A few hours later, at the medals ceremony, as the band struck up the British national anthem, the gold medal was placed around my neck. I had become the first British woman ever to win the European Junior Championship. Beating the best of Eastern Europe in my age group – and as everyone knew, Eastern Europe were the best in the world – I had entered the record books on an important page. I was elated. I was proud. And I was grateful to my coach, my beloved mum, who had taught me so much more than technique. As I stood there on the victory rostrum, grinning, the lights on the scoreboard read for all to see:

MISTRZOSTWA EUROPY JUNIOROV – FATIMA WHITBREAD.

European Junior Champion – Fatima Whitbread.

CHAPTER SIXTEEN

Soldier, Soldier

THE NEWS OF my victory was reported in the national press. And my achievement drew the attention of someone rather unexpected: my biological father, Michael. Just after my victory at the European Junior Championships, he telephoned me out of the blue. He congratulated me, and then told me, 'I have plenty of money now. Do you want anything? I can help you.'

He offered to send me regular payments to cover the food and other expenses of becoming a champion. Athletics was still amateur then, and I and the other young champions were living pretty much hand to mouth.

But I said, 'Thanks but no thanks.' I didn't want anything. I wanted to do it myself. From that day on, though, I thought that one day I would like to see him again, even though we didn't keep in touch after his call. Sadly, it was to be many more years before our paths crossed again, and when they did, it would not be the reunion I might have hoped for.

Now, once again, I focused all my energies on the javelin. The year after the Juniors, I was proud to be part of the British Olympic team that headed to Moscow in the summer of 1980. Though I was encouraged by my victory in the European competition, I did not expect to win, not at my first Games. Getting an early introduction to the Olympic fanfare and tension would be an investment for the future. It was Tessa who was the great British hope.

I found Moscow very drab, the food was awful, and for Tessa and me both the Games were a disaster. In the qualifying round, I threw better than she did, but neither Tessa nor I threw well enough to qualify for the final, even though more than sixty countries, led by the United States, had stayed away to protest against the 1979 Soviet invasion of Afghanistan.

Even though I'd known it would be a tough contest, I was disappointed not to qualify – angry at myself, and sad. But my sense of sorrow was nothing compared to Sebastian Coe's. He had won a silver medal, but had been expecting gold in the 800 metres race. He'd lost by five-tenths of a second to his British rival Steve Ovett.

I remember Andy Norman, who was now vital to British athletics, and one of the key officials taking care of the Olympic team, telling me, 'Sebastian feels terrible because he knows he can do better.'

Nobody seemed to be going over to comfort him, so I went to visit him in his Moscow hotel room late on the morning after. No one was there besides Peter Coe, Seb's father, who was also his coach. Losers don't get many visitors. That's the only advantage of losing: you find out who your real friends are. At the time, I was less a friend than a great admirer of Seb's athletic ability and achievement. There were many fine athletes, but he was already a star.

I went, knowing he would be somewhat upset, to offer a few words of comfort and to tell him that everyone who mattered knew he was a champion anyway and that he would soon show the others. When Peter Coe let me into the room, I got a shock. Sebastian was lying on his rumpled bed, still in his pyjamas, crying his eyes out. I didn't stay long.

I had not realised how much it could hurt to win a lesser medal when you expected to win gold. Sebastian was a winner, so he hated losing. Two days later, though, he recovered. He went out and won gold in the 1,500 metres in Olympic record time, and Ovett had to settle for mere bronze.

I'm a person who can't help showing my feelings, so I guess my disappointment at not qualifying had been very evident to the television viewers. Until bags of post from the British people began to arrive, I had thought of my dismal performance in Moscow as only a private mishap, an embarrassing detour on my climb towards the summit of athletic achievement. But the letters came pouring in. There were so many, Andy Norman and Mum would help me open the mail.

A crusty old Highlander wrote on lined paper from Scotland to say that it was only the Olympics, not a death in the family, and that I should cheer up, adding that her heartfelt wishes were with me for the future. Children wrote, and men who preferred football and rugby, some who admitted that they couldn't even throw a dart. They all said they would be rooting for me whenever I threw the javelin, adding that I should keep it up, for Britain. The support from the public touched my heart. I hadn't realised before that other people cared anything at all about what happened to me in the future or were cheered by my prospects.

Young men of my own age wrote too, many of them soldiers. I received one note from a young soldier called

Steve (not his real name, but I'll call him that). He'd requested a picture of me in his letter, so I sent him the one of me in a bikini entering the sea that you can see in the illustrated section of this book. That kind of shot tended to go down well with the troops who wrote to me. He wrote back thanking me just before I left for China and Japan to attend the Eight Nations Competition, where I came sixth.

Three weeks later, when I returned, there were two letters from him waiting, telling me who he was and how pleased he was to be writing to me. I remember chuckling when he described all the ways the army has of getting and keeping fit. 'Chinnies' a hundred at a time and every day, and, of course, being in the army, he ran with a heavy, bulging pack on his back.

For a few months we wrote to each other, casual letters, this and that, nothing cataclysmic. But I liked the sound of him. One morning, the telephone rang, and when I picked it up, I could hear pips. Steve, ringing from a call box, wondered how I was – and if sometime he might come and see me.

'Yes. Why not?'

'Well,' and he hesitated. 'How about today? I'm in Kent. I could be there in little more than an hour.'

I gave him some instructions to direct him on his way.

At about one in the afternoon, Mum and I were sprawled on the floor, head to head, going over some training instructions she had written out for me, when I saw a broad-shouldered young man with wavy, chestnut hair and a cute, pert nose approaching the front door. He was wearing civilian clothes. Smiling at me through the picture window, Steve knocked on the porch door. Even before he handed me a box of chocolates and gave me a peck on the cheek, I liked the look of him.

Over a cup of tea in the kitchen we sat for an hour chatting about anything and everything. Mum and my brothers said hello and he was pleased to meet them, especially the boys. There was no one thing, no memorable moment, but the time went very quickly. I liked the way he absent-mindedly fingered the cuff of his pale blue shirt when he was asking questions about me. I liked the way he smiled at me over his mug of tea. And his voice. It was not at all gruff but it was soothing – except when he was laughing. Then it was fun. I liked being with him. I found him to be a very nice person. Sometimes you just take to someone. I took to him.

At 3 p.m., though, I had to go training. 'If you don't go now, Steve,' I looked at my watch, 'you will be overstaying your welcome.' I was going running, up One Tree Hill. Steve offered to drive me there and back.

'I have an hour's training to do. You won't get impatient?'

'I won't get impatient.'

One Tree Hill is very steep and slippery and, especially when it's damp as it was that day, is impossible to run up without spikes. Steve stood at the bottom of the slope, watching me run up and walk down, run up and walk down, over and over. I was doing three sets of four repetitions each up that hill, which was a distance of about 150 metres, trying to build up aerobic endurance, stamina, more even than speed. With Steve watching and calling out encouragement, I had to put in a proper run every time. He was good for my training.

After each run, as I walked down the hill with my eyes glued to him, I felt a warmth in his smile. And every so often, he asked me how many more there were to do. On the last one, he decided to race me to the top.

Taking off his jacket and rolling his trousers up so they wouldn't get muddy, he was getting into position when I said, suddenly, 'Go!' and sped up the hill. He had to chase me up the steep slope, which would have been a killer if he hadn't been fit. Although Steve was wearing street shoes, he was as competitive as I am, and he caught up with me. But there was no way I would let him get by.

In a big burst of effort to beat me at the last, Steve pounded forward, but his feet slipped out from under him. I heard a plop and then a laugh.

Craning my neck, I saw him sliding, on his way back down. He looked so funny I couldn't stop laughing. Running back down to make certain Steve was all right, I saw that he was embarrassed and amused at the same time, and didn't at all mind my laughter.

It may have been then that we fell in love. Yes, I think it was then.

Laughter and love were what our relationship was about. But this was not even properly our first date. We moved cautiously. In the car, after chatting me up some more, Steve said softly, 'I have enjoyed myself meeting you. And I think you have too, Fatima. Can we meet again – soon?'

A week later, on a Saturday afternoon, we were strolling together past the Tower of London. Walking, talking, hand in hand, on one of those perfect London days when the sun never seems likely to set and the city seems so romantic, we strolled along the Thames Embankment all the way to Blackfriars. Then, as we paused to gaze at the river, Steve, suddenly realising we were going to be late, hailed a taxi to take us to *The Mousetrap*, Agatha Christie's play, which was on in the West End. We rushed into our seats in the stalls, sitting down just as the curtain was going up.

No wonder *The Mousetrap* has broken the world record when it comes to the number of West End performances. It has a clever twist. The first act made us hungry and we ate sweets during the interval. After the theatre, we went for a meal. I can remember feeling very happy and content to be in his company. My feelings were already quite strong towards him, and his eyes were looking at me lovingly. Near the end of the meal, Steve told me he was going to Kenya.

'Thanks for giving me the elbow. Nice knowing you,' I said tartly, upset that there were to be no more wonderful evenings.

'Don't be so silly, Fatima.' He reached across the table and took both my hands in his. 'I will just be away for a while. I have to go. This isn't the end of us. We've only just begun.'

My heart began to fill with happiness. I had become so attached so quickly. Almost from the moment I saw him striding up to my front door, there had been a magic, a spark between us. I felt happy in his company. I could see he felt happy in mine. But, I realised with a start, I was scheduled to go to the USA for a month's warm-weather training a few days before he got back. I felt a pang of foreboding. It seemed as though circumstances were always going to be against us.

Still holding on to my hands, Steve said, 'We will just have to look at the stars at night wherever we are and remember we're on the same planet in the same universe. That will bring us together until we can *be* together.'

In California, I trained hard and well. The whole family

had come along, including Grandad and Nan. I'd won a Winston Churchill fellowship which paid for my expenses, and the family paid for theirs. Gregg and Kirk and I ran together on the beach.

Mum and I were often away for international events, but it was great to have the whole family together. While we were there, the American university, UCLA, offered me a sports scholarship. I didn't take it because I didn't want to leave my family. We were having a wonderful time, but I couldn't help thinking how it would be if Steve were with us. I often found myself looking up at the stars and realising how much I missed him.

Much later, months later, when we finally met again, at the Tower, almost the first words Steve said to me were, 'Is there anyone else?'

'There's no one else.'

'Then,' his voice went all shy, 'would you be my lady?'

'Yes,' I said, feeling shy too, 'I'll be your lady.'

Again we made a day of it, walking hand in hand, browsing in the shops, seeing a movie, eating. Like me, Steve was always hungry. As the meal was coming to an end and we sat sipping our coffee, Steve handed me a Carpenters greatest hits cassette he had brought for me. Very softly, he began to sing to me the tune he regarded as the best and most apt track: 'We've Only Just Begun'.

You could have used my smile as a torch, it was so bright. After that, I never seemed to be able to get him out of my mind. Nor did I want to. Just thinking about him, about us, cheered me immensely.

Driving out to the family caravan in the Essex country-side one weekend, on the first of our many visits, Steve and

I sang along with the Carpenters tape on the cassette recorder, both of us in high spirits. Compared to his clear, strong baritone, my voice was a shrill squawk. He sang 'We've Only Just Begun' to me over and over. It was our song. 'Top Of The World' was his other favourite. 'That one is your song,' he said, predicting that as an athlete I would top the world.

Steve, who had no doubts at all of his masculinity, felt my sports career was no threat and was keen for me to do well. His greeting when we met always included the words, 'Have you done your training?' I didn't let him know how much seeing him did interfere with training because he was prouder even than I was of my athletics career, although it had only just started to get off the ground.

I began to allow myself to think that he and I had a future together. When I was lifting weights in the garage near home where I did my training, or on a flight to a European competition, I would find myself daydreaming about living with him in our own flat, and then in our own house with a couple of little ones who had Steve's firm chin and laughing blue eyes or his sturdy physique. Because of the army, he was as fit as I was.

The caravan site, which was near Burnham-on-Crouch, became our special place. It was special to me already, of course, being the caravan we'd stayed at on my first family holiday when I first became a Whitbread, but Steve's presence added a whole new set of cherished memories. The site was quiet and peaceful since the summer season was over, and there was no one there except us. Originally the caravan had belonged to my grandad, Mum's dad James, but he had given it to us. I had Mum's permission to go there with

Steve, but my father, who wouldn't have approved even though the first time we went I was nearly twenty years old, was none the wiser.

The setting was lovely, in woodland right near the River Crouch and that little lake where Dad and the boys and I used to go fishing. There was a panorama of trees, but we were in a grassy clearing which trapped whatever sunlight there was. There were always squirrels playing nearby and rabbits running in the distance. But Steve and I allowed no distractions from each other except the ones we wanted.

Breakfast was always fresh eggs from the local farm, with fresh bread and milk which Steve had driven to Burnham to get. Sometimes we played short tennis; sometimes we cycled into Burnham and sat for a long time on the harbour wall, dangling our legs in unison and chatting with the seagulls.

I will never forget the time we arrived at the caravan on a perfect afternoon and wanted to have a picnic, but the grass was too high. We found a mower to cut a picnic-sized refuge. After a lazy picnic, we stayed there for a long time, hidden from the world by the tall grass.

On our trips to the caravan, I always took my running kit with me and he took a pair of trainers and shorts. Our running sessions, sometimes quite arduous ones, would end up with a game of hide and seek. Knowing the terrain better, I would dart behind a tree and, as he passed, jump out at him. It would end up with laughter and cuddles and kisses. We did all the young, foolish things that you do when you're in love.

In his company, I felt pleasure and joy, I felt relaxed and ecstatic, I felt the 'usual' things – but they were not usual to me. Anything and everything made us laugh. I often thought

I was dreaming, a happy dream at last, one I never wanted to wake up from. He had made me come alive.

He told me that he loved me, and I loved him very much.

One day around this time, a surprising letter arrived from America. It was the offer of a role in the Hollywood film *Octopussy*, which would begin filming in August 1982. Andy Norman advised me not to mess around with Hollywood, not if I wanted a career as a javelin champion. I needed to be in England to see Steve too. I declined.

But in the early months of 1982, I had to go away from Steve anyway – this time to Cyprus, for more warm-weather training. We made plans to spend a couple of days together at the caravan as soon as I got back. We were always eager to spend as much time together as we could.

In Cyprus, the Falklands flare-up was in all the papers. Everyone thought it would blow over. Instead, the shooting war started. On 2 April 1982, Argentinian invaders over-whelmed a garrison of eighty-four British marines, and the Falklands War began.

I still did not really appreciate what was going on. Nor, I think, did Steve. Not once did either of us think that his unit would go there – unless he was keeping it from me.

When I came home from Cyprus, I was looking forward to seeing him, but two days before we were to meet, he sent a letter saying his leave had been cancelled. His regiment was to undergo two weeks of intensive training and then they were going to the Falklands. It was a complete shock. To comfort me, he said, 'It won't be for long. At most, a few months.'

Then, by telephone, he asked me to see him off. 'If you don't want to go, I'll understand,' he said, 'because it will be an awkward journey and you won't be able to tell which one is me.'

'Of course I'll come, Steve,' I said. 'I want to.' I could feel his smile down the telephone line at my response.

'Even though I won't see you,' he said, 'it will be nice knowing you are there.'

Mum accompanied me because I needed moral support – and a navigator. Leaving Chadwell St Mary in the early hours of the morning, we arrived in Southampton a bit before 6 a.m. I still hoped there might be a moment to give him a quick cuddle and a kiss to send him on his way.

The noise of the harbour was incredible: loud martial music, marching soldiers' feet, so many people calling out 'goodbye' to passing soldiers … so many people crying. They marched past and on to the ships, regiment by regiment. We could pick his regiment out, but not him. Not only did I not get to see him at close quarters, I didn't see him at all, but I just kept waving all the time in case he spotted me.

When the ship pulled away, I felt empty and afraid.

I was not a great newspaper reader, but I examined the papers carefully every day. And I listened to the war news on television and on the radio. If I heard any of our records playing, I just cried. I prayed to God to keep him safe.

One morning, when I opened the newspaper, I was shocked to see his name printed there. I had never expected to read it in the list of the dead: just a name, a statistic. You can imagine how hard that was to come to terms with. The shock, the anguish. He was such an alive person, and he meant the world to me. I was devastated.

I still sometimes ask myself why he had to be one of the

252 British fighting men who died in the Falklands. Why him? Why us?

All I had left were the letters he had sent me, a tidy stack of them with my name in his small, neat handwriting on the square white envelopes. From time to time, I would take them out of the drawer to reread and to gaze at the snapshots I had: one of him, and a few of the two of us together, which we had taken in a coin-operated photo machine. My thoughts would turn to what might have been.

But, after a time, I knew I had to live in the present. I had to stop reopening the wound, feeling the sharp pain of loss. I knew I had to get on with my life. As clichéd as it is to say, it is what he would have wanted. And I couldn't do it if I kept re-reading his words and looking at his face frozen still in a photograph. Four long years after his death, I made the decision to stop, and I did it the only way I could. I ripped them all up, the letters, the photographs. You can't keep reading the same letter, and gazing at someone's face when fate has decreed it isn't to be.

It was time to let the wound heal as well as it ever could. I know if Steve had lived, my life would have been quite different. I might have settled down earlier and immediately had little ones, never to become world champion. Or, with his encouragement, I might have had both.

Thirty years have gone by since he was wrenched away. That's a long time. I've learned to live with it. But it's true to say I lost a little something of myself when I lost him.

I am putting our story in my book to pay tribute to Steve. I have not given his real name to spare his family, whose grief would be rekindled and who might have to bear the indignity of notoriety. I have, in my time, had unscrupulous reporters camped on my doorstep. I don't want to do that to them. I never knew them when he was alive. I don't feel I have the right to force myself upon them now that he is gone, especially so long after the fact. But I loved their son. He was joyful, exuberant, sensitive … my dearest friend. A loving, caring man. I'm sure they know that. Even after so many years, I sometimes think of Steve and our times together. I knew I would miss him, and I do.

CHAPTER SEVENTEEN

Coming of Age

WITH STEVE GONE, I focused all my need, all my intensity, all my hope on the javelin. Steve had wanted me to be top of the world. I would do it. For him. For me. To hold onto life.

In sweltering Athens in September, I was chuffed when I qualified for the final of the 1982 European Championship, the grown-up one. I finished in eighth place.

The victor was the Greek Anna Verouli, who had suddenly, suspiciously, blazed like a meteor onto the javelin scene. Whereas my own years of hard training had as yet failed to pay off with a major medal – Mum had warned me that the build-up would take years – Verouli had had a swift and unexpected rise to prominence in the javelin. Rumours that she got such fast results because she took muscle-building drugs were confirmed two years later when she tested positive at the Los Angeles Olympics and was disqualified.

In the four years since my victory in the juniors in Poland, my throws had steadily got better. I could now throw 69 metres, but the new world record was 74.76m. It was my secret hope to take home a bronze medal from the first ever World Athletics Championships, to be held in

Helsinki in the summer of 1983, but there was only an outside chance.

When the British team flew to Finland, I was bedridden with quinzies, a throat infection the doctor said was more serious than tonsillitis. I couldn't go. But I couldn't stand the idea of missing the Championships, so even though I wasn't fully recovered, a few days later I got up from my sickbed and flew out with Mum, arriving after the contest had started, but before the javelin competition. Because they no longer expected me to turn up, my room at the official athletes' village had been allocated to someone else. So I had to share Mum's hotel room.

It was quieter in the city than in the village. There were no late parties. Nor did I have to contend with the moods of other athletes. Most of the athletes at any competition are losers. Their depression in defeat could be contagious, and their nerves before a competition could be unsettling too. Winners are too few for their elation to rub off.

The money we had to pay out in Finnish markkas for the hotel room and meals seemed a fortune at the time. But the savings were immense when you calculated the effect on my inner resources. And, of course, you see more of a place. I will never forget going into a local restaurant for a meal and noticing with pleasure that there were javelins as decoration on the wall. Like the Soviet bloc Eastern Europeans, the Finns took the javelin very seriously. In modern Olympic history, nearly a third – seven of the twenty-three – male gold medallists have been Finns. The women have done less well, but that year there was certainly a great one: the world-record holder, Tiina Lillak.

Against the world's best and in poor health, I barely

scraped into the final, qualifying twelfth, the last and least position. After that, everyone thought I was entirely out of the running. There was no pressure on me at all. Not a hint. The best I could do was chalk up experience for the future.

Nevertheless, when I walked out on to the Tartan runway to take my first throw of the six-round competition, I gave it everything I had. You don't hold back. You dig deep. You have to give 100 per cent if you ever expect to be a champion.

I neither saw nor heard anyone as I ran forward, holding the javelin high. Every muscle, every sinew, every centimetre of my concentration was aware only of that javelin in my hand and where I wanted it to go.

As I released it into the air, I could hear the knowledgeable Finnish crowd gasp. They realised my throw was going to be a big one. I watched it soar upward, then sail on the breeze, and then, after what seemed an hour, descend in what felt like slow motion to the ground. The throw was a good one, 69.14 metres.

I had thrown down the gauntlet. Would the towering Finn Tiina Lillak, for whom the crowd was rooting and who was the favourite, be able to pick it up? But after two rounds, then three, then four, then five, no one came near – not even twenty-two-year-old Tiina. She was six weeks younger than me, but at five foot eleven, she towered over me by six inches, and every inch of it was muscle. Those extra inches also gave her extra reach.

People who think of me as the incredible hulk don't realise I am under five foot five, which is a bit of a disadvantage in the javelin. When people see me in the flesh they often tell me they are surprised at how small I am. Oh, those muscles are there all right, but they hang on the runt of the litter.

On my big first throw, I had felt my shoulder go, and realised that I would not be able to throw any further that day. With only one more round to go, the British commentators were getting ready to hang the gold medal around my neck. I could almost see it glittering on my breast. The unbelievable was about to happen. I was on the verge of becoming the world champion.

As Tiina, in her blue-and-white kit, strode out on to the runway to take her last throw of the contest, she exuded determination from every pore. Lillak was thought to be the best javelin thrower in the world, and she was a Finn throwing for the highest honour in the world in Finland. The eyes of the crowd were glued to her, willing her to win.

Tiina stood stock still for one intense moment, all five feet eleven inches of her concentrating on where she wanted the javelin to go. Then she threw.

I watched as the javelin sailed high and wide. The crowd roared. Her throw was longer than mine, nearly 71 metres. She had snatched the gold medal. I would have to be content with silver. The crowd were on their feet. Tiina began to run a lap of the stadium, a victory lap. The Finnish crowd stayed on their feet to applaud.

Her achievement was tremendous. It had so nearly been mine. I could not help myself: I cried. I rushed to the edge of the stadium, where Mum was sitting in the front row, and cried my disappointment into her arms. She ruffled my hair. The television cameras saw. I'm still like that – even when I know I should, I often cannot hide my feelings.

My silver medal meant I was number two in the world,

just one step from the top. I tried to feel delighted because it was an amazing attainment. Having only just managed to qualify, I had nearly won gold and had won my first silver medal in a major championship, despite an aching shoulder and a very sore throat. I had given it my all. As Mum and I walked resolutely back to the hotel, we saw grown men dancing in the street with cardboard cut-outs of Tiina Lillak.

Just a week after the Worlds, fully recovered from quinzies, I won the 1983 Europa Cup with a throw of 69.04 metres. It wasn't as lofty an event as the World or European Championships, but the British team celebrated. Mine was the first gold medal ever won by a British woman in a European throwing event. Mum was chuffed. Me too. Three or four days later I had my tonsils out; I wouldn't miss them.

After my Europa Cup victory and the events at the World Championships, where Tessa Sanderson finished fourth, the press attitude towards the two of us shifted. They were largely ignoring her and interviewing me; I was now the British number one. Tessa didn't like it. Tessa, who I truly admired, told me, 'I haven't worked my arse off to be second to you.'

If it were possible, even now, I would be friends with Tessa – and it was nearly possible. Mum was team manager when Tessa broke the British record in West Germany in 1976. Mum was delighted. We all were. At first, Tessa was an inspiration to me: she was five years older, five years more experienced at our trade. But later, when Tessa felt me creeping up the ranks, she began to throw stones – and not just at me.

What really disillusioned me had happened after the 1981 Europa Cup in Zagreb. The athletes had assembled in the canteen to watch the highlights of the competition on video. All of us were there, East and West, lounging in our tracksuits. Antoanetta Todorova had broken the javelin world record that day, with an – at that time – unprecedented throw of 71.88m, and they showed it on the TV screen more than once. It was the only world record of that Europa Cup: a piece of history. The Bulgarian, who had actually tried to be friendly to us despite her limited English, was the first woman ever to throw 70 metres in a major competition. The only person there who wasn't respectful of this achievement was Tessa.

'That wasn't a woman I was competing against today,' she said in a voice that quite a few people could hear. 'That was a chemical man.'

Todorova had never failed a drugs test. She had no more muscles than Tessa or I did, and we didn't take drugs. In Britain we had – we still have – the best scrutiny of athletes in the world. It would have been impossible to cheat even if you wanted to, and I didn't want to. Todorova wasn't beautiful, but she wasn't ugly either; and even if she was, she was sitting in the room with us, watching the film, and Tessa knew it. Maybe that is why she said in an even louder voice, 'That's no woman, that's a man.'

Todorova's face went red as beetroot. I felt embarrassed for her and ashamed to be with Tessa.

'She's sitting there, Tessa,' I whispered. 'Don't show yourself up.'

At that, Tessa shut up.

But thirty years later, she continues to make the same sort of barbed remarks about me that she did about Todorova. In December of 2011, when I was in the *I'm a Celebrity* jungle, too far away to fight back, Tessa attracted media attention for herself with snide and unkind tweets about my muscles. Even some of the journalists were shocked.

As the 1984 Los Angeles Olympics loomed before us, however, the tension between us was just beginning. Tessa was, unsurprisingly, not at all pleased at media reports that her Olympic prospects were poor and that I was in line for gold. In fact, since fourteen Eastern bloc countries were boycotting these Olympics, both of us had really excellent prospects. At twenty-eight, Tessa was in her prime as a javelin thrower, and I knew she had been training hard and she had a lot of bulk on her. She was two inches taller than me and on the eve of the Olympic final, for which both of us had qualified, she outweighed me by a stone. I had to give her credit. She was all muscle.

My only edge was that I was getting better with every throw, but my training had been hampered by still more illness – severe pelvic pain and fibroids, which had had to be cauterised twice. Then, just two weeks before I was due to depart for the Games, I had to undergo fibroid cauterisation for a third time. I felt weak and wobbly. The doctor told my mother it was not advisable for me to compete in the 1984 Olympics. But I had such a good chance at a medal, even in my weakened state, that I just couldn't put the Olympics on hold for another four years. I disobeyed doctor's orders. It may well have been the wrong decision because I did have a lot of medical trouble until the following year, but I don't regret it at all.

LA, the smog capital of the world, was hot, humid, choking. Although physically the weather was annoying, technically, it was fascinating. Because humidity expands the javelin and gives it lift, that high humidity could, particularly if there was a little wind, make for record-shattering throws.

But the final was not until early evening, when the stadium had cooled off. Not a lot, mind you, just a bit. There was a hint of a breeze. I knew that my throw would have to be high and dead centre to float the javelin on so tepid a current of air.

This time it was Tessa who threw down the gauntlet on her first throw. Running fast, holding the javelin high, she hurled it hard. I could see at once from the angle of release that it would be a long throw.

The javelin plopped to the ground at the 69.56-metre mark. That was impressive. I was excited for Tessa, honestly. I also felt a twinge of sadness for myself. Then I remembered: I had five more rounds to beat it. So did the world champion, Tiina Lillak, who now held her second world javelin record, and who was, at the time, without a doubt, the best thrower of the three of us. But Tiina was walking gingerly, suffering from a stress fracture of her foot, which was disastrous for her run-up.

In the second round, I inched closer to Tessa's mark with 65.42 metres.

Then Tiina gritted her teeth and let go a knockout throw, which landed just short of victory, at 69.00. One more and she might have transmuted silver to Olympic gold, but Tiina had injured her ankle and took no more throws.

I kept trying. On my fifth throw, I moved into bronze medal position with 67.14. There was only one more throw. I knew I had to make it count.

It was getting dark. The floodlights went on in the

stadium. The crowd was as tense as I was, even though it was an American crowd, and there was no American in the running. Holding the javelin aloft, I ran with it, and let it go. But at the moment I released it, I knew it would fall short.

Tessa was the Olympic champion. She had become the first British woman to win an Olympic throwing event. A disappointed Tiina had won silver. I had to make do with bronze. Despite the achievement of making it to an Olympic podium, I could not help myself. I cried, once again with the cameras watching.

Pulling myself together, I went over and congratulated Tessa.

Later, as Tessa, Tiina and I stood together on the victory podium, medals hanging like necklaces around our necks, the sound of our national anthem being played and the sight of Tessa crying touched me. I just had to reach up and give her a little tweak on the cheek. We were both Brits; we had known each other a long time. Her joy, her big smile, brighter than a toothpaste advert, was contagious. At that moment, I felt happy for her. But even as Tessa cried for joy, despairing tears streamed down Tiina's cheeks.

Mum and I were thrilled that Britain had a gold and a bronze, not to mention the silver in the men's event – won by none other than Mum's protégé, the handsome Dave Ottley, who had been one of my first reasons for sticking with javelin throwing.

After that, there were the ups and downs of competition that marked the rhythm of my life. For me, mostly ups. Then, in December of 1985, something entirely unpredictable, something terrible, happened.

CHAPTER EIGHTEEN

Quietly Brave

FOUR DAYS BEFORE Christmas, as my fifteen-year-old brother Gregg got out of bed, his legs buckled under him. Unable to stand up, he lay sprawled on the floor, helpless. Mum drove him to casualty within the hour and our GP phoned to say she was on her way. But by the time they got to Oldchurch Hospital in Romford, Gregg's hands were useless too. Only the day before, Gregg had been a strong, apparently healthy young lad, running around doing this and that. Now he was paralysed. The suddenness of what had happened was terrifying. The doctor said he had Guillain-Barre syndrome, which is sometimes fatal. There was no known medication. You just had to hope for the best and wait it out. Mum and Dad were badly shaken and worried, as were my other brother Kirk and me. Gregg himself, who didn't know if he would ever have any strength in his limbs again, or even if he would live, was remarkably composed. I have never seen anyone be so quietly brave.

About 1,500 people in Britain come down with Guillain-Barre syndrome every year, but no one knows what causes it to pick those particular people. Three years earlier, Tony Benn had had it, and scientists now think it was this rare disease that put Franklin Roosevelt, the American president, into a wheelchair.

If Gregg had been diagnosed in the first three days, the doctors would have tried complete plasma change, but now it was too late.

For four months, Gregg lay in bed in Oldchurch Hospital, a horribly run-down-looking, depressing place that inspired little confidence. But appearances can be deceptive – the nursing staff were superb. We went to see Gregg in hospital twice a day. He was amazing. As we sat around his hospital bed, he told *us* not to worry and tried to hide the anxious look in his blue eyes.

We had BUPA insurance and wanted to transfer him to a cheerier hospital immediately, but we had to wait those four months until he was out of danger, because private hospitals like Hartswood-Essex in Brentwood, where he spent six more weeks, only do general nursing. They don't offer the specialised nursing skills you get in an NHS hospital.

At Oldchurch the attitude was to just give the disease time and the paralysis would slowly lift. Eventually, they did send a physiotherapist in to see Gregg three times a week, to help him re-educate his limbs and to stimulate the nerve pathways. But my instinct was that it was too little, too late. Of course, Oldchurch, being a National Health hospital, was under financial strain. There were too few physiotherapists available to treat too many patients. But I had only one brother in hospital.

Against the doctors' better judgement, weeks before the NHS physiotherapy began I massaged Gregg's limbs two or three times a week. More would have been too tiring for him. Having had so much manipulation for my own injuries, I felt I knew what I was doing, even though I realised all too well I was not medically trained. I would raise Gregg's legs for him to help his tummy muscles. I also gave him some exercises he could do in his hospital bed, and did some of them with him. Eventually, he could reach up to the iron bars of the headboard and stretch a little. He did it as often as he possibly could. I would leave him a sponge ball to squeeze and later, when he was able, a squash ball. I felt such joy the first time he had strength enough to pick up a small cube. I could see he felt immense relief.

The exercises were very important. Otherwise, lying in that bed like a vegetable, he would find that when he did walk again – we always said when, not if – his muscles would have atrophied and recovery would be harder than ever. The doctor and the hospital physio did not ban my ministrations. They merely said it wouldn't help him. I persisted anyway.

Visiting Gregg was taking a lot of time from my training at a crucial period. Winter training lays down the foundation that will build into the summer's success. But I decided my brother was more important than a gold medal at the upcoming Commonwealth Games and European Championships. The Whitbread family had always given emotional support to me. For the first time, I could be an emotional support to them. My father, who is a sensitive soul, a lovable softy, was very upset. My mother needed a shoulder too. Kirk was as shocked as the rest of us. I felt I had to try to be strong for them.

The months that followed were very traumatic for every member of the family – arriving at that dreary hospital, helping Gregg with massage and exercises, later bathing him and urging him to use the wheelchair. Gregg was enduring the agony of not knowing when or if he would ever walk again. I had always loved him. Now, as I saw how he bore his debilitating illness, I gained a new respect for him.

He fought to get well, insisting on exercising even a little finger as soon as he possibly could. He was worried because he was missing his GCSEs, and he was worried that I was losing time from my training.

'That's not a problem,' I reassured him. Then an idea occurred to me, an idea that I thought might give Gregg, and indeed the whole family, a real boost. In a rash moment, I promised I would win the Commonwealth Games gold medal for him.

It was a crazy idea. I was under-trained, emotionally vulnerable and, because I had been so worried about Gregg, lacking the single-mindedness about my sport that every champion needs. But seeing him lying there – a shadow, physically, of his former self – I felt I wanted to do something for him. I wanted to put his enormous grin, which I loved so much, back on his face.

In May, Gregg and his wheelchair accompanied Mum, Dad, Kirk and me to Cyprus for warm-weather training. Often recovery from Guillain-Barre syndrome is in two years, or never. But already Gregg was leading almost a normal life. Our instinct to start him immediately on massage and exercise and to keep it up was correct. That's the current NHS recommendation too.

The warm weather of Cyprus and the change in environment were a boon to us all. In the summer, Gregg went in his wheelchair to take his GCSEs. His handwriting, which never had been a calligrapher's dream, had deteriorated badly and Mum got a certificate from a doctor explaining the circumstances to the examiners. Despite having been so ill, and still not fully recovered, he took and passed five GCSEs. I was so proud of him.

At the end of July, I flew to Edinburgh for the Commonwealth Games. Winning there is no big accomplishment, as the Commonwealth standard isn't that high. But I wanted that gold medal for Gregg. Silver wouldn't do. When Tessa won and I came second, I couldn't help myself. I cried. Again, the world saw me in tears, and Tessa celebrating.

As I sat sobbing into the plaid blanket I had brought to dry off from the rain, the hurdler Wendy Jeal, who was one of my closest friends on the athletics circuit, rushed over to comfort me. Mum hurried over too.

I had let Gregg down. I felt guilty. Mum said that that was nonsense. Gregg said it was nonsense too. I had done my best. 'You can't,' he said level-headedly, 'do any more than that.'

It was now made clear to me – by Mum and Gregg and Andy Norman – that promising to win the gold medal for Gregg had been a tactical mistake. He had not asked me to, I had offered. But I don't like to break promises, so the pressure I had put on myself to win was tremendous. I had felt like a pressure cooker when I walked out on to the field in Edinburgh, when I should have been a razor-sharp carving knife.

The fact was, though, that things had been going wrong for a long time in my life. Disaster seemed to be following upon disaster. What with Steve's death, my medical problems and my second-rate performances on the international stage, I had no luck. Even more horrifying, those near and dear to me seemed to have no luck either. Was my misfortune rubbing off on them?

Mum said that I wasn't causing any bad luck and that thinking it was nonsense.

'The javelin throwing will come right,' she told me. 'Javelin throwers mature like wine.' She said that she was speaking not only as a mother but as a coach, the voice of authority. 'On both counts,' she said, 'you had better listen, Fatima. And while you are at it, stop that whinging and whining.'

Four weeks after the Commonwealth disaster – that's how I viewed that silver medal – without much hope, on a cloudy August day, I flew to West Germany with Mum for the most prestigious javelin event of the year, the 1986 European Championships.

I had stopped whinging, and I had stopped whining, but I couldn't help wondering: was heartbreak on and off the competition field going to be my lot in life forever?

CHAPTER NINETEEN

A Weekend to Remember

L OOKING OUT OF the window of our Stuttgart hotel room at 6 a.m., I saw that the day was not inviting. It was cold, dull and damp, classic British summer weather; apparently also classically German. Six a.m. was earlier than I needed to get up, but I just couldn't sleep. Mum made us each a cup of tea and we munched a few plain biscuits she had brought from England. Then we left for Neckar Stadium for the crucial but unglamorous qualifying round. Only if I qualified this morning could I compete in the final tomorrow.

The stadium was nearly empty, the stands entirely deserted. Only the prospective competitors, their coaches and advisers, and a handful of schoolchildren were at Neckar that grey summer's morning. The journalists were still asleep or breakfasting at their hotels.

There is no energy boost from an empty stadium, whereas a crowded one is electric.

East Germany's Petra Felke, a lanky, pretty blonde who currently held the 75.40m world record, was the favourite. I was to throw in the first pool of qualifiers. But Petra was throwing with the second pool. She would have no trouble qualifying; nor, did I expect, would I. To qualify, we each had to throw a distance of 62 metres, much less even than my silver-winning throw at the Commonwealths. Although I had three throws in which to qualify, I hoped to do it on the first throw, so that we could get out of this wintry summer weather and back to the warmth of the hotel. Then I could lounge around and rest up for the real job of the weekend, the final.

It was an almost windless morning. The West German thrower Ingrid Thyssen was just before me and threw 65 metres looking very comfortable. I thought if she can do that distance, I shouldn't have any problems at all.

Picking up the javelin for my first throw, holding it high, I began my run-up, eleven strides, fast, faster, even faster. Every instant of my run-up flowed, and at the power-packed moment of release, everything felt just right. I let the javelin, which was now pointing skywards, explode like a missile from the gantry of my hand.

As the javelin soared away, I knew it was going to be a long throw. I watched the javelin soar higher, slicing cleanly through the bread-thick air. Looking across the field at the yellow line marked at 65 metres, I waited for the javelin to land, but it was still sailing on that damp air. It was going to be a *very* long throw.

The judges scampered further out on the field. I bit my lower lip, and after what seemed a century but was only seconds, my beautiful javelin began its swift descent, landing softly on the turf. The judges put the marker down at 77.44 metres, which was 254 feet. Ecstatic, I could hardly believe it. Not only had I set a new world record by a gargantuan 2 metres 4 centimetres – that's fully 6 feet 8.5 inches – but I had shattered a psychological barrier in my sport. I was now the only woman in the world who had ever hurled a javelin 250 feet or more; a feat many people had thought no woman would ever be able to do.

I gave a whoop of victory and smiled and smiled and smiled.

By now, my tears were almost as well known to Britons as the gymnast Olga Korbut's were to the world. But, at last, on this dreary morning, 28 August 1986, I had reason to smile. At 8.18 in the morning, British summer time, in an empty stadium in Stuttgart, I had hurled my javelin further than any woman ever had before. These things happen when you least expect them.

Mum was as thrilled as I was. She signalled to me to grab my kit so that we could get back to the warmth of the hotel and maybe have a celebratory meal, but then we both realised that was no longer possible. Because I had set a world record, I had to undergo a drugs test. Instead of hurrying back to the hotel, we had to wait about an hour for the testers to get to the stadium. All world records require that test.

By the time the staff had arrived with their beakers and, under their scrutiny, I had provided a urine sample, word of my achievement had reached the media. They were everywhere, full of goodwill, but bombarding me in a dozen languages. Was I happy to have set a record? Was it a surprise? And, *Fraulein*, do you like Stuttgart? You know the sort of thing. The answers were obvious. But it was their job to ask those questions, and I replied to all of them. The athletics correspondents, the specialists, asked a few more astute questions. I tried to give them good answers.

Later, Petra Felke, who was the second highest qualifier,

told the man from *The Times* that she had been less surprised than I was at my throw. 'I always thought that Fatima had got one or two really great throws in her,' she said, 'but I still think I can win tomorrow with 74 metres.'

Mum told the journalists that Petra, who had been as consistent a thrower as I was, but at a slightly higher standard, was still the favourite. What Mum didn't say was that I had wrenched my arm in the qualifying round.

As soon as we could, Mum and I hurried back to the hotel, where we ate a takeaway lunch. Mum had hastily arranged for Arne De Jong, the most respected physiotherapist in athletics, to treat my shoulder. Because athletes frequently receive massages, me being seen coming out of the massage area would not reveal that I was injured. I spent the rest of the day in bed, lazing about and watching German TV. Often my world record was shown – it was in the introduction and at the end of each sports programme. In between, there was me winking happily and blowing a kiss, which, evidently, is what I did at the height of my jubilation.

Our evening meal, which we also had in our room, was as unexciting as lunch – rolls stuffed with ham and cheese, biscuits and a mug of hot chocolate. This was all part of the strategy for staying calm for tomorrow's final. That was the only problem now. There was no worry about the drugs test because I never took any illegal drugs. And, as I expected, my world record was fully ratified.

But my wrenched shoulder was worrying. It still hurt. With an injured throwing arm, how could I even hope for a medal, let alone victory? Was the price of my world record going to be the gold medal? Was gold in major competition going to elude me yet again?

Just such a catastrophe had happened over twenty years before to the greatest javelin thrower of her time, the Russian Yelena Gorchakova. In the qualifying round of the 1964 Olympics, Yelena set a then world record of 62.40 metres, but in the final she couldn't manage any more than 57.06 metres. She didn't get a medal. Gold went to a Romanian, but Yelena Gorchakova's world record remained unbroken for fully eight years – the longest time any javelin record has stood. Every serious javelin thrower knows Yelena's story.

I went to bed that night with more than an aching shoulder; I had a mind full of anxieties. I didn't sleep well. The next morning, I stayed in bed until 11 a.m., and had nothing but a cup of tea until Mum and I walked over to a nearby restaurant. Although we were in Germany, I ordered a big plate of spaghetti Bolognese for lunch. I couldn't eat all of it. My stomach was in knots. The day was as grey as my prospects.

Back at the hotel, I had a fitful little nap. At 5 p.m. we left for the stadium.

The warming-up area was very crowded. As I strode on to the field, Petra Felke, a gracious opponent, rushed forward to congratulate me on my world record. Hugging me, she said, 'To me it was not a surprise. I believed in your ability.' Petra's coach Helmann congratulated me too.

Before the bell sounded for the end of the warm-up, I had a couple of delicate throws, concentrating in turn on the positioning of my hips, shoulder and arm. As the other final-ists and I made our way to the reporting room for the start of the final, I could see that Mum was a bundle of tension.

She was quivering so much she could barely talk. She told me after the competition that she had a little cry and a pray before making her way to her seat behind the javelin run-up.

As the competition began, the rain was hammering down. I was used to throwing in the rain, but I wondered how Petra would cope. Well, she took an early lead, and my arm hurt. After each throw, I held my shoulder to keep it warm. Mum, who was watching on the huge stadium television, which shows the action larger than life, realised that it must be throbbing. For rounds one, two, three and four, Petra, who was throwing ahead of me, led the competition. I tried to keep the growing sense of hopelessness off my face.

Between throws, I bundled into my tracksuit and huddled under the small, roofed, open-walled shelter, rather like a bus stop shelter, which they had there. I watched as between rounds the West Germans brought on a big machine to sponge the water off the runway.

The throws in the rain were not impressive, but Petra's were more impressive than mine. My throws, though, were, I realised with some comfort, going further with each round. I was beginning to click. The rain let up, and on the fourth round I took the lead by a few centimetres, with a throw of 72.68 metres. Petra's best throw was 72 metres. In the last two rounds, she could not better that. Even with my shoulder aching, I had squeaked to victory. I did not even need to take my last throw.

But the story was not over yet.

I did not want to win the European Championship by a hair. I didn't want anyone anywhere – including myself – to think my victory was an accident, a fluke. I was entitled to one more throw at this competition, and as I had nothing to lose and everything to gain, I decided to take it. If it was a good throw, it would underline my superiority, giving my future opponents a little lesson; giving me a decisive win, not a near one. And it would also show me just how well I could perform when I was relaxed, even if I was hampered by injury.

With no further need to protect my arm for an answering throw, I stood on the runway and let rip. Yes, yes, I was right: it was going to go far. My sixth throw, which I had been under no obligation to take, landed at 76.32 metres, making it the second furthest throw in the world – bettered only by the world record I had set the day before. I had not only won, I had won well.

All the years of training had finally come to something. What a weekend I was having! I went on my lap of honour, with the photographers running backwards in front of me, trying to get their shots. After the victory lap, I would willingly pause for them, but not during my victory lap. Exultant, throwing kisses to the cheering crowd, I thanked God every step of the way.

Spontaneously, I wiggled my hips in happiness, a victory wiggle.

I stopped briefly to shake Wendy Jeal's hand and to hug and kiss Arne, the Dutch physiotherapist who had given me treatment before the final. When I got to where Mum was sitting in the stands, I saw that she was smiling and crying at the same time.

Petra, ever gracious, came over and congratulated me on my second achievement of the weekend. She had arrived in Stuttgart as the world-record holder and as the hot favourite for gold. She would leave with neither. I felt for her. But mostly I felt joy at my triumph. It healed a lot of wounds.

Now I was the champion of Europe and the world-record holder in one fell swoop. What a weekend. I was the first Briton of either sex to hold a world record in a throwing event.

With only one exception – and that was my own Europa Cup victory – no British woman in history had ever succeeded in winning a major throwing event in which the best javelin throwers, the Eastern Europeans, had competed. Tessa's and my Olympic medals in Los Angeles had been won in their absence. But the Soviet bloc were here at the European Championships. And, as ever, they'd been the ones to beat.

Yes, I told the German journalists who asked me, *Fraulein* Whitbread was enjoying her stay in West Germany.

CHAPTER TWENTY

A Roller Coaster Ride in Rome

S PORT CAN BE a roller coaster of emotion. A year after my triumph in Stuttgart, once again everything looked bleak. On 4 July 1987, at the Bislett Games in Oslo, I had defeated Petra Felke soundly, which ordinarily would have caused me to celebrate, but I fell on my throwing arm during the competition, cracking a bone in my wrist, and aggravating the old injuries to my back, arm and shoulder. Three weeks later, on 29 July 1987, Petra set a new world record. Her throw of 78.90 metres eclipsed my record by almost 1.5 metres. That news didn't help my aching shoulder one bit. Neither did cortisone or soft tissue manipulation.

Unable to train, unable to sleep properly, I felt like an old lady, not a twenty-six-year-old international athlete. I dared not practise throwing.

I'd have to give the World Championships a miss. Unless I could throw at 100 per cent in Rome, there was no point going. I wasn't whinging or whining, but I was very glum. Mum and Dad and the boys were too.

All the other British athletes flew out, and I was still in Britain, getting treatment from my osteopath. Because my event wasn't till the very last day of the Championships, with qualifying the day before, if the extra treatments worked, I could turn up late. I clung on to that thought as I endured the latest set of gruelling manipulations.

It was Andy Norman, who had been smoothing the way for British athletes for more than a decade, who helped me to make my decision to fly to Rome just four days before the javelin competition started. It was clear I would never be perfectly fit in time, but I was so hungry for victory that I might be just fit enough. I longed to become world champion, and competing in Rome was the only way I could achieve that goal.

I'd found that Andy was an increasing support to me. He now managed the careers of many of the top British athletes, including mine. He was a tough taskmaster, but he could also be a very calming guy. More and more, when I needed to talk to someone, I would talk to Andrew. My mum was instrumental in my life but like anybody she could get rattled, especially at times like this. I'd called Andrew to talk the decision through, and after two minutes on the phone I felt much more secure. Andy drove me and Mum to Crystal Palace for a final check-up with Dr Ken Kingsbury, medical adviser to the Sports Council, who gave me a cortisone injection. It helped a bit. It would have to be enough.

As we got on the plane at Heathrow, I could see worry in Mum's blue eyes. There would be no time to acclimatise to the heat and humidity, and the shoulder was still very painful. I felt in my heart it was the right call though. No matter how much it hurt, I could always grit my teeth, couldn't I?

This is the nightmare I had in Rome. I am driving the car as carefully as I can because it is a winding road and there is a sheer drop. All of a sudden, one of the curves is too sharp.

The car veers out of control and over the top of the cliff. It is falling, falling, and I am trapped. The door won't open, or there is no door. The glass of the windscreen is as hard as lead, or is made of brick. The windows are locked, permanently sealed. I can't get out. I can't escape. The car, with me in it, is about to crash into the mountainside.

Waking up suddenly in my hotel room, a mass of jangling nerve endings, I told myself this dream signalled only one thing: I had to make myself relax. It was a classic anxiety dream, the sort of dream so many athletes have in the days before a big competition. I lay there in the dawn light, taking deep breaths and forcing myself to calm down.

In the morning, I qualified for the final – but only on my second throw. At least I knew I would have no bad dreams that night. I never had nightmares on the eve of a competition ... because I didn't sleep much.

On the morning of the final, even Mum's constant chatter couldn't keep my mind off the forthcoming competition. I could tell by her cheerful prattle that Mum was wound up even tighter than me. This was the World Championships, after all. It was a huge deal. We had both slept badly, plagued by the buzz and bites of whirring mosquitoes most of the night. We were eager, both of us, to get out of that room. Lunch was my usual, a small portion of spaghetti Bolognese, five hours before the competition. I wouldn't have another meal beforehand. The five-hour interim, I had learned from experience, was about right for me.

It was a sweltering day. I spent the afternoon in bed, resting and listening to tapes. The mosquitoes had taken the afternoon off. But there were butterflies in my stomach.

Then it was time to go. The Holiday Inn we were staying

at was about two miles from the stadium. Our taxi driver burrowed through the crazy Roman traffic, and dropped us at the warm-up area. There were no live spectators in the stadium where the athletes warmed up, but we were watched by statues of the gods of Rome.

As I walked onto the field in my GB tracksuit – which, despite the heat and the killing humidity, I wore out of habit and pride and to keep my muscles fluid – I did not feel confident. I had no reason to feel confident. But I felt better than I had expected to.

Dozens of track and field athletes were stretching, twisting, jogging on the spot and taking little practice throws that would whizz past your ear. It was actually dangerous. The chaos of the field was potentially as lethal as driving on the streets of Rome, where, it was my impression, drivers shut their eyes and stepped on the accelerator.

I began to jog around the stadium. Petra arrived with her coach Helmann. In her blue vest and white shorts, her hair a shade blonder than it had been last year, Petra looked very sure of herself. At nearly five foot seven inches, she carried her musculature well. Her knee was swathed in the bandages that were almost her trademark – I wasn't the only one plagued by injuries – but she was walking well.

As I jogged round, I stopped and walked over to her. It was the first time I had seen her since she had set the new world record, the one that had been mine. I congratulated her. Petra, gracious in victory as in defeat, said that she knew the record would not stand still. 'I have not heard the last from you on this issue,' she said in her broken English, 'and think you have not heard all from me.' We shook hands, and I carried on jogging.

I liked her so much. We could spur each other on, to see how far a woman could throw. Like me, Petra would do everything she could to raise the standard of achievement. She was a worthy opponent. If not for the geographical distance between us and the political distance between our two countries, we might even have become close friends.

The day before, Petra had qualified with the furthest throw. Mine was second furthest. That was worrying, though with my injury I was lucky to have managed even that.

I saw Tessa warming up with her coach, Wilf Paish. She was much, much thinner than she had been in Los Angeles; too thin, I felt, to be much of a threat at this level of competition. For the past year, Tessa had let it be known that she was training for her former event, the heptathlon, which required less weight. When her hopes in the heptathlon seemed unrealisable, Tessa had switched back to the javelin. Sixteen days before, when my arm hurt so much that I could throw only a pitiful distance, she had won an event in Britain with just 64 metres, a fairly paltry throw by the current international standards.

Now, I did a little throwing, and then I went down to the reporting area. Soon, the other athletes and I were shepherded into the tunnel to await the moment when we would be called into the stadium to compete. It was damp in the tunnel. Because of some delay, we were kept there for much too long, and some of the athletes bounced a ball against the metal walls to keep limber. The sound of the ball ricocheting against the wall began to give me a headache.

At last, we were allowed to go into the stadium. I grabbed a spot under an umbrella out of the sun and sat down to wait for my turn to throw. I took a deep breath. The final was about to begin. Petra and Tessa were as keyed up as I was. Looking up at the stands crowded with people and beyond to the hills of Rome, though, I wondered what I was doing there. There was little chance I could make a respectable throw in my condition. Why had I come to disgrace myself?

Stop it, I told myself sternly, these are not the thoughts of a world champion. It was time now to commit myself to the competition, to put aside my doubts. Winning was what being in Rome was all about. Becoming champion of the world. And considering that my arm hurt and my stomach was restless, I felt remarkably good, even in that sapping heat. Staying away from Rome till the last minute had turned out to be a clever accident. No athlete who didn't live with it could fully acclimatise in a few days or even in a few weeks to the heat and humidity. At least I had given the Italian September less chance than it might have had to wear me down.

I had been a tangle of nerves in the run-up to the Championships, especially when it looked as if I would not be fit in time. Now, in comparison, I was calm. No doubts, no second thoughts. I was there to do a job. Determination bubbling in my veins, I stepped up and took my first throw. But, to my dismay, I managed only a pathetic 61.80 metres.

Then I watched with trepidation and some admiration as Petra bounded up the runway, and gave her javelin a mighty throw that soared just over 70 metres. She increased her lead to 71.76m on her next throw. But although I improved dramatically to 69.02, she still held the lead.

On my third throw, I inched up even closer, with 71.34. I was only half a metre behind her now, in silver medal position, but my arm was throbbing. Oh God, I thought, have pity on me now – and on my aching shoulder.

Waiting for my next turn, I lay under the umbrella in the heat of the sun, apparently resting, but in fact willing myself to win. The moment I mentally accepted what appeared to be destiny, the moment I accepted second place, or third, or worse, the competition was over for me. No matter what the odds, I must not give in. Muscle is only half of winning; mind is the other half, or possibly even three-quarters. But there is a fine line between believing you can win a competition, and mentally putting a medal around your neck before you have won it. The latter leads to over-confidence, cockiness, carelessness – and that is likely to lead to defeat.

Now, as I stepped out of my tracksuit again and walked over to pick up the javelin from the stand for my fourth throw, I knew I had to hold onto my belief in myself. Although I almost had not even come to Rome, although this was definitely the hardest competition I had ever encountered, I had to keep believing I could win. I could not bow under the pressure. I had to go for it.

I felt no anger at Petra; none of the aggression at the enemy that can win you through. For Petra, I felt only respect. It was a pity we could not both be world champion – but we could not. And if it had to be just one of us, it was, if I had any say in it, going to be me.

Squinting into the bright light at the people in the stands – there were so many of them there, watching me – I looked for Mum, who was chain-smoking. She gave me the thumbs-up sign. Picking up the javelin, holding it loosely in the fingers of my right hand, I walked to the red Tartan runway to take my fourth throw. I looked out over the green field where my javelin would land. These were the World Championships; apart from the Olympics, the greatest occasion in sport. For a moment, I felt too much awe. How did I get here? Fatima Whitbread, child of a care home, a girl who had been told she was unloved and unwanted, how could she be standing here, with the world at her feet, potentially one throw away from making history?

In that moment, I made up my mind. I had to show everyone – the Smiths, who had told me I was a troublemaker and that no one would ever want me; those classmates who had known I was from the home and wouldn't let me forget it; the woman who had given birth to me, but had let me grow up lonely and unloved in a children's home – I had to show them all what I was made of. When I went out there to throw, no matter how much my arm ached or how frightened I was, I had to, I must, give it my all. This was my chance to prove myself to the world.

Taking a long, deep breath, I let my anger at the past flow out of me. Then, becoming aware of every muscle in my body, forgetting the crowd, forgetting the occasion, I thought only of the throw I was about to make. Striding forward with my arm held high, the javelin aloft, but pointing downwards, I felt a rush of determination flow through my veins like a hypodermic of adrenaline. Running now, quickly, surely, I raised the point of the javelin heavenwards, and with a swift, strong whip of my arm forward, bowled it like a molten cricket ball into the sky.

The roar from the crowd, not just the British contingent, soothed the sharp stab of pain in my shoulder. The scoreboard registered 73.16m, a metre and a half further than Petra. The British contingent were applauding wildly. I was in the lead.

But Petra still had three more throws. Anything could happen. I bit my lip.

Petra, her blonde hair darkened with sweat, tried not to look defeated. She was sure of silver, but she too wanted gold. She picked up the javelin and ran with it, gritting her teeth as she let it go. But her answering 71.56-metre, fourth-round throw did not increase her distance. I was still in the lead.

As I stood on the runway ready to take my fifth throw, I was full of confidence, but my shoulder was throbbing. There are six throws. Petra would have two more chances to increase her distance. I must underline my lead. Concentrating only on the task in hand, I no longer thought of Petra or saw the crowd. Aware only of the javelin, of the turf in the distance and myself, aware only of the feat I had to accomplish, I held the javelin aloft, and began to run. And then I let go. At the precise moment of release, I knew it would be a good throw. The angle of release was right and there had been power behind it. I watched the javelin soar 76.64 metres into the distance before it landed. I was elated. It was the third longest throw in history. Only Petra's world-record throw and mine, which she had superseded, were further. I now led the competition by nearly 5 metres.

The crowd roared approval. Then it became hushed. Like me, the spectators were wondering what Petra's answering throw would be.

With relief, I realised her next throw was a foul, a no-throw. I was still in the lead. My own final throw was another pretty good one, 72.28 metres. My arm was aching, and when Petra stepped up to take her sixth and last throw of the competition, I held my breath.

Anything could happen. As her throw sailed through the humid air of Rome, I exhaled slowly. It was embarrassingly short. I felt for her. Then, suddenly, I realised what that meant. I had won! There were tears in my eyes. I had won! I had won Britain's only gold medal at the World Championships. Spontaneously, as before in Stuttgart, I wiggled my hips in happiness, a victory wiggle.

As I stood on the grass, arms clasped behind my back, with the East German Petra Felke on one side of me and the West German bronze medallist on the other, I thought of Steve and the song he had said was mine, 'Top Of The World'. I wished he was here to see it and share my joy, and to hear the words that were coming over the loudspeaker: '*Prima et Championesse Del Mondo: Fatima Whitbread.*' First and champion of the world, Fatima Whitbread.

At last.

My face wreathed in smiles, I waved to my father and brothers and grandparents at home and to the rest of my friends watching on satellite TV. Then I took one big step onto the white victory platform. As I thought again of Steve's wish for me to be top of the world, the orchestra struck up the British national anthem.

As I had been instructed to do, I leaned forward so that the gold medal could be hung by its ribbon around my neck.

And once again, as I had done so many times over the years, I felt gratitude to Mum, my coach, who had taught me far more than technique. (Which is not to knock the technique – I was more than grateful for that too.) I felt gratitude too to Andy, my manager and good friend, for spurring me on despite my injury. And I felt proud of my achievement, proud for myself, proud for the British people. Just in the nick of time, on the very last day of the Championships, we had won a gold medal at the Worlds. I felt a wonderful, joyful, rare elation.

Instinctively, I put that gold medal, the size of a biscuit, in my mouth and bit on it, hard – to make sure it was real. I wanted to make sure *I* was real. The medal was, I was, and my victory was. As I stood there sweating in the Rome sun, knowing I was number one in the world, *Prima*, I was tired and my arm ached, but I had never felt better in my life.

CHAPTER TWENTY-ONE

On Top of the World

T HE WHOLE NATION, I was told, was celebrating my victory. Ecstatic British well-wishers found me even in Rome. Many of them said that by winning our only gold medal, I had saved British pride. I knew that was an exaggeration – British pride may on occasion need boosting, but it certainly doesn't need saving.

I couldn't wait to get home.

But when I arrived at Heathrow, the first question I was asked – by the man from *Panorama* – was: do you take drugs? The David Jenkins drugs scandal had just broken. Jenkins, who was British but lived in Los Angeles, had been named as the brains behind a drugs ring that was supplying anabolic steroids all over the United States. British athletes were not even named in the case but to the man from *Panorama*, evidently, anyone was fair game. I felt my homecoming was the wrong moment for the drugs question. If I had been a man, I would have bopped him one, but as a woman I had to be polite.

I explained yet again that I had been tested five times that year, winter as well as summer. I had even put myself in for a test at a meeting where I wasn't competing, to set an example. Not only are British athletes tested at events during the season, but Britain has year-round random testing, and was – as it still is – among the most rigorous testing countries in the world.

It is sheer prejudice to think that women can only build muscles with chemical help. It is a notion that comes from the stereotype of the weaker sex. Our genes may have a lot to do with sporting potential, but in the end, you get your muscles only from sweat and hard work. I had been pushing myself hard to put in the sets and reps I needed to, whether I felt like it or not, for a dozen years. That's how I'd achieved my physique – and how I maintain it, even to this day. I no longer train full time. But I still do a run with my dog in the morning and I do regular workouts at the gym – whether I feel like it or not. It's a way of life that, in my opinion, more of us should embrace.

Luckily, the man from *Panorama* was the exception to the rule. My homecoming was, overwhelmingly, a resounding endorsement of both me and my achievement. After more than a decade of blood, sweat, pain and tears, it was amazing to feel that all that hard work had paid off. It was also a revelation. My parents and my brothers Kirk and Gregg – who had recovered and was no longer in need of a wheelchair – were thrilled for me. I was inundated with incredible honours and awards, even having a waxwork made of me at the world-famous Madame Tussauds.

I soon learned that being world champion brought with it a whole host of responsibilities. And awards ceremonies. One of the first events I attended was the Thames Television sporting awards at the Savoy Hotel in London. The room was full of sporting celebrities – cricketers Denis Compton, Derek Underwood and Mike Gatting; the footballer Ossie

Ardiles; the champion horsewoman Virginia Leng. Snooker champions Steve Davis and Jimmy White, who had faced each other in Preston just the night before in a match that went to the final frame, were chatting to each other intently.

At lunch, I sat next to the pop star David Essex, who was utterly charming. It was stimulating to have a conversation that for once did not involve sport. The well-known businessman Richard Branson was also at our table, and I also enjoyed chatting with the golfer Nick Faldo and the boxer Frank Bruno. The year before, when I had set a world record and won the European Championships, I had been the female runner-up for this award. To my delight, this time I was a winner.

A few weeks later, I attended the most important awards ceremony of the season: the BBC Television Sports Personality of the Year Award. I had always wanted to join the ranks of my heroes and heroines as a winner of this prestigious prize. At the children's home, when sport was already important in my life, I had dreamed of it. What makes the BBC award so special is that it is the public who choose the winner. It's not chosen by men in grey suits, it's a vote from the people – the men, the women, maybe even the kids – who watch sport.

Sitting through the long awards ceremony at BBC Television Centre that evening, I could feel myself becoming more and more nervous. The year before, I had been runner-up to Nigel Mansell, the Formula One motor-racing driver who had nearly won the World Championship. Nearly winning doesn't usually get many votes, but Nigel had obviously won the hearts of many people. I loved the British public, and it was gratifying to know that they also cared about me. I had been so proud to be second, finishing ahead of Kenny Dalglish, the popular Liverpool footballer, and also ahead of all my track and field colleagues, many of whom had had fine years. Some of them had been none too pleased that the first-placed athlete was female. How would they feel if I now actually won the BBC award?

I glanced over at the runner Steve Cram, who was seated beside me. He immediately smiled. In fact, Crammie, who had won this award in 1983, had been rather sweet all evening. I was seated on the aisle, and my black-and-white polka-dot dress, which was slit to the thigh, was riding up well over my knees. I had had the dress made specially, but now I was a bundle of nerves, and began to worry that as the camera scanned the aisle, the dress would seem too revealing. Momentarily, I considered asking Steve to change seats with me. Deciding that moving in the middle of the proceedings was not a good idea, I sat tight instead and listened to the presenter describing the exploits of the runner-up, none other than the brilliant world snooker champion Steve Davis, who had had a fantastic year.

I applauded enthusiastically, and then I held my fingers to my mouth as I waited for the name of the winner. At last I heard it: Fatima Whitbread.

The applause was thunderous. I could feel my grin spread literally from ear to ear. I was not just overcome with elation, I was stunned. So many people had told me a woman couldn't win. I could barely believe my good fortune.

I was the first woman in ten years to win the most prestigious popular sporting award in the land. Sport was still a man's world. My most recent female predecessor was none other than Virginia Wade, who had won it in 1977, after becoming the Wimbledon champion in the year of the Queen's silver jubilee – on the very same day I'd won my Victorix Ludorum at the District Schools Championship. Now, *I* had won the big one, but inside I was feeling the same emotions I had as a schoolgirl: hopeful, grateful and proud.

Somehow, I managed to walk up to accept the BBC Television Sports Personality of the Year award. Thank goodness I was dressed up to the nines. I was amused to hear the commentator say that this was the year of the wiggle. I said a few words that I meant sincerely – thanking every one of the British public, and sending them all good wishes for the upcoming New Year. 'Please,' I added, 'make a little wish for me too.'

Two days later, I went to Buckingham Palace to receive an MBE. Months earlier, I had been told that my name was being put forward for an MBE in the Queen's Birthday Honours list. I was so thrilled. Me, Fatima, the girl from the home, on the Queen's Birthday Honours list. I could hardly believe it.

I wrote back immediately, accepting the invitation and saying how privileged I felt. The invitation had stressed that the nomination was confidential, and for once I kept a secret to myself, not telling anyone, even my family, the news. When the nominations were at last announced, on 13 June 1987, I was at Gateshead in the midst of a javelin competition. A message of congratulations was displayed on the electronic scoreboard. I felt very emotional when the crowd in the stadium gave me a tremendous round of applause.

The MBEs are presented at Buckingham Palace in alphabetical order. Since 'W' is the twenty-third letter of the alphabet, it wasn't until 15 December, two months after the

World Championships, that I was to go to the Palace to receive mine from the Queen. I asked my mother and my Grandma Maud to accompany me. We drove swiftly through the morning traffic, but at Canning Town, on the perimeter of the East End, we came practically to a stand-still. The flyover was blocked. My blood pressure rose to new heights as I thought I might miss the ceremony. But we eventually found an alternate route through the drab back streets of Stepney and Limehouse, a stark contrast to the elegance that awaited us at Buckingham Palace. After what seemed like hours, we arrived at the Mall with ten minutes to spare and joined the queue of cars.

Security was very strict. A policeman leaned into the car to check that we had invitation cards and the letter of infor-mation. Then we were waved along into the Palace's central courtyard, which is not visible to the public. Another policeman checked the boot, looked under the bonnet and even examined the bottom of the car to make sure that there were no weapons or bombs.

When Mum, Nan and I walked up to the door of the Palace, our credentials were checked once more, and then we were allowed to enter. Leaving our coats in the cloakroom, we descended a spiral staircase to the plush toilets to freshen up. We had been on the road for over two hours. I was wearing a blue dress, which I had designed myself and had had specially made for the occasion. In the mirror, I saw with relief that the dress had travelled well and was not creased.

Upstairs, where the presentations were to be made, I was captivated by the works of art that were displayed on the walls. Mum and Nan were ushered to their seats, and I to mine in the area cordoned off for the prospective MBEs. We were from all walks of life and from all over the realm. As we waited, members of the Palace staff and many of my fellow recipients came over to congratulate me on my athletics achievements, to shake my hand and to get my autograph. I was very astonished and moved to be regarded as a celebrity in such distinguished company.

Now it was almost time for the ceremony to begin. One of the Palace staff attached a small pin to the front of my blue dress. The Queen would use the pin to attach the MBE. The first name was called, then another and another. When at last I heard mine, I walked forward three paces as I had been instructed to do, and turned left to face the Queen. Her Majesty was wearing a very elegant yellow outfit. I curtsied.

Her Majesty said that she was delighted to meet me, and that she had watched me receive the BBC Sports Personality of the Year award on television two nights before. I told her that to receive the MBE was the completion of a wonderful year.

Her Majesty attached the MBE to my dress, and then she shook my hand. I curtsied once more. On the way back to my seat, I caught a glimpse of Mum and Nan beaming. I felt elated and a little solemn. This was one of the great honours of the land, one of the highest honours I would ever receive. I savoured the moment.

When the band struck up the national anthem, memories of the gold medal ceremonies at the European Championships in Stuttgart and at the Worlds in Rome came flooding back to me, making me feel so proud to be British. Her Majesty departed, and then there was a gentle, excited melee as the hugging and kissing and congratulating by relatives and friends began.

Outside the Palace, the sun was shining brightly. In the courtyard, I held up my MBE for the television and newspaper cameras. I signed some autographs, and then we drove across the area where the changing of the guard had just occurred, and out of the grand gates of Buckingham Palace. As we drove down the Mall towards Trafalgar Square, I felt immensely proud.

We stopped for lunch at the Tower Hotel. After that, it was immediately back to training. I put in the weight-training session I would normally have done first thing in the morning. Then I drove my Mazda RX7 to Blackshots playing field for a session of strenuous running, concentrating on bounding. As I drove home along the A13, I noticed a lone man walking along the road. He was carrying an air rifle. Suddenly, he turned and shot at me, shattering the windscreen.

I didn't stop. Once home, I alerted the police, but I didn't give my name because I didn't want the media to hear of the incident. Some of them would have let their imaginations run down ugly corridors. I didn't want them camping on my doorstep either, asking how I felt when the bullet struck, and what it had to do with my MBE.

Even though I knew that the bullet had been fired at me only by the merest chance, I was a little shaken. All in all, it had been quite a day. But I was not going to let a moment of random viciousness poison my memories of the day I met the Queen.

Nor will I ever forget the day I went to Number 10 Downing Street to have cocktails with the Prime Minister. As soon as I arrived, all semblance of nerves disappeared because I saw so many familiar faces from the world of sport.

Golfers Nick Faldo, Tony Jacklin and Ken Brown were there with their spouses, as was Nigel Mansell. But I didn't mind a bit that I was on my own. Everyone was very chatty, and I felt terrific in the conservative royal blue outfit I had on. It was another of those I had designed myself.

Mrs Thatcher was wearing blue too, a darker shade than mine. As ever, she seemed very cool and in complete control of the situation. Her husband Denis was standing beside her. She welcomed me and told me to make myself at home. Peeking into the cabinet room, I could sense almost palpably the power the room had. So many decisions which had changed the world had been made here. So many more would be in the future.

I munched a few sandwiches and talked to Colin Cowdrey, the former England cricket captain. Then one typical pain-in-the-neck – and there is always one at these functions – tried to corner me. He went on about how important you had to be to get an invitation and therefore how important he was. I was rescued by a member of the Prime Minister's staff asking me to join Mrs Thatcher for photographs.

I had almost reached the Prime Minister when I was waylaid by another guest. Mrs Thatcher herself then stepped in and took me aside for the photo session. There were a number of pictures taken, and the one of me and Nigel Mansell with the Prime Minister eventually appeared in the press.

When we had completed the photos and were well out of the Prime Minister's earshot, Nigel said wryly that he was pleased to have been photographed with the two most powerful women in Britain.

'I hope you don't mean brain and brawn.'

'Certainly not,' he said, and we had a good laugh.

But my shoes were hurting my feet. I found a little room off the main one, and wriggled out of them. Sitting there in my stocking feet, surrounded by history but very much at ease, I had a chat with one of Mrs Thatcher's staff about the pressures that are placed on a prime minister and those that are placed on a world champion. Hers, as you can imagine, made my pressures pale into insignificance. It was good for me to realise that.

As I was leaving, I was introduced to Willie Whitelaw, who had been Home Secretary and was currently leader of the House of Lords. By now Mrs Thatcher was greeting her advisers. I thanked Denis Thatcher for his hospitality and extended my gratitude through him to his wife.

My next chat with a prime minister was nearly twenty years later, in June 2006, only this time I was wearing a T-shirt and trainers. And so was he. Tony Blair ran that year's Sport Relief mile in 7.56 minutes alongside the Olympic rowing champion Steve Redgrave, Sebastian Coe, and me.

Mr Blair, puffing a little during the run, said he couldn't do his job as prime minister without a certain level of fitness. He tried to train two or three times a week. I remember him agreeing with one of us, I think it was Sir Steve, that the older you get, the more important it is to keep yourself fit.

But that wasn't yet an issue for me during that stellar period after the Worlds when I was being welcomed at Buckingham Palace and Number 10. I was on top of the world, and I expected to be at my peak for the upcoming Olympics.

CHAPTER TWENTY-TWO

Heart and Seoul

I T WAS AT the unveiling party for my Madame Tussauds waxwork that I first noticed something was wrong. I felt way under par, down in the dumps. Gone were my usual energy and high spirits. In fact, there were no jokes being cracked during training anymore at Chadwell St Mary. I felt listless all the time. That lassitude, that lack of vigour, depressed me far more than the pain in my shoulder.

Some days I couldn't even get out of bed. When I collapsed during a training session, I was diagnosed with glandular fever. But there was more to it than that. I knew what was wrong, but I didn't know how to fix it.

My Olympic odds were getting worse and worse. Many people suggested that I should go out at the top as world champion and not risk disgracing myself at the Olympics in Seoul, where in my listless state my chances of qualifying let alone winning a medal were close to nil. But I knew I could never ever respect myself if I simply gave up. I knew too that my problem was psychological as well as physical.

Before the World Championships, one of the red-top newspapers had printed a double-page-spread interview with the woman who gave birth to me, in which she said she wanted her blood daughter back. That's when John Rodda, the most respected athletics correspondent of that era, told Andy, 'I think you better have Fatima write a book to tell her side of the story. Otherwise these people will keep on.' John told me I had to protect myself because some of the public might start to believe that I was shunning a deserving family.

So in January 1988, in the midst of winter training for the Olympics, I wrote out the main events of my life to go in the autobiography, and then I sat down with Adrianne, my co-writer, who would ask me questions, hard questions, detailed questions about what my life was like in my child-hood, which had been so terrible. I would try not to weep, but I couldn't help it. It still hurts a lot when I think about it, but at the time it was completely horrendous because inside me everything was raw. I had to go back into my memory and become that child in a children's home again, long enough to remember the details. It was like being in a cine-film. I didn't want to relive the hatred shown to me by the woman who gave birth to me or the rape at her home, nor remember the children's home matrons who had no love of children.

It's good to move forward instead of staying locked into the past. But now I had to do it. John Rodda was right. So I went to see Cory, who had been so good to me when I was very little. And one day, we drove over to my last children's home, the one in Ockendon, to see if that would bring back some memories. It did, and that really took it out of me. I started having panic attacks. I would go tongue-tied and start to sweat. Then I just sort of fell apart.

I refused to go to a psychotherapist. The one I had had as a young teen had prescribed throwing myself into sport, which had worked ... but it wasn't working now. Also, we couldn't risk it getting out that I was seeing a shrink before the Olympics; that would give a huge boost to my rivals.

There's never a good time to have a breakdown, but for it to happen to me during my Olympic preparations was sheer disaster. I was too depressed to do much of anything. And when I did train – for a few minutes instead of a few hours – there was the additional danger that my poor shoulder would jump out of place. It happened more than once. So I had to practise technique without throwing, and do much less than I normally would. It was frustrating and painful and scary. It was like catch-22.

All we could do was keep our fingers crossed that after each truncated training session I would come out unscathed. When you are training flat out for the Olympics, you need to train and sleep, train and sleep, or train and relax, sitting in front of the telly with nothing on your mind. I knew that. Mum, my coach, knew that. Andy, my manager, knew that. Yet I couldn't relax. The pressure on me was enormous. As world champion, I was the favourite, and with all the new sponsorship opportunities and the charity work and the honours I was receiving, plus the injury and the psychological stress, well, I just had too much on my plate.

The sponsorship appearances in an Olympic year meant I was getting good money, which I would need for my future – especially if my shoulder let me down and I couldn't continue my career for another four years till the next Olympics. Making the most of the moment, I had just moved to my first home of my own, a mews cottage in Essex. I'd wanted a place of my own where I could have private times, but I also loved being part of a family, so I was of two minds even about that. Nothing was simple.

At this point, I still thought my shoulder was my biggest problem. In a way it was: my shoulder was never really going to be right again. I was getting frequent cortisone injections from Dr Ken Kingsbury, the Sports Council doctor who looked after the British internationals in several sports, not just athletics. I was seeing the osteopath for massages frequently too. Ken wasn't a psychotherapist, but he realised that there was far more than my arm bothering me. The injections took about ten seconds, but we would talk for about an hour on each visit. On one occasion, when I rang him at home early one morning, he gave me good advice. Then he told Mum it would be a good idea to get me a dog for distraction, and he recommended a shitzu because they like a lot of love and attention.

I remember Mum arriving at my cottage with this cute, affectionate, fluffy, mischievous little black-and-white puppy, aged about eight to ten weeks old. I named her Champ. I would hold and cuddle Champ and tell her all my troubles, and she always understood.

Now, slowly, I began the task of rebuilding myself, starting my season's training again almost at the beginning. It was July. I was months behind schedule. I would give it everything I had, and I had my years of dedicated training to call on, like muscle in the bank. I could only hope it was enough.

Mum said it was my decision, but I knew she wanted me to go to Seoul. She and Andy – who was still managing my career and pulling out all the stops to find help – had not given up on me, despite my months of physical and mental trouble. They made sure they were always available to encourage and help me. In mid-August, I competed at

Gateshead, then at Brussels and Zurich; all necessary to become razor-blade sharp. My shoulder hurt, but I was victorious. That reminded me how much I like winning. Three weeks before the Games, I had my last hard competition, at Crystal Palace against Tessa. I won with 69.40 metres.

My shoulder had been flaring up after every training session and every competition, but I was throwing further every day. Although I had not achieved my previous standard, and I was living in constant pain, I felt I was in with a chance at the Olympics, even when on 6 September, just twenty days before the javelin final, Petra Felke again shattered the world record with a throw of 80.00 metres. I reassured myself with the thought that the year before, when Petra had broken the world record shortly before the World Championships at Rome, I had nonetheless beaten her for gold.

As I got on the plane for the long journey to Seoul, I knew the odds were against me, but no one could possibly want to win as much as I did. In world-class competition, you need the muscle, you need the technique, but the will to win is tremendously important. I'd need a lot of focus, and a lot of will to have any chance of winning, but one thing Fatima Whitbread had always been was wilful. This contest would require me to call on all my reserves of inner strength.

It was pleasantly hot in Seoul. After our chill British summer, you couldn't fault the weather, but Seoul was, many people thought, a strange place to stage the Olympics. It was a centre of political turmoil. Riots in the city had been front-page news for months. North Korea, which had been refused the right to join South Korea in hosting the Games, threatened to disrupt them. With the border between North and

South Korea just 35 miles north of Seoul, an artillery shell lobbed at the stadium from north of the border would easily hit its mark. There was a lot of talk, people were frightened, but it was pointless to imagine dire possibilities. I could only hope that those in charge were acting responsibly.

My own responsibility was to focus on the task before me, and to do my best, no matter what. Yet even after the Games had started, there were riots just 15 miles from the stadium, between radical students, who threw firebombs and stones, and the police, who responded with violence and tear gas.

The Olympic village was, of course, well insulated from disturbances, but Dad was worried about Mum, who was staying in the city at the Seoul Plaza Hotel, where I would join her as often as I could, relishing the time not only to see her, but also to escape from the pressure-cooker environment created by a village full of tense athletes. Luckily, neither of us got a whiff of tear gas.

In the days before my event, I spent my time training in the big throwing field near the Han river, chatting with friends from all over the world, and trying to avoid queuing – even for breakfast at the Olympic village you had to wait for forty minutes. Every day, I got treatment from Arne, the Dutch physiotherapist, for my throbbing shoulder.

Whenever I could, I got well away from the stark, new, modern Olympic complex and stood in the quiet serenity of the gardens beneath the ancient pagoda called the Namdaemum. It was a place to meditate, to feel quiet inside. On the way back to the Olympic hubbub, I would look for the wizened old woman with smiling eyes who sold chestnuts for 1,000 Wong.

At last, on 25 September, came the javelin qualifying round. Tessa failed utterly to qualify for the final. Surprisingly, so did Tiina Lillak, the former world champion from Finland, who must have been battling a serious injury. But Petra Felke, East Germany's best hope, was on top form. She qualified easily on her first throw. Now it was down to me.

With dismay, I saw my first throw land short of the 63 metres qualifying standard, and felt a stab of pain in my shoulder. I was just a little shaken, I told myself, because during the warm-up, a Chinese thrower's javelin had skidded crazily along the ground, nearly jabbing me. I threw again and watched my second throw also peter out. Usually, even at the worst of times, I could throw 63 metres. I had to pull myself together – now – or it would be a rerun of the depressing Moscow Olympics eight years before, when Tessa and I had both failed to qualify. That time, I had mainly gone to the Olympics to gain experience. But this was my time.

You get six throws in the final, but only three in the qualifying round. I had just one more chance. I couldn't let myself and Britain down. I wouldn't. Silently, I told myself: you *will* throw the qualifying standard, plus 5 bloody metres more. You can do it; *I can do it.*

And I did, qualifying on my last throw with 68.44m, the best throw of the day.

Meanwhile, in London, unbeknownst to me, I was at the centre of a tempest in the tabloids. The *Daily Mail* had printed an excerpt from my autobiography, revealing that as a girl I had been raped. My book, which I'd finished except for the Olympic chapter, was to be published six weeks after the Games. But now the *Sun* printed a front-page story about the rape, featuring a photograph of a man who denied raping me. What was extremely odd about this was that the man had never been accused, not by the *Daily Mail* and not in my book either. If I ever knew it, I do not remember the name of the man who raped me. And I knew too little about the housekeeping arrangements of the woman who gave birth to me to know if he lived with her on a long-term basis or was just 'visiting'.

On the day before I was to compete in the Olympic final, the *News of the World* got in on the act. The woman who gave birth to me was quoted as saying of me, 'I pray that she loses.'

But in Seoul that night – the night before the final – I knew nothing of all this. Andy and the other British officials had skilfully protected me from the press. But as Mum was preparing to meet me for an evening meal, the *News of the World* rang through to Mum's hotel room – even though she was registered under another name. Mum says the man from the *News of the World* was insistent at first, then quite rude. He told her he had to have a quote about the rape and an answer to the woman's malevolent wishes for me, and that she or I had to do it then and there. Mum said, 'We can't deal with this now,' and hung up. Mum never even mentioned it to me until well after my event. Can you imagine thinking about all that when you are trying to win an Olympic medal for yourself and for your country?

During our evening meal at the Seoul Hilton, I was apprehensive about the final, which was scheduled for late the next afternoon. I was so anxious that I didn't eat as much as I have been known to: a sure sign of my nerves. I didn't say as much as usual either, I just sat there listening vaguely to the background music, a pleasant medley. I perked up though when the band began to play 'We've Only Just Begun', the song Steve used to sing to me. Recognising the tune, Mum grinned at me and said, 'This is an omen.'

The Olympic stadium was deeply impressive. It was bold, modern architecture, framed by a blue sky. As I picked up my javelin and went out to throw, I felt a proper sense of occasion, but I was in no way intimidated. It was impossible to be, what with a lively British contingent of fans seated right behind the javelin run-up, cheering my every move. I gave them a big smile, and then, after noting that the sky had become cloudy, which could affect the javelin, I became oblivious to everything but the competition, which began with a flourish.

Petra Felke, on her first throw, threw further than 70 metres, breaking the Olympic record.

My first throw was rubbish.

On her second throw, Petra, in the midst of her best season ever, increased her distance to an astonishing 74.68m.

Well, no matter, I was still going for gold. Self-doubt was a luxury I could not afford. I shut off from it and from the stabbing pain of my shoulder, and with a yell I threw 67.46m, which put me, for the moment, in silver medal position.

The weather changed. The air seemed to go out of the stadium. The breeze was now unpredictable. My next two throws were close to rubbish. Petra's next two throws were, on average, worse than mine. The other East German, twenty-one-year-old Beate Koch, who was in bronze medal position, was now throwing badly too. On my penultimate throw, I increased my distance slightly, but not enough; and then came the sixth throw, my last.

Wrapping my mind round the javelin, visualising the perfect shot, one in which every muscle was instructed correctly and did as it was told, regardless of whether it hurt or not, I held the javelin aloft and began to run. Then, with a loud shout, I whipped my arm forward, and let the javelin go. I could feel it was a good throw; not my best, but a good one. Would it be good enough?

The javelin rose high. I held my breath. Where would it land? Would it be far enough? My shoulder was throbbing. I kept my mind entirely on the flight of the javelin, willing it to go further, even further. Please, I muttered. Please. And the javelin continued to soar. Right, I said, javelin, you just take your time. After what seemed a millennium, it nosed towards the ground, landing gracefully at 70.32 metres, my longest throw of the season.

But not quite good enough. I had gone for gold, but it wasn't to be. I'd have to be happy with silver. That's sport. That's life. I tried not to be disappointed. It had been such a struggle all the way, even just to throw at Seoul. I'd come to the Olympics on a hope and a prayer. Really my arm was pretty much rubbish – my shoulder was shot – but my will had recovered. I won that medal on technique, muscle, daring ... but mainly on a will of iron.

I hoped no one at home was disappointed.

At the Olympic Games in Los Angeles four years ago, I had won bronze. In Seoul, today, it was silver. In Barcelona in four years' time, why wouldn't it be gold? Maybe something new would be discovered that could repair my shoulder. I was still the world champion, and still enamoured of my sport. My mum had always told me javelin throwers mature with age, and I was only twenty-seven.

But all that was in the future. Now that these Games were over, I was looking forward to some quiet times with the people who were close to me, and some playful times with my dog, Champ. Shortly before Seoul, I had moved into my eighteenth-century cottage, not too far away from the family. The cottage, with its crushed raspberry carpeting and, in the lounge, a chandelier with fifteen glittering lights, was my first home of my own. I intended to cook many, many delicious meals there for Mum, Dad, my two brothers, Grandad and Nan, and other special people. And for one special person in particular.

CHAPTER TWENTY-THREE

Andy

OVER THE YEARS I had known him, I had slowly grown closer to Andy Norman, and Andy Norman had grown closer to me. Yet I don't think it occurred to either of us, certainly not to me, that our friendship could bloom into a relationship. For one thing, he was married, and I even knew his wife. For another, he was much older, eighteen years my senior.

Of course we had always been reasonably close; he was my manager. I looked up to him, I admired him. I felt I could rely on him. People working together in sport spend a lot of time together. They do get close. But just like the friendship he had with Steve Ovett, his first big star, at whose wedding Andy was best man, our friendship was platonic.

Andrew was a former police sergeant – the very same one who had acted as a character witness for the Whitbreads all those years ago when they first fostered me. As far as I was concerned, that immediately made him a force for good. Andy left his police career after twenty-two years to work full time for British athletics; but way back in 1972, he had become AAA Southern counties co-ordinator, a time-consuming position, which like most jobs in athletics at that time was unpaid.

All us athletes adored Andy. He could be blunt, and sometimes rude, but to us athletes it was clear he had a caring nature behind that tough-guy exterior. Although on occasion he would say things you'd rather he hadn't, he was a lion when it came to helping and protecting us – and, like a lion, he would bare his claws if his cubs were under attack. Andrew managed the careers of the greatest names in athletics – Steve Ovett, Steve Cram, Steve Backley, Linford Christie, Colin Jackson, Jonathan Edwards, Sally Gunnell and Kelly Holmes. And that's just some of them. He influenced the careers of Alan Pascoe and Brendan Foster and Paula Radcliffe. I could go on. He was one of the first to spot Paula's great talent. Andrew knew his athletics, he loved athletics, and he gifted his life to it.

I remember his green eyes flashing as he told me how he hated 'shamateurism', which forced the world's finest sports champions to turn to subterfuge to survive. Paying athletes was strictly forbidden under the amateur rules, but if you didn't train full time, you had virtually no chance of winning at major international competitions. The Soviets put their people in sports academies and the military and controlled their every move. In the West, so that athletes could survive, brown envelopes were handed out under the table. The fastest men in the world, the star runners, earned the most. It was, as Sebastian Coe rightly said in the *Independent*, 'a situation which makes honest men dishonest'.

It was Andrew's speech to the 1982 congress of the IAAF (International Amateur Athletics Federation), and his campaign for legalising trust fund payments to British athletes, that ended the sham. The rules were changed so that athletes could be paid without deceit. Andy even saw to it that at British meetings male and female champions were paid equally.

But I can't stress enough that, at that time, no athlete's main motivation was money; it was winning and representing your country. We'd gone into it before there was much money to be made. Our families made big financial outlays kitting us out and paying for travel and high-protein food. Even today, when the Olympic 100-metres champion, as the fastest man on Earth, can be sure of making millions, he's not paid an awful lot compared to some of the footballers. And he's got the rest of his life to lead. A career in sport is short-lived.

As part of his job with the British Amateur Athletics Board, Andy travelled to competitions with us athletes. Sometimes Gerd, his wife, came along. She was there in Helsinki when I won silver at the World Championships. Whenever we travelled, and not just in the early days, Mum was there too. She was the national javelin coach, after all (at that time, this too was an unpaid position). Even in the later years, if I wasn't staying in the athletes' village, I shared a hotel room with her. I never shared a room with Andrew until after his divorce.

I met Gerd for the first time when I was seventeen or eighteen. Gerd was an attractive lady, and I was pleased for Andy. I assumed she was a good wife to him. Then I began to hear gossip and to notice things, and Andy told me he loved his children but that the state of his marriage saddened him. I felt bad for him because Andy Norman was a good guy who helped athletes and I wanted the best for him. I could see that he was hurt. Of course, I felt for him. But it didn't occur to me to have a relationship with Andrew myself. He was older. He was married – and I would never go with a married man. I value family, and stability, far too much ever to cheapen them.

For reasons of her own, Gerd confronted Andy with unfounded suspicions about him and me in 1985. As she admitted in the *Mirror* a quarter of a century later, Andrew was lost for words. On 20 November 2011, in a long, anti-Fatima interview in the *Mirror*, Gerd said of Andy's reaction at the time: 'He was speechless.' And ask anyone, Andy was never afraid to open his mouth. No, as he told me himself, he was astonished at her claims. Gerd also said in her interview: 'He adored his family and he was a joy to be around.' I agree there.

That newspaper article came out while I was away in the Australian jungle appearing nightly on *I'm a Celebrity … Get Me Out of Here!* Just like the woman who gave birth to me had done decades earlier, Gerd bad-mouthed me at a time when I couldn't reply, and was vulnerable and trying to make something of myself.

During their bitter year-long divorce, Andy often cried on my shoulder and that led to a new closeness between us. Until Gerd's accusation, Andy had never even broached the subject of having a relationship with me, and the thought did not ever enter my mind. You could say Gerd gave us the idea. When Andy suggested it, during the divorce proceedings, I said, 'Andy, there is no way I can have a relationship with another woman's husband. I can't do that.'

Everybody in athletics knows that Andy and I were very close during that period. I was always seen with him at athletics meetings. People drew their own conclusions. Some may have thought we were sexually involved, but nobody was in a bedroom with us. We cared about each other, but we weren't intimate until after his divorce came through. Of course I didn't feel about him the way I'd felt about Steve; that was first love. But for the next twenty-one years, Andy and I were together and were emotionally very, very close.

The age gap of eighteen years didn't matter to either of us. We knew the same people in the same world. We shared a love of sport. Andy had gifted his life to sport, and I was gifting mine. I already loved Andy. Now I would just love him in a different way.

He wasn't threatened by my muscles. Andy was a big, powerful man. Just like Mum, he was proud of them because he knew how hard and how many years I'd had to work to build them up. All three of us thought they were attractive; or to be more exact, my muscles were very attractive to us because they were the fruit of so much joint labour. Mum directing the training; Andy managing my schedule, so that I competed at just the right time to build to a peak for the big championships; and me sweating it out in the gym.

Soon after her 1986 divorce, Gerd Norman married the solicitor who had handled the divorce for her. Gerd got custody of the children: Stephen, then fifteen, and Kirsti, then thirteen. Over the years, Andy did everything he could to stay in touch with them. I remember him telling me, sometimes tearfully, of the times he was told the children wouldn't come to the phone, and when he had arranged to go and see them, more than once he was left standing at the door and came home and wept. I felt terrible for Andy, and it impacted on our relationship, because it made him so sad.

Nevertheless, he kept phoning and sending birthday cards to his children. I encouraged him to keep on with this when he was depressed about seeing the kids so rarely. Andy often told me he missed his children. He loved them and was immensely proud of them. He willingly paid their private school and university fees even when it left us short of money, and I didn't complain because I respected his love for his family.

As our relationship blossomed, Andy came to mean a great deal to me. We were spending a lot of time together. After his divorce, Andy said, 'I want to move in with you.'

I said, 'No, you can't do that.' I was living in the cottage in Grays, my first home of my own.

He said, 'It has two bedrooms.'

But I said no, I had to have something that was mine. So he bought a flat in the adjoining mansion block in Coppid Hall in Grays. In effect, though, he did largely move in with me, using his own flat for telephoning at all hours to set up athletics meets all around the world.

Andy and Mum and I had worked as a team during the triumphs and disasters on the way to my winning the European Championship, the World Championship and two Olympic medals. After Seoul, I'd had surgery on my shoulder. It was a last-ditch hope, and it failed. Unfortunately, the four-hour operation to repair my rotator cuff damaged the fast twitch muscle. The pain was gone. So too was my ability to make championship throws. Andy sat me down in the early months of 1990, and helped me see that as much as I loved my sport, it was time to retire from competition. I had to face the fact that my shoulder was no longer up to it, and if I kept on, I would destroy my self-confidence too.

With tears in his eyes and mine, reluctantly I agreed to retire.

I was just twenty-eight, a couple of weeks shy of my twenty-ninth birthday.

CHAPTER TWENTY-FOUR

A New Life

N
O LONGER COMPETING, I had time on my hands. I needed a life. I am a great believer that life is what you make it. If one opportunity goes, you go for another. I made sure I had all of my coaching qualifications. People had heard of me so I was in demand, and began coaching in Britain and internationally from Norway to New Zealand, and as far afield as Tonga and Fiji. I ran training groups for ordinary Essex and London kids, as well as for talented young athletes coming up all over Britain. I continued this satisfying work, much of it for charity, even when I took on a fascinating new job, which I negotiated for myself.

There was a new housing estate in Grays being developed by private builders. It was called Chafford Hundred. It now houses thousands of people, has two primary schools and adjoins the big Lakeside shopping mall, but at the time it consisted of two gorges that were in the process of becoming a building site. I got the idea of starting a club of elite athletes called Chafford Hundred to create awareness of this new development and to gain sponsorship for top British athletes. In that way, the housing development could help sport and sport could help the development. There were

245

clubs like this in America, most famously Carl Lewis's Santa Monica, but this was the first in Britain. The athletes wore Chafford Hundred on their vests when they ran, and we got other sponsors too. I would meet with people from big corporations and some local companies to 'sell' them on the idea of sponsoring athletes, who would appear in adverts and at events for the sponsor. This would bring in good money for the athletes and the sponsors, and a commission for me.

As the marketing manager of the Chafford Hundred athletic team, I looked after Linford Christie, Jonathan Edwards, Steve Backley, Colin Jackson and Sally Gunnell, and later Kelly Holmes and Paula Radcliffe – in all, thirty-four top British athletes. The job was great, but it was tricky. When Linford was the fastest man in the world, he had so much going on, just getting him to show up on time for a Lucozade photo shoot could be a nightmare.

Andrew and I now had a house on one of the most sought-after roads in Brentwood. I bought the house with my winnings from athletics, and we gave it the name Javel Inn. It had a horseshoe drive and a massive entrance. A red-brick, Edwardian mansion, it had an enormous kitchen and a huge conservatory. The big garden was beautiful: mature, with a rockery, and I had my vegetable patch in the rear. I grew runner beans, peas, tomatoes, lettuce ... you name it.

As soon as we got the keys in June 1993, we had the downstairs gutted, knocked down walls, and did it up thoroughly, before moving in just in time for Christmas. The parquet floor was in such a terrible state that I carpeted the house all the way through. Upstairs, Andy and I had separate bedrooms but he often stayed in mine. We got on well. So well, in fact, that we now felt we had a secure enough base to have some little ones. To my delight, we began trying for a baby.

But then, unexpectedly, all hell broke out on the work front for Andy. He was a man who had always had enemies, but now was the time they chose to show their hand. The end of 'shamateurism', which Andy had initiated, meant athletes were now less at the beck and call of sports officials. Some of the officials didn't like it, and therefore they didn't like Andy. Andrew was a unique man, who made no attempt to charm his adversaries. Only the sort of man he was, with his great abilities and his lack of a bedside manner with those who disagreed with him, could have succeeded, as he did, in bringing athletics into the modern world. The media often said Andrew was the most powerful man in British athletics. And British athletics was thriving. It was a golden age.

Andrew's demise ultimately came about due to the sad death of an athletics correspondent, whose suicide was made use of in a power struggle going on within athletics. Andrew had been typically direct, indeed harsh, in a telephone conversation with this correspondent, warning him that his actions towards a certain female athlete could be viewed as sexual harassment. (Her lover had actually asked Andy to intervene.) Without telling Andy, the athletics correspondent recorded their conversation, an act which is illegal, and then he played it for his colleagues.

When, some months later, in the January of 1994, the correspondent walked under a moving train, his conversation with Andy was blamed as a contributing factor. Andy was accused of bringing athletics into disrepute. By the time the dead man's psychiatrist told a coroner's inquest that his client had a compulsion to pat young women's bums, had psychotic episodes, had previously tried to kill himself, and that his clinical depression stemmed from his divorce, it was too late. Andy had already 'resigned' from his job as promotions officer and signed a gagging order which meant that he never told his side of the story. He received a year's pay, but he was banned from working in athletics in the UK, and even from attending UK athletics events. Linford, Sally Gunnell, Colin Jackson and several other top athletes tried to get Andy's unfair dismissal overturned, but there was nothing anyone could do. It was the end of an era.

New people took over the reins of the sport. The man who took on Andy's job had to learn a lot fast. He surprised many when he said publicly that Andy was 'very, very helpful' to him. But it didn't surprise me. Nothing would ever be more important to Andy than British athletics.

Understandably, it was not a happy time. Andy's green eyes stopped twinkling. Gone was that beautiful smile – until, fortunately, word got around that the brilliant man who was no longer busy looking after British athletics might be available to help out the rest of the world. Not only was Andrew soon promoting major events in Eastern Europe, but by 1996 he was welcomed in Mandela's South Africa, where he took on the job of helping post-apartheid South African sport make a name for itself on the world stage.

Before long, Andy was spending about four months of every year in SA. Mum and I went too, for shorter periods. As well as their elite athletes, we coached township kids in places like Soweto. We went regularly for years. In that first year, Mum and I did a joint interview for South African TV. When the presenter asked about family, Mum got a bit upset. After the interview, Andy put his arm around her, and said, 'I know how you are feeling, Margaret; don't worry, you'll get better.' He was always such a supportive man.

The sad thing was that there was a reason behind Mum's emotion. After thirty-seven years of marriage, Mum and Dad's marriage ended in 1996. It jolted all of us. They formally separated in January. Both parties were considerate, and the divorce came through in November of that year.

Like the rest of the family, I was saddened by the situation. For me, the Whitbread family had been the port in the storm, the one family I could rely on when I was traumatised and believed no one wanted me. Both Mum and Dad had always been perfect to me. I didn't want either of them to be unhappy. Seeing what I regarded as the model marriage of the century break down was discouraging to say the least, even though Mum and Dad were divorcing in the nicest possible way.

I have said a lot in this book about Mum, less about Dad, so let me say here that I will never forget what a good father he was. When the boys and I were growing up, he was always a warm, reliable, calming influence and, despite everything that's happened, I owe him a lot. I still love Dad, and always will.

The breakdown of Mum and Dad's marriage was tremendously upsetting for us all. But it wasn't the divorce that was keeping me awake at night. It was the worry that, after years of trying, we still didn't have a baby.

CHAPTER TWENTY-FIVE

A Pregnant Pause

THE BIOLOGICAL CLOCK was ticking away. I was thirty-five. For years now, we'd been trying for a child of our own.

We tried, but I didn't get pregnant. As the reality of our problems became clear, I said that if we couldn't have children naturally, I wanted to go through IVF.

We assumed that I must have some type of fertility issue. As happens to many – maybe even most – world-ranked female champions, my period had stopped for a number of years during my career. I didn't worry because a doctor had explained why. For similar reasons, women's periods often cease during great famines. The highly trained woman, like the malnourished one, has so little fat on her body that nature thinks there's a famine that would cause any newborn baby to starve. But I'd stopped competing eight years ago, and my periods had long since come back. The Harley Street specialist we went to found that my fertility was normal too.

What we didn't know then is that in about 40 per cent of British infertile couples, the issue is the sperm. Andrew had already fathered two children, so he was surprised and somewhat shattered to be diagnosed with low sperm motility. If he had not had so strong a sense of self, it might have been a devastating blow. He had plenty of sperm and they were of good quality, but they could not swim fast enough and far enough to fertilise my eggs.

At the age of fifty-four, Andy was so busy taking care of athletes that he didn't take care of himself. In the years since his two children had been born, he had begun to suffer from diabetes and heart problems. He couldn't run as well as he had when he was a younger man; and his sperm couldn't either. If Andy had got more rest and switched to a better diet, if he had taken exercise and vitamins and minerals, eventually things might have worked on their own. But Andy had never taken care of himself and he wasn't about to start now, so we opted for IVF treatment.

It was a very emotional time for both of us. Ever since I was young, I had wanted children. There's no whys about it. It's just how you feel. We sat in the waiting room at the doctor's surgery nervously. When we were ushered in, the doctor said that they couldn't guarantee that we would have just one baby; should the treatment succeed, there was a good chance it could be two or three. But both Andy and I said it didn't matter how many. I would have been perfectly happy to have twins. Three would have been a handful, but we would have managed.

First, they gave us drugs, which we had to take for a while to ready us for IVF. Then we went back to Harley Street, where they harvested the eggs. They give you something that blocks the discomfort, so I didn't feel any pain.

I didn't see it, but I know what happened next. Hand-picked sperm which Andy had provided were injected into the egg waiting in a petri dish. It sounds so scientific when you spell out the process, but it certainly didn't feel like that as we anticipated having a baby of our own.

Now all we could do was hope and pray and wait for this 'sample' to take. When it did, the fertilised egg would be implanted into my womb.

When the time came, we went back to Harley Street expectantly, but as soon as the doctor sat us down in his office, we knew. Andy reached over and took my hand. The first attempt had failed. I felt terrible, so did Andy, and not just because the treatment I would have to go through again was unpleasant.

Yet there was no question that we would try again. I had always wanted to be a mother, and I was scared it would never happen. We were fortunate, of course, because we could afford to pay for another go. Andrew went with me to Harley Street for all my appointments, even when he wasn't needed. He was very, very supportive in that way.

On the second attempt, I did get pregnant. I was elated. I carried my baby for nearly four months – but then, sadly, I had a miscarriage. I lost my child in a pool of blood.

It's the most terrible thing to lose a baby. I was devastated. People expect you to just get on with things, but you can't because a child has died. And I feared it might be the end of my chance to have a family. I began taking medication to thicken the lining of my womb, in preparation for a third attempt, but I was broken-hearted.

At about this same time, my brother Kirk and his wife had a baby. When I held my brother's lovely little baby boy, James, in my arms, I was overcome with yearning for one of my own. Even as I blinked back the tears and congratulated them, I could feel that yearning inside me like a hollow wound. I could only hope that, next time, my luck would change.

All this time, I was reading baby books – all sorts of baby books. I couldn't think about anything else but having a baby. For me it was so important. Having been brought up in children's homes, in close contact with so many children, I thought I would make a good mum. And Andy no longer really saw his two kids; he was so sad about that. I wanted to give him back through our marriage the chance of being a father. For both of us, we realised this was proof of our living, and a chance to offer love to a little one.

Andy and I had now been together for a decade. We had been talking about getting married for years – but now we actually did it. The wedding, which took place on 24 May 1997, was in West Sussex, so that Andy's elderly parents could attend. I loved his mum and dad, loved being with them. They had been so supportive of our attempts to have a child; it was so important to them to have a grandchild they could watch grow up. They had told me they missed Kirsti and Stephen, Andy's two children, whom they'd seen less of since the divorce.

Of course, we invited Andrew's children to the wedding. They didn't come, which was a shame. Andy felt hurt by that.

We also invited Dad and his new wife to the wedding. They didn't come either, which was probably for the best because it was just six months after my parents' divorce, and our family's wounds were still pretty raw. Still, it was sad not to have my father at my wedding.

The vicar was wonderful. This was an unexpected bonus because the church, St Johns the Evangelist in Copthorne, had been chosen largely for Andy's parents' convenience and because it was near an airport, Gatwick, so guests from around the country and abroad could arrive easily. The Reverend Alistair Cutting interviewed us both first and, fortunately, he agreed to marry us, which he might not have done because Andy had been married before.

I wore a white dress with a veil, and Andy a new designer suit and swashbuckling tie I helped him pick out. He looked so handsome. With Dad absent, my brother Gregg gave me away. Sven Arne Hansen, a distinguished athletics colleague of Andy, was his best man. Happily, Cory was there, and so was Mrs Peat, my Auntie Rae. It was great seeing them both again. Lots of people from the world of athletics attended too. Sebastian Coe was there, as was Brendan Foster.

I had not realised before how right it was for us to be married. Not just because our child – should we have one – would be born in wedlock, which I think is important, but also because it was a very public pledging of our commitment to each other.

Andy and I had been a couple for a long time by the time we wed, but being married did immediately feel special. In his speech at the wedding, Andy said so too. We decided then and there that our future child, should we be fortunate enough to have one, would be christened in the same church. It was a very happy day.

And, just a few weeks later, I was pregnant again. I was overjoyed. Mum was holidaying at the Mayan ruins of Chichen Itza in the Yucatan of Mexico at the time I found out. She was with my brother Gregg. They were on the coach when I got through on the phone and I said through the static, 'Mum, I'm having a baby.'

'Only one?' Mum asked. With IVF, it could easily be more.

'Only one, Mum.'

That day, she and Gregg went into a church and they both lit candles for the baby. The whole family was terrified of losing this baby too.

I was so scared. Every day, there was the fear that this would be the day I would miscarry again. I decided not to train at all during the first four months, till I passed that worrying period where I'd lost the baby before. My training during that first pregnancy had been very low key, just a bit of jogging or walking and some exercise, which the doctor had told me would be fine, but now, for the first time since I was fourteen, I didn't do any training at all. I didn't want to risk a thing with this baby. I had check-ups all the time, scans. I wasn't taking any chances.

During my early pregnancy, Andrew was frequently away in Budapest or Strasbourg or Russia or South Africa, planning major competitions and then helping world-class athletes to get ready for them. I was still running the Chafford Hundred athletics club, representing some of the biggest names in British athletics, and was beset by morning sickness. I decided to stay in England while he travelled. We spoke on the telephone every day. It never occurred to me that his being on his own so much without me would turn out to be bad news for our marriage. I reassured myself that Andy would be home for Christmas.

Then he phoned from South Africa to say he didn't have time to come home. He was flying to Helsinki, with a stopover for more work in Russia, and then he'd go straight back to SA.

I was distraught. Christmas had always been so important to us and to our families, and this was a particularly special one: our first Christmas as a married couple, and our last before our precious baby came.

Eventually, Andy realised the effect his going AWOL at Christmas was having on me. Because he loved me (though perhaps – while I didn't realise it yet – was no longer in love with me), he did come home for the holidays.

But it wasn't a great Christmas. He seemed moody and restless. I thought he missed working. Finally, I said to him, 'What's wrong?'

He said, 'Nothing,' and as soon as the holidays were over, flew back to SA.

Andrew had always travelled a lot for his work, and it wasn't a problem when I was competing; we'd travel together. Even with my Chafford Hundred job, I still had reason to travel to international meetings. But now I couldn't go with him because of my morning sickness, which was dire, and the care the doctor had told me to take because I had already lost one baby.

I wasn't complaining. I knew the drill before I married him; of course I did. To love Andy was to accept him as he was, and to understand that he had dedicated his life to athletics. He was a workaholic. Once, just once, in all the thirty years I knew him, we went on holiday, to Egypt, and the whole time he was on the phone arranging a sports meeting. We went to the pyramids, but it was 'Hurry up, get on the camel, get off the camel, hurry up, I have to make some calls.' That was Andy. You had to take him as he was.

And I loved him. It was partly loyalty, but I loved him. He'd been the centre of my world for a long time. We always had an enormous amount of respect for and cared about each other. There had been a long period when both of us were very happy together. We were still happy now, but we were less passionate. We might have been newly married, but we were an old couple, with old routines. Sport was an obsession we shared. Sport was our life. But, for me at least, that was changing now. A new life was growing inside me. It took all precedence.

We had planned for Andy to be there when the baby was born, so he could cut the umbilical cord. But as Andy's trip to South Africa was extended again and then again, I realised that in order for that to happen, I'd have to be in South Africa too.

Family was and still is my most important value. I was willing to do whatever it took to hold on to our happy home. I hoped that a new arrival in the family would be not just a joy in itself, but that it would also bring back the joy that seemed to be fast disappearing from our marriage.

The baby was due in March. I flew out as soon as I could, in early February, because I didn't want to endanger the unborn baby on the flight. We were staying at a lodge close to training facilities and a ten-minute drive from Pretoria. Lots of champions stayed there, including Jonathan Edwards and Kelly Holmes, whose first manager had been Andy.

Athletes from a number of nations hung out with us while we stayed there. I carried on with my light exercise routines, which I'd started again once I'd passed the danger point in my pregnancy, helped out with the athletes, and enjoyed the clean air and the African sun. Coming to SA had been the right decision.

While I was carrying the baby, I went jogging every other day. On the non-jogging days, I did aerobics, sit-ups and cardiovascular exercises. It might seem strange to some people, but I was an international athlete for twenty years. If I don't exercise, I feel terribly under par. While pregnant, I was doing much lighter workouts than I would otherwise do, but I couldn't give up exercise entirely. Nor would it have been healthy to; I think my body would have gone into shock.

Three weeks before the baby was due, I did my usual light workout in the gym and then Andy drove me to the obstetrician in Pretoria for my regular check-up.

The doctor examining me suddenly looked startled and asked, 'Are you in any pain?'

That scared me. 'What's wrong? Why would I be in pain, Doctor?'

'Because you are four centimetres dilated and this baby will be arriving tonight. You better get to the hospital right away.'

We sped back to the hotel, grabbed the valise that was kept packed just in case, and rushed to the hospital. But the doctor hadn't rung to tell them to expect us, and as the baby wasn't due for three weeks, it took us an hour to convince the receptionist to admit me to the maternity ward. The only way was to pay in advance for my stay in hospital, which we did, on the credit card.

We were expecting Mum in three weeks, just before the due date, and she already had her ticket. I phoned Mum from the hospital to say I was in labour. Just three hours later, Ryan Andrew Norman, weighing in at 4lb 9oz, was born. It was 25 February 1998.

Unbelievably, I didn't even have any contractions until two hours before the baby was born. But when they finally came, it was agony. I tried not to scream, but I did. Andy was there with me every step of the way, and he cut the umbilical cord; he looked a little pale, but I insisted. I was six days shy of my thirty-seventh birthday, and I was a mum at last.

CHAPTER TWENTY-SIX

Bliss

B EING A MUM changes you. As long as I live, I will never forget that feeling when they laid Ryan on my stomach after he was born. The moment I touched him, I felt instant love, instant warmth. He was the most beautiful baby I had ever seen. He gave this little whimper, and in a moment I fell totally in love. You carry this little thing for nine months and you know it's a baby, but you can't actually visualise what it's going to be like. I smoothed his fair hair, I smoothed his delicate skin. He was the best thing that had ever happened to me. He was worth a million gold medals.

He seemed to be breathing deeply, but he was so tiny I was frightened. During the delivery, the doctor and nurses had sometimes spoken to each other in Afrikaans, a language I didn't understand. Had they done that to keep the worst from me? Suddenly my elation turned to fear.

'Is the baby all right?' I whispered.

'He's perfect,' the grinning South African doctor replied.

Andrew kissed my brow and the baby's little head. 'We finally did it, Fatima,' he said. 'This time we crossed the finish line.'

*

I was instantly besotted with my son, and in the weeks that followed, as he grew and grinned and gurgled, he seemed to be besotted with me too. I could hardly believe he was mine. And he looked so much like Andrew, although he had brown eyes like mine. We all three were besotted. Mum arrived when the baby was already three weeks old. Now Ryan had two women caring for his every need. Andrew saw and sang to baby Ryan whenever he could. But he was a busy man.

I said, 'These years will fly by and you need to integrate and bond with your son.'

He did bond, but not enough in my opinion. Andrew loved Ryan dearly, but he had to work. His passion for athletics didn't wane when his son arrived.

From the start, Ryan was a good traveller and we had an easy flight home to the UK. The three of us went to Oslo in July for the Bislett Games, which was Ryan's first flight since we returned from South Africa. I felt safe to do it once he had had all his jabs. Also in July – when Ryan was five months old – the Norman family drove up to Birmingham for the British AAA Championship, where Linford's baby girl and baby Ryan instantly took to each other.

Ryan and I often stayed at home in England while Andy flew back and forth to Europe, South Africa and the Far East to work. When I worked, I was either arranging sponsorship deals for my thirty-four Chafford Hundred champion athletes and getting them to photo shoots for TV commercials, or I was staging young athletes' training sessions and events, from which a charity usually benefited. Once, I went up to Yorkshire to film the studio piece for the *Through the Keyhole* programme, which featured our Javel Inn.

And, of course, I was busy doting on Ryan. At his first swimming lesson, at the Blackshots municipal pool, he took to water like a baby duck. The instructor said to dunk him a couple of times so he would understand how to overcome the danger of going under the water. I did it reluctantly, but it worked. At seven months, he could swim reasonably well and float and kick on his front and back. We'd go for a swim nearly every day.

In August, when Andy flew off to Budapest for the European Championships, Ryan and I drove up to visit Andy's parents in Ipswich. I had known them for years, of course, and loved them dearly. I had been involved in their lives, and they in mine, for all the highs and lows of the past few decades. Ryan and I stayed for two nights on that visit. They loved seeing him: at last they had a grandchild they could see regularly. Andy's younger brother's children lived abroad, too far away for frequent visits, but Ryan could now be a big part of their lives.

Grandad Russell, who'd been poorly, really came alive when he saw Ryan. He was good with our dog Champie too. While I helped Billie with her shopping at Tesco, Russell took Champie for a walk. Ryan came with the ladies. We all went out to lunch and walked together in the church garden till the rain came pelting down. It was a special time. It was important to me that Ryan knew and loved his grandparents. I, who had had no family until the Whitbreads, knew how precious every single relative could be.

We did accompany Andy to Zurich, the last important meeting of the year, where he looked proud as punch to be pushing Ryan's pram along the riverbank of the Danube. Ryan seemed glad to see some of our greatest champions.

The triple jumper Jonathan Edwards and the javelin thrower Steve Backley were especially brilliant with him.

When Andrew returned home from Budapest, as usual he was hungry, eager for my homemade shepherd's pie and for some company. We talked late into the night about Ryan's future. It meant so much to us both that he have the right start in life, including private education. I had quit school as soon as I could, and Andy, a grammar school boy, missed out on uni because his family needed him to go to work.

Andrew immediately began researching schools. There seemed to be a good one near us, and that very September we went to the Brentwood School to check it out. We'd read all the literature about it. Now we met the head and viewed the school, and decided it was the right one for our son. In September 1998, when he was just seven months old, we registered Ryan for admission in 2001.

We were still going to South Africa every year to work with elite athletes, and Ryan would accompany us on these lengthy trips. As before, I worked in the townships too, encouraging the children to come out and have a go at athletics and coaching them. Toddler Ryan would run up and down with all the township children.

We took Ryan with us everywhere, even on safari to see the wild animals roaming South Africa's vast Kruger Park. We made sure he was well and truly safely ensconced in the jeep. On one trip, we went out with Mum and four young British trainees I had brought over from England for the experience. While we were driving through Kruger on a dusty pathway, one of the trainees, a somewhat macho boy, kept standing up in the jeep, even though he had been told by the ranger not to. Finally, the ranger said, 'Last week one of the Japanese tourists insisted on standing up like you are, and the lion really enjoyed him.' The kid sat down. Of course there was no real danger. All the lions we saw were napping or lazing about.

What I loved best was teaching in the townships. The kids were an absolute joy – keen to learn, enthusiastic and so warm and friendly. Some of their mothers worked as maids at our somewhat luxurious hotel, which was so close to the woefully impoverished townships that it was embarrassing.

On one occasion, I invited the maids' children back to the hotel. At first, the kids were crouching down, visibly nervous. I tried hard to make them welcome. We had big tables set up and a meal for them. They were mainly seven to ten years old. But there were some littler ones too. It was touching to see that five-year-olds had already learned to share and take care of the even younger ones. It reminded me of us children in the care homes in Hertfordshire and Essex where I had grown up. Like us, these African children were used to not having anything that was only theirs. They played a game we had played too, where one child runs and then tags the other, but in their version they were chasing a lion.

Twice, the mums challenged me to a run. They ran tactically, cutting across in front of me like a team. I would have to dodge around to win, and we laughed and laughed throughout the race.

One of the hotel maids brought us home to her tiny house in the township one day, where we had tea and biscuits. The government was building new houses, but most of the township people were living in shacks put together with whatever could be found. If they were lucky, the houses had a tin roof. There was no electricity in the township and the sanitation was awful. It was hard to know how they got the washing hanging on the line so white.

The township ladies had a crèche, and when I was working, Ryan sometimes stayed there. There were a lot of children, but they all seemed happy. Mum and I returned one day, when Ryan was a baby, to see that they had propped him up on pillows with his bottle propped beside him on another pillow. Mum asked the ladies, 'Wouldn't he choke if he was sick?'

But they showed us that the angle of the pillows was set so he could easily spit the bottle out. If he was sick, it would be all right. At our hotel, we tried out their technique, which worked really well.

Nelson Mandela was chuffed that his township children were getting some athletics training. He told us that himself in Soweto. Mum and I were there working with the local youngsters when – and what a surprise it was – the great man himself just turned up. He and his retinue stood watching the kids' training session for a while. We had them doing some stretches and some callisthenic-like movements.

During a rest break, Mr Mandela came over and told us that he was pleased that we had put ourselves out for these children. But we didn't think of it as putting ourselves out at all, and we told him so. Later, he sent over two signed copies of his autobiography *Long Walk to Freedom*, one for me and one for Mum.

Ryan and I stayed on in SA when Mum went back to England. Because of the excellent weather and training facilities, there were lots of British and foreign athletes around, so there was plenty of company. Nonetheless, with Mum gone, it was more noticeable that Andrew wasn't home enough … although when he was home, he was very much there. He was attentive, he loved his son, he loved me. I'd known when I married him that he was a workaholic, so I couldn't complain.

Take hold of yourself, Fatima, I told myself. You have a good marriage. It's a good sign, isn't it, to miss your husband? Things are fine, aren't they?

But something was nagging at me. Something felt wrong.

CHAPTER TWENTY-SEVEN

News to Me

I GOT THE phone call at around 6.30 a.m. I was still in bed. Ryan was still sleeping.

Every day, Andy would leave in the morning around 6 o'clock, drive to his Athletics South Africa office, and come back that night at about 7 or 8 p.m. It was roughly an hour's drive each way. That morning, fifteen or twenty minutes after Andy had left, the phone rang. I thought, oh, he's forgotten something. I got out of bed to answer it quickly before it woke Ryan up.

A voice said, 'Hello Fatima, I tell you Andy does not love you anymore, he does not wish to live with you, he wishes to live with me and we are going to be married and live here in South Africa.'

I said, 'Who is this speaking?'

She said, 'It's Olga Nazarova.' I thought for a moment and remembered which one of the foreign athletes she was. I had seen her around the pool with her teenage daughter. She was a Russian runner at the very tail end of her career.

I said, 'Well, thanks very much, we'll see about that.' I was jolted. The conversation ended abruptly. What do you say to somebody who rings you up at 6 o'clock in the morning and tells you your marriage is over, your husband is having an affair?

I rang Andy. I said, 'I need to talk to you. Can you get home earlier tonight? If you can, come home earlier because I'd like to talk to you.'

'What's it about?'

'It's not a subject to talk about on the phone.'

He went quiet and then said, 'OK.'

Meanwhile, I was devastated. When I went out to the pool with Ryan as usual, a couple of people asked me what was wrong, but I couldn't tell them, of course.

I realised now that whenever I'd been in South Africa with Andy, we'd spent time with Olga and her daughter. They were both in the photos we took around the pool. Yet there were a lot of international athletes we were friendly with. I hadn't taken any special notice of her. Olga had run on two Soviet gold-winning 400-metre relay teams, at the Olympics in 1988 and 1992, and running as an individual had won a 1988 Olympic bronze. She was blonde and four years younger than me. I hadn't minded her following my husband around because she had made no secret of the fact that she wanted to learn to be a sports manager so she could have her own company. Fool that I was, I didn't realise she wanted my husband too.

Andy and I had been together for more than a decade. We were both older, his health was declining, and things were less passionate than they had been, but I thought that was all part of married life. I knew he loved our son and I had thought he loved me.

I hadn't realised that he had fallen for Olga's charm and beauty – and maybe flattery. A picture formed in my head.

Andy was being chased by this Russian ex-runner who was using Andy to introduce her to all sorts of people so she could find a new career in sports management. It wasn't love. It couldn't be love.

In a gut-wrenching moment, I realised that he must have been playing around with Olga while I was pregnant with Ryan. I felt like a fool. I began to catch on as to why he hadn't wanted to come home that Christmas.

I'd felt hurt and sad, but now I was also angry. What I'd learned made me grow up fast. I said to myself, you'll just deal with it. You'll face it and make him face it, and what will be will be.

Andy got back at about 4 o'clock. I said immediately, 'Olga says that you are in love with her and if you could, you'd get a double-barrelled shotgun and shoot me.'

He looked like he'd been shot. 'What are you talking about, Fatima?'

'If you're in love with her, then go and let me get on with my life.'

'I'm not in love with her.'

'That's not what you told her.'

Andrew denied everything.

'Andy, I've put up with you being away year in, year out. You've got time for everybody but me and the boy. We rarely see you. Why should I give up my whole young life and be insulted into the bargain? That's it. Finished.'

He said he wanted us to stay together. He begged me. 'We're good for each other,' he said.

But as good as things might once have been, they weren't any more. Andy clearly wasn't happy. Well, neither was I. I hadn't been for a long time. Taking a deep breath, I admitted how it really felt having a husband I never saw, who was often not even on the same continent as me. 'I feel lonely,' I confessed. He stared at me. He insisted what he wanted most was for our marriage to work. Then I thought of the one thing that might save our marriage.

'In that case, we need to go to counselling, Andrew. We need to admit to each other that something's wrong.'

It had to be done quietly. I didn't want the national press getting hold of it; neither did he, of course.

Well, we tried. When we got back to England, we found a therapist not too far from home. Andy went half a dozen times. But he kept saying it was a waste of his time. We loved each other, wasn't that enough? Then he said it was stupid; he didn't need to go to counselling, he knew his own mind, he knew he loved me and Ryan. And anyway, he had to fly back and forth to Europe for work; he had no time for this. He told the counsellor the same thing. He avoided me and spent a month visiting Olga in Russia and, I suspected, travelling round Europe with her.

Linford called to tell me, 'You should watch out who your husband is keeping close company with.' A couple of other athletes took the trouble to mention it too. At one point, the press were camped outside the house at all hours asking: were Andy and I separated? Was Andy having an affair? The pressure was immense.

When Andrew deigned to come home, he insisted our family was still his priority.

I said, 'If you don't go to counselling regularly, we can't solve our problems.'

The counsellor realised before me that he wasn't going to make any more effort about our relationship, and said, 'He does love you. Don't you think it best sometimes just to accept the relationship for what it is?'

'It's what I have done these last few years,' I replied sadly. 'But I don't think it's right any longer.'

I was still young, after all. I wanted a life. A life in which I was loved; in which I didn't have to share my husband. If Andy wanted Olga, I felt he should make a clean break and let me be free. He couldn't have a foot in both camps. For me to have a chance at a meaningful relationship with somebody else, I knew I had to resolve this one first. I wasn't the sort of person who could keep emotional balls in the air, juggling loyalties. My absolute first choice would be to get things right with Andy but, as time went on, I realised that wasn't going to happen.

Yet Andy refused to see my point of view. He said he still cared about me and knew I cared about him. And we both loved our boy. So why change anything? Things were OK as they were, he said.

But they weren't OK. And, finally, Andrew admitted that he was in love with Olga.

CHAPTER TWENTY-EIGHT

Broken-Hearted

I T TOOK ME a long while to get over that. I was very sad for a long, long time. I never stopped loving Andy, but I did fall out of love with him.

Andy was away most of the time. Although we were officially still married, I was already living the life of a single mum, home alone with a young child I was devoted to, or taking him with me whenever I went out, even to work. But I needed someone to chat with from time to time, someone to make me laugh.

I felt strongly that I didn't want to let my life slip by and not have some kind of a relationship in the years I had left. Andy had Olga; well, I deserved the chance to find someone too. I decided I wasn't going to just sit around twiddling my thumbs. I wanted to step out and meet people; I wanted to have the opportunity to converse with the opposite sex. If I was honest, I was keen to find somebody with whom I could share some special moments.

But, as every single mother knows, that's easier said than done. Every evening after my son went to sleep, a long lonely evening stretched ahead of me at home. Then one of my girlfriends at the gym where I worked out suggested I go on the internet. A few of the girls I knew from the gym –

some of them were single mums – and one of the guys started talking to me online from time to time in the evenings. It was fun, and I didn't feel quite so isolated anymore. Then one of my girlfriends suggested I try a chat room. My brother Gregg said I should do it, but he warned me to be careful about who I talked to and what I told them. My friend from the gym said never invite them to your house unless you have met them a few times and are sure. Be careful.

I was a bit green behind the ears even though I was over forty. With my marriage in the state it was, I was feeling vulnerable. I was very wary, but where else was I going to go? I was immersed in loneliness, and I wanted to do something about it. That's why I started communicating with people on the computer. At bedtime, I would read Ryan to sleep, and then I would sit on my bed talking to people on my laptop. That's how I started. Then all of a sudden other people were trying to communicate, and I started clicking on websites. I came to a website that tells you how to meet people online, how to go out with them in a safe environment, how to get to know somebody. They had a database of 'approved' people, with names and pictures and other details. So, I talked to a few people there.

At first, I was careful not to tell them who I was. It was scary for me, because I had this whole thing going on in my mind that I mustn't divulge who I was. I just said: I am Kaye. There I was online, trying to live behind this mask with a false name, while simultaneously looking for friends I could share my life with. Being an open person, that just didn't feel right. But I knew I had to because you really don't know who you are talking to, and it could be dangerous. It was a really big gamble for me – but it started to pay off. I met a couple of quite pleasant, chatty people online.

Bram was one of the guys I communicated with. He seemed the most genuine. It was clear most men were just looking for sex. I was looking for someone I could chat with, someone companionable, a friend. Bram told me he was newly divorced and had family in South Africa, and he was over here working because his family life had fallen apart. He particularly missed his son, who was half a dozen years older than mine. When Bram asked to meet me, I suggested a walk in Thorndon Park in Brentwood.

He was there at the gate when I arrived, a tall, good-looking, well-built six-footer in his fifties, with silver-grey hair and that lovely soft accent some South Africans have. This fellow was more than nice. We walked together through the parkland, chatting and listening to the birds singing. He liked the outdoors.

It was enjoyable too to get all dressed up to go into London for lunch. But mostly we walked in the park or I would cook us a meal. He was a really lovely chap. Some months into it, I went to a sports shop with him and helped him choose a cricket bat for his son.

He even came up to Boston in Lincoln with me to see my Grandma Maud in hospital. She had moved north to live with her sister after Grandad James died. When the trip seemed to be taking forever, and I mean hours and hours, I finally realised we were going the wrong way. I said, 'Bram, I don't know where we are.'

'Don't worry,' he said, 'just drive into a petrol station, we'll ask.'

It turned out that the Sat-Nav had been taking us up to

Boston, Scotland. Modern technology, eh? I was the one who had mis-set the system. Bram was fine about it. We got to the hospital eventually, hours late. Grandma Maud, who I felt was a soul mate to me, was pleased to see me. But she didn't like him. She knew Andrew and I were in trouble, she knew we had an arrangement now our marriage was over, but she didn't like Bram. I now think my grandma was really shrewd; I think she knew instantly there must be some catch to him.

But I was taken with him.

We were together for six months. It was six months; it felt like six years. Six good years. Emotionally, it was over-whelming. I was in love with him. It was a big turning point for me. I spoke to my lawyer about what I should do if I wanted to end my marriage with Andy formally and move on. I thought in time I would marry Bram. I wanted to seize control of my life. I had matured out of all recognition from being the vulnerable, insecure girl from the children's home to being a confident, determined woman.

Bram was going back to South Africa for Christmas, and he kept saying, 'When I come back, I will be able to spend more time with you.' I said that would be good. By now, he knew I was Fatima Whitbread, but to his credit, he didn't take advantage of that. He seemed decent. A strong, South African guy.

Then, a month before Christmas, things went quiet. I didn't hear from him. I tried to track him down, because I was already committed emotionally. Maybe he had to leave suddenly for South Africa, I thought, and had been too rushed to tell me. I rang his workplace to find him. I asked for him, saying he was a director of the company. It turned out that he wasn't a director at all; he was an ordinary factory worker. He'd lied.

I didn't know what else he might be lying about.

I didn't ever go into it with him, because when I saw him again, it was only briefly, and he was going away. He said he'd be back and would explain a lot of things. I never saw him again. I rang him in South Africa a couple of times, and he was distant. I told one of my girlfriends and she said, 'He's got to have been lying about everything to you.' 'Why would he lie to me?' 'Because he has a wife or something.'

He went home that Christmas and never came back. I was devastated, to be honest, because I cared for him. Maybe I should have realised he had been living a double life. He probably was still married. He had probably come over here, like a lot of South Africans do, to earn better wages, and while he was here, he had cheated on his wife. But I didn't realise it. You cloud your judgement when you commit yourself emotionally.

I had truly thought that Bram was my future. I'd thought he would be a good father to Ryan; not to take Andy's place, but to be a kind of plus factor. I would never have entered a relationship I thought might in any way compromise my relationship with Ryan or his happiness. I wouldn't do that even now.

Before Christmas, my lawyer had advised me to get divorced in case I wanted to marry Bram. I really was that serious about him. After Christmas, when I realised he wasn't coming back, I was distraught. The only good thing to come out of it was that I now knew I needed to be free if I was ever going to have a caring relationship with someone. That's when I first broached the subject of divorce to Andy.

But we continued to play happy families for a long, long time.

We did it because we cared about each other, even after everything that had happened. In fact, I literally cared for him, seeing that he had a clean shirt and tie, making him buy new clothes, and cutting his hair and all that. We continued as we were because we still loved each other, even though we were no longer in love. We did it mostly because we both cared for our boy.

In time, Olga went off with someone else who could help her advance in the IAAF, though I'm not saying she chose him for that reason. How could I know? When Andrew woke up to it, he tried to walk back into my life as though nothing had happened. I knew that couldn't be, but he was still Ryan's father. As ever, when he was there, he was a good father.

And so, Andy continued to stay over at our house in his own room. He'd always had his own room in the house; he just didn't always sleep in it before. It was a big house, and I was glad he was there for Ryan, and I was even glad to be able to look after Andy, as his health was going downhill fast. Andy had never monitored his diabetes properly, sometimes missing injections and frequently eating what wasn't on the approved list. Now that inattention was catching up with him.

In the last few years, the doctor had prescribed dialysis. But Andy wouldn't hear of it. Mum's dad had had to have it. Andy's dad did too. So Andy knew how dialysis would interfere with his life. Even at a minimum, he would have to stay in England hooked up to the machine twice a week. The doctor said, 'Your travelling days are over.' Andy didn't want to know.

I tried to talk to him about it. I said, 'You're being selfish because Ryan is young and you have to be here while he is growing up.' But Andrew was in denial about his health. And as he said himself, he was strong as an ox.

Ryan was nearly five when I had a date with another man. My son never said anything, but it was clear to me he didn't like it. I stopped seeing the guy. With my background, I wanted to give Ryan the best possible of everything, and I didn't want to put any unnecessary stress on my boy.

Andy didn't like it either, although, in theory, we had an understanding. He no longer even liked me going out to see friends when he was at home. He wanted dinner on the table and all the attention on him. Eventually, things got too stressful. I filed for divorce. Twice.

The first time, we got as close as the decree nisi. When the court gives you your decree nisi, you have to wait six weeks and one day before you can make your divorce final. This is to allow time for anyone who objects to the divorce to tell the court why they object. Andy begged me not to go through with it. He said he loved me and would totally change. I withdrew it.

But a year later, in 2006, I started divorce proceedings again. There was altogether too much stress in the house. Andy was being more and more demanding and I didn't feel, given the situation, that it was fair. This time, I went through with it.

But, practically speaking, nothing changed. Ryan and I saw no more or less of Daddy. He stayed over in his room at our house as he always had. There was nothing different to explain, so Andy and I didn't even mention to our eight-year-old that Daddy and Mummy were now divorced.

CHAPTER TWENTY-NINE

Hard Times

Y OU ALWAYS THINK the people you love will be
around forever. When they're there, so solid in your
life, it's impossible to imagine a world without them.
But every now and again, fate reminds you that they could
be snatched away in an instant. I was horrified when, at the
sixth-form college she worked at, Mum got knocked down
the stairs. It happened on an open night at Palmers, the
college where she taught PE and business studies. Most of
the parents had not yet arrived. In the corridor on the way
to her classroom, Mum saw a young man carrying a laptop
and her rucksack. Actually it was Gregg's rucksack, Mum
had borrowed it, and without thinking, she attempted to
grab the rucksack back.

The young man didn't hesitate. He punched her. Then he
pushed Mum and kept on pushing till she fell down the long
flight of concrete stairs. A couple of vertebrae were fractured,
and Mum broke a small bone in her shoulder too. It didn't
do Mum's knees any good either. They were a bit dodgy
anyway, after all the sport she'd done, but that fall down the
stairs meant she needed new knees. They stayed painful and
swollen until she got new ones.

Mum was driven to A&E by her head of faculty, Allison

Ross, and a policeman. He was hopeful that they would get the guy because at the college there were CCTV cameras everywhere. But later, once he'd examined the footage, the policeman told Mum the cameras were such poor quality that people only had to move quickly and they became a blur. They never got the guy.

Getting seen at A&E took a long time. Allison drove Mum home, and I didn't hear about the assault till past midnight.

I said, 'I'll be right over, Mum.'

But she told me: 'Don't you come rushing round, you have Ryan. I am not critically ill.'

So, I went over first thing in the morning instead – and took Mum straight back with me to Javel Inn. I didn't let her go home for ten days. We had four bedrooms in the house, so there was plenty of room, and I wanted to keep my eye on her.

Sadly, the incident forced Mum into early retirement. I was just glad she was still with me. I couldn't help thinking that I should have been there at the college with her that night. It's everyone's instinct to protect their loved ones, but with all the first-aid knowledge I've accumulated over the years, through my own medical treatment and through my coaching courses, I felt I might really have been able to help.

A year after the attack on Mum, I was in the right place at the right time. At a petrol station not far from where I lived, a six-year-old boy was helping his mum fill her car with petrol when the nozzle slipped and petrol shot into the boy's eyes. He screamed, and his mum rushed him to the women's toilet to throw water in his face.

But I knew from one of the safety courses I had been on

that water would make things worse and that milk was the best antidote, which I quickly told the boy's mother. I hurried to the little shop at the petrol station, grabbed some milk, and poured it onto the boy's swollen eyes. In seconds, he stopped crying and the swelling started to go down to normal. I was so glad I could help. I knew how I would have felt in that mother's situation.

Meanwhile, at home, Andrew was – as usual – working too hard. He returned totally exhausted from Osaka early in September 2007, after two weeks of working relentlessly on behalf of Sebastian Coe. I knew what Andy would do when he was lobbying – he would stay up till all hours of the morning, leaning on his contacts from all around the world. Partly thanks to Andy's endeavours, Seb had been elected vice-president of the IAAF, a powerful position in international athletics.

Two years earlier, Andrew had worked just as strenuously to support the London 2012 Olympic bid. He'd rung me on his mobile each night, and told me how he was doing everything he could, so that London would get the Games. During that time, Andy was in close communication with Sebastian, who was leading the bid. As everyone knows, we won. Andy, who loved nothing more than British athletics, was elated. But he was no longer a well man, and the trip took its toll.

When the Osaka engagement came up, I had urged Andy to stay at home because I thought he was too ill to go – he almost certainly needed to start on dialysis – but Andy had promised Sebastian. He told me he was putting himself out because he not only regarded Sebastian as a personal friend, he regarded him as a friend of Olympic sport. He packed his bags and went.

For the next two weeks after his return, Andrew could do little but sleep. Even young Ryan recognised the difference in his health. As I dropped my boy off at school on the morning Andrew was to fly to Germany for the last athletics event of the season, Ryan asked me to go right home so I could look after Daddy.

I did go back that morning. I well remember Andrew standing in the kitchen. He looked tired, and though he was a heavy man, he looked almost frail. But then he flashed that appealing smile of his, and said, 'I can be back here the middle of next week. Maybe we could start over, Fatima, and I can be a father to my son.'

'You are a father, Andy. You sang to him when he was a baby. And when you get off the phone and look up from your work, you have even been known to kick a ball with Ryan in the garden. He loves you.'

'I want to be more of a father though. My little man deserves more of my time. I want to watch him grow up and help him with everything. Like a father should. And maybe you and I could … maybe things could be like before.'

'Ryan could do with seeing you more,' I agreed. I took a deep breath. 'And so could I. But I'm not sure things could be like before. I'll have to think about that. But it would be lovely to see more of you and have a family dinner now and then – when you're in the country – especially at times like Christmas. I'll think about it. Maybe we could try.'

He was pleased at what I had said, but he wasn't full of his usual bluster.

'Is something wrong, Andrew?'

'I'm just not feeling too well, but nothing serious. It's the end of the athletics season. I need a rest.'

I called him Sunday morning. He was having breakfast at his hotel in Stuttgart. He told me he wasn't feeling well and asked if he could come home to us sooner.

I said yes, we would like that. He'd booked an early flight to Birmingham on the Monday and said he'd now drive down to Essex later that same day. He was looking forward, he said, to seeing his little man and to finishing our talk about the future.

Yes, I said, we would talk more when he returned.

He never did.

On Monday morning around 9 a.m., I received a call from one of Andrew's colleagues. He was at Birmingham Airport. He was brief. Andy had collapsed – but there was nothing to worry about as the paramedics were with him.

A paramedic got on the phone and began to ask me questions.

My voice shaking, I told them about the diabetes and the insulin injections and the likelihood that Andy might need dialysis. He said Andy was responding and it looked like he would be OK. I asked them to keep me informed.

Ten minutes later, the terrible phone call came. They were sorry, Mr Norman had passed away. It was 24 September 2007, three days after Andrew's sixty-fourth birthday.

I couldn't take it in at first, or make sense of it at all. Then it hit me. How was I going to tell Ryan? How was I going to tell Andrew's sick, elderly parents that their son had died? How would they withstand the shock of outliving their eldest son?

Ryan was at school, so I had a bit of time regarding him. But I rang Andy's mum and dad right away. The last thing I wanted was for them to hear it from a stranger or on the radio or TV. They were heartbroken. He was a son who had visited often, and who brought the only grandchild they regularly saw. They loved and were wonderful with Ryan. I promised we would keep visiting them, no matter what. Then I had to hang up, and leave them to their grief.

It had been so hard to tell them. I was sorry I had to do it over the phone. For them, as for Ryan and me, Andrew's death was a calamity. They would never be totally reconciled to his death. Nor would I. But now was not the time for my tears, my loss. Now I had to tell my son.

CHAPTER THIRTY

Harder

H OW DO YOU tell a nine-year-old child his father has died? I knew that Andy's death would leave a hole in Ryan's life that no one could fill. I vowed to do whatever it took to make it up to him as much as I could. I decided I had to tell him today, before he left school. I rang the Brentwood School and arranged a meeting that afternoon for Ryan and me and the headmaster.

With that done, I rang Mum on her mobile, and I fell apart. I was crying. 'He's died, Andrew's died, he's dead, Mum,' I said, over and over.

She was in the middle of having lunch with a friend. 'I'll come right over,' she said.

'No, come tonight,' I said, trying to be practical. 'I have too much to do now.' Still weeping, I rang off. It took me a long time to pull myself together. I couldn't stop thinking about him. At least I knew he had died doing what he loved. Andy's heart stopped at Birmingham airport at the end of the season. Horrible, but fitting too, because athletics had been his life, and he loved Britain. I think, sick as he was on the Sunday when I'd last spoken to him, he held on till he was home, on British soil.

I wiped the tears from my eyes. I tidied myself up. Then I went over to the school to tell Ryan.

I decided I wanted to tell him there because if sometimes, later, he was upset when he was at school, they would need to know why. I knew kids could be devastated by life-changing events like the loss of a father. I knew they needed stability. Ryan had been at Brentwood since he had started school, so that was a stable factor in his life. And I wanted him to have the school's support. If there were any problems emotionally that he couldn't cope with over the next few days or even months, the school would need to know what the problems were. I knew all too well how it felt to cope alone, and I wanted Ryan to have the support of every caring adult in his life.

The headmaster had asked Ryan to come to his office at the end of the school day, so I could talk to him there. The headmaster promised to offer his support too.

I was seated in the head's office when Ryan arrived. He was wearing his red blazer and red tie. He was only nine years old, and he had no idea why I was there at the school. I could see his little face wondering as he made his way into the office and sat down. Wanting to spare him his confusion, I got straight to the point.

Taking a deep breath, I said, 'Ryan, Mum's got some not very nice news to tell you. It's bad news. I'm sorry – but Daddy died today.'

He said, 'What? Grandad?' He thought I meant Grandad Russell, Andy's dad, who wasn't well. Ryan knew we were expecting Grandad to die.

 'No, darling. Daddy.'

Ryan went pan-faced.

'You know Mummy's here for you, and also the teachers are here. That's why Mummy is telling you here – because when you come to school, if you feel upset, the teachers will be here to help you just as Mummy is there to help at home.' Telling him that, I broke down.

Ryan didn't say anything. He just put his head down and you could see he was very upset. I tried to comfort him.

The headmaster said in a solid, reassuring voice, 'We're here to help you, Ryan. If you want someone to talk to, any time at all, you can come and see me.' The school also assigned a teacher to keep an eye on him. They were very good. It was important to me that Ryan had a good safety net around him. He was so young to suffer this loss. I knew I had to make sure he had continuity, security.

But he was remarkably brave and strong. He was like his dad. In the weeks and months that followed, Ryan used to come and put his arm around me, and he'd say, 'Don't cry, Mummy.' Fortunately, Ryan and I had always had a very tight relationship. I'm sure that helped.

Even now, thinking about it so many years later, I feel upset. It is a loss. Andy and I were still very close even after the divorce.

That first evening, Mum came and stayed over, and we three, all three of us, cried. Andy was Andy and we just thought he was going to go on forever. No matter how many doctors' orders he ignored, it seemed he could get by. I had known he wasn't well; of course I had. He didn't walk as fast as he used to, and his clothes were a bit bigger on him, but he used to come back to his room in our house, and I would wash his clothes and get everything shipshape for him, and then he would go off again, and I thought that would just continue.

Many people think that for me Andy was a father figure, but I became a mother figure for him. I used to check his medication and put it into little boxes marked for each day, and he would come back from his trips and I'd see that for some of the days the pills were still there. Before we became a couple, he wore the same blazer and shiny trousers every time you saw him. I had to buy him nice clothes and all his ties. I bought him the new suit he wore for our wedding.

He loved it that Ryan was so intelligent and he took a real interest in his education. We had a lot of happy times together. In Hungary, in the summer, he would take us off to the local spa for the day, and in the evenings we would eat together in Budapest. He would always drive and take the scenic route – he loved driving – and he would always laugh and say, 'Oh, I'm like an Australian, 500 miles is just down the road.'

In that first year after his death, if Mum was staying overnight, sometimes Ryan would ask her to tell him a story about his daddy. From time to time, she and I still tell him glowing stories of Andy's exploits, of which there were many.

I weep sometimes that there's no daddy to watch Ryan play football. I go and Mum goes to watch him all the time. My dad John Whitbread, who was such a good dad, doesn't do 'Grandad' often, which is a pity because he was a great dad and would be a great grandad for Ryan. But to be fair, my dad has had to slow down a lot now, ever since he had a heart attack a few years back.

After Andy's death, I tried to say only good things about him, although at the time I was feeling both sad and angry.

For many months, I struggled mentally and physically. I felt bereft without Andrew. Even divorced, we remained close.

But I was angry too – because Andy had left his son, who wanted him and needed him. I knew I shouldn't blame Andy. He didn't plan to die, he certainly didn't want to die – but on the other hand, if Andy had looked after himself better, looked after his heart and diabetes instead of rushing around the world promoting athletics, he might be alive today.

It was hard to believe he wasn't there anymore. I would ring his mobile. I would hear it ring and then I would say to myself, 'What are you doing, Fatima?'

The day Andrew died, Kelly Holmes, Britain's 2004 double Olympic gold medallist, paid tribute to Andy, who was her first manager. 'He ran British athletics at one stage and he played a big part in my career; he got me into races, and was instrumental in me going to train in South Africa, which is now like my second home. My thoughts are with Fatima and Ryan.'

I arranged the funeral. It was just for family and close friends, and was held in Suffolk so it would be easy for Andrew's mum and dad to get there. I invited his first wife, Gerd, and Andy's now adult children. They did come, accompanied by two friends. Gerd sat in the row right behind Mum and me. It was a sad occasion, and I was at a loss for words. I couldn't talk to anyone much, because I was crying. So was Mum.

The following April, at St Giles-in-the-Fields in London, we had a big, more public memorial service, and the whole world of sport turned up. Jonathan Edwards generously paid for the memorial. He gave a touching speech too. Sebastian

Coe also spoke, and he spoke well – including a joke, where he looked heavenwards, and said that Andy should take note that this time Seb Coe was appearing without being paid a penny in appearance money.

CHAPTER THIRTY-ONE

Financial Straits

TWO WEEKS AFTER Andy's funeral, there was a letter from the bank. It explained that at his death, Andrew had left a debt of some £40,000. That debt, the bank revealed, now fell squarely on my shoulders.

Some years ago, I had signed a document, a guarantee, for a loan of £2,000, which Andy had taken out when his finances were at a low point; he'd had money due that hadn't come in. What I hadn't realised when I co-signed the document was that Andy then had the right to continue borrowing again and again. I suspect the bank must have told me, Andy must have told me, but I didn't take it in. And I never read contracts.

Over the years, Andy had re-borrowed whenever he needed to, most recently for the trip to Osaka, and the amount had grown. I know he would have paid me back – but now, he never could.

Unfortunately, Andy's death coincided with the world-wide economic downturn. Our finances had been tight before. Now came four and a half more lean years. Andy left no insurance, and by insisting on a divorce, I had signed away my right to a policeman's widow's pension of £900 a month. The Chafford Hundred club had long since been disbanded, and since then I had had little luck finding work. I had dipped deep into my savings to buy sheltered accommodation for Mum after her knees were ruined in the attack at the school, and although my investments from my athletics winnings were bringing in a reasonable income, my day-to-day expenditure now exceeded it. Ryan's school fees alone were more than the investments gave me. Yet there was no question of changing my son's school. I wanted the best for him, as had Andy.

It soon became clear that I had no choice but to sell our home. Six months after Andy's death, Javel Inn went on the market. It was too big for just Ryan and me really, we rattled around in it, and it was time for a fresh start. I needed to sell for financial reasons, but it was equally important for Ryan and me to have a different look at life, a new beginning. I am not one to live in the past. We both needed to move on and breathe fresh air into our lives in order to evolve.

In the old days I would have curled up on the sofa with Champ on my lap to tell her my troubles. But sadly Champ was no more. I'd had her for thirteen good years and she was really old and ill when she'd died, a few years earlier, but it had been upsetting nonetheless. I still missed her. I'd buried Champ in the pet cemetery in Brentwood and thought of her often.

I didn't get another dog for a long time. I was travelling a lot, and there was the baby and I felt I just wanted to wait. But lately I'd been thinking that Ryan and I both had need of a puppy. I definitely didn't want another shitzu because I felt I would betray Champ if I went back to the same breed. So now, when I was supposed to be downsizing, I found Bertie, a black-and-tan Jack Russell who is lovable too, but in his own way. We go running together most mornings.

I had hoped for a quick sale on the house, but after months on the market, we had received only ridiculously low offers. Amidst the stress of trying to sell the property, I also had another duty to deal with. Grandad Russell and Grandma Billie, Andy's aged parents, became my responsibility on Andy's death, as Andy's sole brother was living abroad. With Russell and Billie in poor health and devastated after their loss, I began making the 120-mile journey to Ipswich to see them three times a week.

Billie was left even more isolated when, as had been expected for some time, Russell passed away. My life had become a stream of worries: the money, the house, Billie, my concern for Ryan, my fears for our future … Then, in the summer of 2009, that stream overflowed.

I was stopped for speeding at 116 mph. It wasn't the first time I'd been stopped for speeding, but I am ashamed to say that this time I had my son in the car. I knew there was no excuse, but it would be a catastrophe to lose my licence. I had little choice but to explain the circumstances and the stress I was under, and hope the court would be sympathetic.

I broke down as I told the court that the deaths of my husband and, more recently, my father-in-law had been hard to bear. I was the person responsible for Grandma Billie, Andrew's now severely disabled mother. Yet she lived so far away. Ryan and I had been driving back from visiting her at the Felixstowe nursing home where she now lived when we'd been stopped. To make ends meet, I told the magistrates, I was having to sell my home. I needed my licence, I explained, because with the importance of visiting my mother-in-law and keeping up with any opportunity that might arise to earn income, I was heavily reliant on my car.

Thankfully, the court showed mercy. I was lucky to be let off with a fine of £220 including costs, six points on my licence, and two weeks' suspension.

And then for a while it seemed that everyone was dying. I went to Rae Peat's funeral and to Billie's. I mourned them. A journalist rang to tell me that the woman who gave birth to me had died of a stroke, and asked if I had forgiven her. But it wasn't a case of forgiving. I'd long since accepted that things happened as they happened and not always for the best. If anything, I felt sad because we were related, I was of her flesh, even though I would never regard her as my mother.

I also heard word of my biological father, Michael, through a note put under my door. Years before, a young lad at one of the sports training sessions I was running had told me he was my half-brother; Michael had married and had several children in the intervening years. The lad seemed proud to be related to me, but it was too much for me, so I just gave him a hug and said, 'It's best that you have your life with your daddy and I keep my life separate.' Now, he contacted me with this note, asking me to call him. When I did, he told me that Michael was in a coma. The lad – he was now a man – hoped that a visit from me might bring Michael out of the coma.

I went immediately. I suppose I wanted something, maybe a sign that Michael did love me or was at least proud of me. As I sat beside the bed where he was hooked up to a breathing machine, showing little sign of life, I remembered our last conversation, just after I'd triumphed at the

European Junior Championships. It seemed a very long time ago.

Now, as I sat beside his bed, I told Michael how sorry I was that we didn't have our time together in later life to talk. I told him I loved him, which I realised I did. He wasn't moving, but I hoped he could hear. Then a nurse came in and told me he was brain dead.

I began to sob. As I was leaving the hospital, one of Michael's sisters came up to me and said, 'I don't know why you should care, you were only the result of a fuck.' She walked off and that is the one single thing that has stayed in my mind ever since.

Around this same time, a phone call came out of the blue with an unusual offer of work for me. I was asked if I would like to take part in an upcoming BBC TV show, *Total Wipeout*. I said, 'Yeah, I'll have a go at that.' Frankly, I jumped at the chance to bring in some cash.

I flew out to Argentina for the four days of filming while Mum looked after Ryan. It sounds glamorous, but one reason they filmed it in Buenos Aires is because there's no health and safety there. *Total Wipeout* was a physical game show – jumping over red balls, running on floats, that kind of thing. At first, some of the male contestants felt threatened by me being an Olympic athlete, but they were OK in the end. I didn't win, but it was tremendous fun.

Total Wipeout aired on Boxing Day 2009. After that, a producer, a young woman, said she felt I would be quite good on *I'm a Celebrity*. They would call me, she said. But I didn't hear anything more for quite a while.

At the end of 2009, the situation with the house came to

a head. I dropped the price by a quarter of a million pounds, and a buyer snapped it up. There are other houses on that same street for sale that remain unsold because the owners have not cut their price. But I was ready to move on with my life, and made the call.

We left Javel Inn in the springtime of 2010, and lived in rented accommodation while we waited for the bungalow I'd bought to be ready for Ryan and me. It wasn't until October 2010 that we moved into our new home. It was worth the wait.

The kitchen is ultra modern, and so is the furniture. There are just two bedrooms, and there's a little study that adjoins Ryan's room. Roof windows throughout the house bring in lots and lots of natural light. The lounge looks out on to the garden, which is small but big enough. We have a table out there so in the summer we can dine al fresco. I love gardening and do it all myself. I love cooking. Ryan sometimes cooks too.

I put a lot of effort into getting and keeping my new house just right.

Nevertheless, despite my happiness in my new home, the idea of life in the *I'm a Celebrity* jungle really appealed to me. I could only hope they'd call.

CHAPTER THIRTY-TWO

The Waiting Game

I N FACT, MY relationship with the celebrity jungle had begun many years before. In 2002 or 2003, the very first years of the programme, an *I'm a Celebrity* producer had contacted me about it, and I'd gone up to the South Bank studios in London to be interviewed. I was quite keen. I knew that, at that time, programmes where you have to rough it had never had a female winner. I said, 'I think I could be the first.'

They actually laughed. They said they were not necessarily looking for the winner. They were looking for a suitable mix of personalities and someone who would get on with all the different characters.

I didn't get on that series. But with their renewed interest in me in the wake of *Total Wipeout*, I was keeping my fingers firmly crossed.

In the meantime, Channel 4 invited me to do a celebrity *Come Dine with Me* special. Four Olympic medallists from the golden era of athletics would cook for each other. I love cooking, and the dinner was for old friends. For the main course, I did one of my specials, baked monkfish wrapped in Parma ham. Kriss Akabusi, the 400-metres hurdler, and I flirted as we always do, but it's just for fun. Dalton Grant, the high jumper, who lives half in Nigeria and half here, had some good stories to tell. And the white South African barefoot runner Zola Budd, who had a British grandfather and ran for Britain in the 1984 Olympics, surprised us all by saying, 'When I came to Britain to run aged seventeen, that was the first time I had heard of Nelson Mandela.' The guys did a better job than Zola, who says she dislikes cooking, but I was in paradise in my new kitchen, and I won.

Finally, in January 2011, I got the call back from the *I'm a Celebrity* producers that I'd been hoping for. Would I like to come for another interview?

By that time, I was seriously in need of work. I'd tried for the last four or five years to get work in athletics. I'd seen coaching jobs come and go, which no one had told me about till after the post was filled. I do realise, naturally, that there are a lot of us former athletes who have a lot to offer, and there aren't enough roles for us all. Even with the opportunity of London 2012, the committee couldn't possibly have involved us all. While I still did whatever I could for Sport Relief and other Olympic-linked charity events, I also needed to put bread on the table. Maybe reality TV was the answer. And I could speak about that subject with a voice of authority. Out of work, I was spending far too much time watching TV, especially reality TV, which my son and I love. Ryan and I watch sport – football, athletics, you name it. We also watch *I'm a Celebrity*, *The Only Way is Essex*, *Come Dine with Me* ... the lot. What I like about reality TV is the honesty of seeing real people. As I now know, sometimes the producers set up situations, but there is no script.

But some of my friends and my brothers were sceptical when I mentioned that I might be joining a reality show.

They said you never know how this is going to work out. They warned me that the producers can edit the programme so you look bad.

I said, 'Well, I'm just going to be myself. That way, how can it be so bad if you are what you are?'

They interviewed me in June 2011, and said it would take a while to see who would go well together. I used to ring the producers frequently – there were two guys I really felt I could talk to. I'd say, 'How's it going, am I still in the mix?' They'd say, 'Yes, you're still in the mix.'

It got to be October, and I said, 'You must know.' The show was starting on 13 November.

The reply was, 'All we can say is you're the twelfth, and we're still trying to persuade the powers that be that they should take you.'

I replied, 'I desperately want to go and I'll do a good job.'

A few days later, a producer rang me back, and said, 'Get prepared, just in case you do go. Arrange the babysitter.'

So I did. If they wanted me, even at the last minute, I'd give it a go.

Then Lady Luck smiled on me. I got the call from *I'm a Celebrity*. Four days later, I was on the plane to Australia. Ryan would be flying out with a chaperone – *not* a babysitter – ten days later. It was an exciting opportunity for us both. I couldn't wait to get started.

CHAPTER THIRTY-THREE

I'm a Celebrity

G OOD INTERCONTINENTAL FLIGHT, excellent Australian hotel. But after just one night, we were airborne again in a helicopter – and obliged to parachute into the jungle.

For the jump, each one of us was attached to an experienced parachutist. I actually found it exhilarating, but it was a terrible trial for *Coronation Street*'s Antony Cotton. Mark Wright and I tried hard to help Antony overcome his paralysing fear, and he did it and was glad. But he seemed to have it in for me after that.

In the jungle, with not enough to eat, and stomach cramps and heat rashes and worse, nobody is on their best behaviour. Nobody is at their best, and of course there are some people you like more than others. Let's leave it at that. There were some terrific people in there, who will remain friends.

I was heartbroken when Stefanie Powers was voted off. She is such a courageous lady, and fun. Not only has she starred in Hollywood films and in plays and on TV, but Stef also showed us that lung cancer, which she had just recovered from, can be defeated.

Her knowledge of camping in the wilds was invaluable. Stef has spent a lot of time camping out in the African jungle, not just for reality TV, but for real. She runs a major charity that protects endangered animals. She warned the cook that our water for drinking and cooking needed more than just bringing to the boil, it had to boil for several minutes, to protect us from serious stomach bugs, but there was some resentment at 'orders' coming from a woman. Some of us did get ill.

The first few days in the jungle were really tough. Then, if anything, it got tougher. The problems were psychological as well as physical. You're thrown together with complete strangers in quite severe conditions. You're cut off from the outside world and you're not allowed to get in touch with loved ones. It's hard. I hadn't been away from my son before. So I tried to cut off emotionally from my ties at home, my friends and family. Rather than torment myself emotionally, I embraced the life in front of me. Instead of my normal workout at the gym, I carried the heavy logs we needed for the fire.

I did a lot of work around the campsite, but with the lack of nutrition – some days there were only 300 calories – I'd come crashing down quite quickly. Not just me; all of us were suffering. Yet we were finding out about ourselves – and we were building up camaraderie.

Pat Sharp was a great guy, but in the last bushtucker trial, we were face to face, and I had to beat Pat to stay in. He'd been a good influence in the jungle – Sinitta told me how he had helped her through her fear when they absolutely had to sleep in the cave that the rest of us had refused to kip in. It's a pity he later decided she was faking her fear. Sinitta was the bravest of us all in my opinion because she really was scared of so many things, but she did it anyway.

Crissy Rock, recently of *Benidorm* fame, was supportive of everyone, particularly me. She's a good friend. We know we both sort of made fools of ourselves screeching and swooning like schoolgirls when Peter Andre arrived unannounced in the jungle. But I'm a long-term fan of Peter. He's a terrific singer and he was so sweet to us that neither Crissy nor I felt foolish. Well, not very foolish. Getting to know Peter was the high point of my time in the Aussie jungle, and it's a friendship that's continued ever since.

I admit that sometimes I did approach the *I'm a Celebrity* challenges a bit like an Olympic event. That's the only way I know to be focused and to move forward, and it works for me. Actually, it would work for everybody.

Maybe occasionally I was bossy, too, but I wouldn't ever ask anybody to do anything I wouldn't do myself. Fair's fair – some of the guys could have done more wood carrying and less swearing.

From the start, everyone expected Mark Wright, the hunk from *The Only Way is Essex*, to win. After twenty-one days, we were down to the last three in the jungle – Mark, Dougie Poyntner, who is the bassist in McFly, and me. I was the last woman standing, the queen of the jungle. I came away with the bronze medal. Then when the public voted for the silver and gold medallists, we got a big surprise. Dougie won.

But Mark, because he has character as well as looks, was happy for Dougie, who is light-hearted and quietly strong: all good qualities in a king of the jungle.

When I came out of the jungle, my son Ryan was in Australia waiting with his chaperone, Toni Purkiss, at the luxury hotel. Ryan was two months short of turning fourteen.

He said he was very proud of me, though perhaps a little embarrassed at how I had swooned over Peter Andre.

But I wasn't quite the same mum I had been. I had lost 12 kilos, roughly two stone – and that was without trying. The ITV doctor said that was too much. He thought I might have picked up some bug in the jungle – literally. To tide me over, he gave me some electrolyte fluids, but he said that as soon as I got back to London, I must have tests to see what parasite I'd picked up.

After the doctor left, I took a bath and scrubbed and rescrubbed the brown algae off my skin. In camp, we bathed regularly, but not in potable water. Then I took a power shower to get some more of that stuff off. Then … I collapsed. Ryan's so-called babysitter now had to babysit me.

For the next few days, Ryan looked after most of the practicalities. I was in too much of a state to do much myself. He is so careful and thoughtful. He arrived in Australia a boy; he went home a man. Gone is my boy now.

The day after I got back to Britain, I had the medical tests the doctor had recommended, which showed that I had the giardia parasite in my stomach, probably because the lads didn't boil the water long enough. The specialists gave me some pills and said it would take six months to fully recover. The parasite may have lingered, but very soon I was working pretty much flat out, doing talks and television and appearances for charity. Things hadn't been this hectic and exhilarating, and I hadn't been so in demand, since my triumph at the World Championships.

Before Christmas, I appeared on a celebrity version of *Who Wants To Be a Millionaire?* The programme was, as usual, hosted by Chris Tarrant, whom I was happy to be facing, but as I told him, I would have enjoyed it even more if he'd been Peter Andre. Chris took it in his stride and the studio audience laughed heartily, just as I'd hoped. We are just friends, Peter and me – respectful friends. If you ever hear rumours otherwise, there is nothing to it.

For the quiz, I was paired with the singer Russell Watson. We won £75,000, half for the charity I started in 2007, 21st Century Youth, and half for The Prince's Trust. We won more than any other contestants that night, but I hadn't seen it as a competition against the others. It was for charity, so I was hoping every team would win the maximum possible.

Christmas itself was a rather different celebration in 2011. Following our shared jungle experience, Peter Andre and I had stayed in touch, and Peter invited Ryan and me to join him and his extended family for a traditional Christmas dinner. It was turkey with all the trimmings, including bread sauce, served buffet style.

I sat down at the table next to Katie Price's son Harvey, who is blind and autistic, and helped him eat. He's a nice boy. Katie and Peter have two children, Junior and Princess. I think it's wonderful that they share the love of bringing up all three. They are doing a great job, even though they are now divorced. The divorce saddens me because in 2004, I was one of the millions of viewers who watched Katie and Peter fall in love on *I'm a Celebrity*. That's when I decided Peter is not just a good singer, he is a lovely man. I am still wearing the bracelet Peter Andre gave me in the jungle. It's a power balance bracelet, and I think it does me good.

When Christmas dinner was over, Junior asked his daddy to put on the Michael Jackson CD, and he danced on the table to that music, like his daddy used to do. His sister soon joined in. Of course, they both took their shoes off first. Then the party moved to the movie room. We were all gathered around the telly when I got a text on my BlackBerry. It was from my sister-in-law Claire – Mum was at her and Kirk's house and they'd been eating turkey too. Claire wanted to know what was going on.

So I texted back, 'We are watching *Braveheart*. Lovely meal, and Peter is a charming host.' And he is.

The next day, Boxing Day, our whole family got together at Kirk and Claire's and took a big family picture, which is in this book. Boxing Day is our big family occasion, and I have often been the hostess myself. On New Year's Eve, Ryan and I generally stay in with friends and family. We sit up late and watch the celebrations round the world, and that's just what we did in 2011 too. As we watched the fireworks explode over the River Thames, I made a wish for good fortune for us all in the year ahead.

It certainly started well. In January, at the National Television Awards, *I'm a Celebrity* was named Best Reality TV show. Dougie, Mark and I were invited to attend the awards ceremony with Ant and Dec, and to go on stage to pick up the trophy. I wore a brand new, floor-length, mocha-coloured dress and spent the whole afternoon getting fitted into it and having my hair and make-up done. It was worth it. I even met Jonathan Ross.

I also started a new job, as the fitness guru for 'Fatima's Fat Fight', my slot on *This Morning*. When I was offered the work, the producer said I would be a kind of Ms Motivator, but it turned out that the participants weren't just people who had put on a bit of extra weight, they were seriously obese, which meant there were psychological as well as fitness issues. ITV ultimately set up a boot camp in Norfolk to help them kick start their training, and a nutritionist and psychologist were brought in as well as me. I really wanted to be of help, not just front the programme, and some progress was made, but it was hard-going for all of us.

In late February, we were filming 'Fatima's Fat Fight' at the big Croydon shopping centre. It was packed, with people lined up everywhere looking down at us. We were all set up, the participants were on the stage, when suddenly, the music stopped, and the next thing, over the tannoy, I hear a voice: 'Hello, gorgeous.' It was Peter Andre. It was a total surprise.

He said to me, 'I'm sorry I haven't been in touch, but being someone who doesn't keep secrets very well, I had to stay away.'

ITV had set the whole thing up to surprise me. Peter came down on the stage, and they filmed us both exercising to music with the contributors and the audience, which made for a brilliant programme. As I danced on that stage and watched the world spin by, I thought quietly to myself, 'The girl done good.'

CHAPTER THIRTY-FOUR

Home Truths

I AM SITTING in my lounge looking out the window at the garden. I have just come back from running with my little dog Bertie. Ryan is watching the football on our 50-inch TV. The iconic cockroach is on its shelf. The sky is that crisp, unpolluted blue we get here – they don't get it in London – that makes you think you are miles from anywhere. It is almost a countrified life in this part of Essex.

When I was sent to a care home in Ockendon all those years ago, a home with plenty of green fields to run and play in, it was the best thing that could have happened to me. Essex has been good to me, and I am still here. You could say that, for me, the only way *is* Essex.

Ryan was born in South Africa, but he has grown up here too, and he still goes to Brentwood, the nearby school that Andy and I enrolled him in years in advance.

Even if he wasn't my own son, I would have to say Ryan is a nice young man. He's very good at sport and has a very competitive streak. (I wonder where he gets that from?) He is also good at his studies and is very intelligent, a good thinker. He takes after Andy in that department. He's very thorough with his studies – doesn't rush to finish and put in a half-hearted attempt, like I did at that age – and he researches well. Ryan has asked me to stop showing visitors his glowing school reports, so I'll stop there.

This winter, when Ryan's school football team was playing in the under-15s Essex Cup quarter-final, I was filming for 'Fatima's Fat Fight' on *This Morning*, so I couldn't go. To be honest, boys his age don't greatly like their mothers hanging around anyway. But his nan doesn't take no for an answer, and Mum drove over to watch Ryan play football.

Ever since Mum was pushed down that flight of concrete stairs, she can't stand for very long. She wanted to find out which pitch at the Brentwood School the match would be played on, so she could park her car close and get a good seat before the stands filled up. She asked some girls which pitch to go to, and mentioned that it was her grandson Ryan who was playing.

The two girls' eyes widened and one said, 'Are you Ryan Norman's nan?' And when she said yes, Mum says, they seemed willing to *carry* her to the best seat in the best stand. My boy is already a big hit with the girls. He can cook too. His signature dishes are ratatouille and pasta Bolognese and hamburger.

Brentwood won 5-1 that day. Ryan was playing on the wing. He really knows what he is doing, but his nan, who is after all an ex-PE teacher, not to mention the former national javelin coach, told him he needs to pass into space more. Deep down, she knows he is an excellent player. Skilful, good footballing brain, a great team player. I love him so much – he is wonderful, caring, loving, kind, happy, full of fun. He is my son. We have had so many joyful times together.

He doesn't say so, but it's been tough for Ryan without his dad. I've filled in where I can. I've played golf and tennis with him, and sometimes football in the garden. Now he is older, of course, he prefers to play with his mates. Also, he's much better than me.

Sometimes, I feel I've lived a charmed life, because so many times, bad things have become good things for me. That cockroach that crawled up my nose was bad luck that turned out to be good. I wouldn't wish growing up in care on anyone. I always felt the absence of a family. But it did have its good side. It taught me discipline and the certainty that I had to work hard to have any chance of getting what I wanted in life. It was in those care homes that I learned to love children. I was encouraged to care for the younger ones and I loved it because when I was with them, I felt needed. I promised myself then that one day I would have a family, and that no child of mine would ever have to feel the emptiness that I did.

And what a family I got. Four generations of Whitbreads – my brothers and their wives and children, my parents and the grandparents until they passed on – embraced me and my son. We're part of a large, caring, exuberant family. Things were a little awkward in our family after my parents' divorce, but they are better now. I can't tell you what a relief that is to me personally. I see a lot of Mum and Dad, although I tend to see them separately these days. I understand that my fantasy of the perfect family and the perfect marriage was too good to be true. While things will never be as they were, it means a lot to me that we're all in touch, and supportive of one another. That bond of love still connects us, and it always will.

As a single mum, I'm always juggling lots of balls in the air and wearing different hats. In the Australian jungle and on the plane back, for the first time in years I had time to think about who I really am, and I learned a lot about Fatima Whitbread. Not the athlete, not the mum – just the person. We were up against physical and mental hardships in that jungle. I liked facing the new challenges in a new environment with new people, and finding out I could do it. I got to know Fatima the person, who I had forgotten. The experience in the jungle actually made me quite like myself again.

Since then, I have had more challenges, more opportunities. Many of them have been on TV. The new all-singing, all-dancing Fatima Whitbread was actually quite nervous dancing Cuban style for Sport Relief on *live* TV. Wearing that swirling red dress and the fringed wig they dreamed up for me, performing with the Cuban Brothers – who are not Cuban – was good fun, but I had to stretch myself.

I try not to live my life in chains. I believe it's a choice – you can chain yourself to the ground, or you can fly free like a bird. When things seem tough, I tell myself, don't chain yourself down with past history. Cut loose those shackles. Let your spirit fly.

I think that's why I'm a survivor.

At fourteen and a half, I started a new life, even though social services had labelled me as beyond help. At twenty-eight, I reached a crossroads – sport had taught me the focus and discipline needed to succeed in life, but my career as a javelin thrower was over. I had to re-invent myself. I had to find a life. I did it, and just before my thirty-seventh birthday, the most important event of my life occurred. I gave birth to my son. At forty-nine, I embarked on a new career that's finally taking off.

Yes, I loved my athletics career and I'm sorry it couldn't go on longer. But I love the life I have now. I have a beautiful home, work I enjoy, a wonderful family, and most of all a son who has transformed my life. I really think this is my very best time. Ryan is the best thing that's happened in my life. He is a lovely lad, becoming a man. I hope I will have the strength to loosen the apron strings fully and to let him go when he grows up. But if I get clingy, I'm sure Ryan will set me straight.

Acknowledgements

This is a very personal book. Even so, it could not have been written without the assistance of many people who gave freely and generously of their time and knowledge. Nor could my life have been lived without some of them, including Rae Peat and Andy Norman, who, sadly, are no longer with us. I want to say thank you to Cory Boswell, Edna Dennis, Peter Orpin, Alma Riley, my brothers Gregg and Kirk and their families, Mum and Dad and Ryan.

My warm thanks, too, to Adrianne Blue for helping me probe into the often painful past, and for making the manuscript a reality.

In a few instances, we have omitted or changed a name to avoid embarrassing anyone.

My thanks also to my agent Juliet Mushens and my publisher Kate Moore for guiding the book through to publication. Above all, I would like to thank the public, who I have always found to be an inspirational help.

Picture Acknowledgements

Page 1 – all pictures courtesy of Fatima Whitbread

Page 2 – all pictures courtesy of Fatima Whitbread

Page 3 – Tony Duffy, Allsport (top left); all other pictures courtesy of Fatima Whitbread

Page 4 – Getty Images (top left and right); Ted Blackbrow / *Daily Mail* / Rex Features (bottom)

Page 5 – © Press Association Images (top); Press Association (bottom)

Page 6 – Jamie Wiseman / *Daily Mail* / Rex Features (top left); all other pictures courtesy of Fatima Whitbread

Page 7 – ITV / Rex Features (top left); Getty Images (top right); courtesy of Fatima Whitbread (bottom)

Page 8 – Claire Whitbread (top), used courtesy of Fatima Whitbread; Mike Daines (bottom left); Rex Features (bottom right)

If you were inspired by *Survivor*, you might also like …

Zara's stepfather, Hassan, mercilessly bullied her brother and sister. But at just seven years old Zara knew she could never tell anyone about what Hassan was doing to her. For the next nine years, she kept the terrible secret, until eventually she found the courage to fight back. But was she too late to save the people she loved?

Secret Evil is the moving and inspirational true story of a little girl who tried to protect her family against the evil that pervaded their lives.